Hot Coal, Cold Steel

Hot Coal, Cold Steel

Russian and Ukrainian Workers from the End of the Soviet Union to the Post-Communist Transformations

STEPHEN CROWLEY

Ann Arbor

THE UNIVERSITY OF MICHIGAN PRESS

Copyright © by the University of Michigan 1997
All rights reserved
Published in the United States of America by
The University of Michigan Press
Manufactured in the United States of America
⊚ Printed on acid-free paper

2000   1999   1998   1997   4   3   2   1

A CIP catalog record for this book is available from the British Library

Library of Congress Cataloging-in-Publication Data

Crowley, Stephen, 1960–
    Hot coal, cold steel : Russian and Ukrainian workers from the end of the Soviet Union to the post-communist transformations / Stephen Crowley.
        p.   cm.
    Includes bibliographical references and index.
    ISBN 0-472-10783-6 (acid-free paper)
    1. Trade-unions—Coal miners—Russia (Federation)—Political activity.   2. Coal Miners' Strike, Soviet Union, 1989.   3. Trade-unions—Coal miners—Ukraine—Political activity.   4. Trade-unions—Iron and steel workers—Russia (Federation)—Political activity.
    5. Trade-unions—Iron and steel workers—Ukraine—Political activity.   I. Title.
    HD6735.15.Z65C76   1997
322'.2—dc21   96-45812
                                                                           CIP

For Cynthia

Contents

Acknowledgments

My debts are many and deep for the realization of this project. A first and rough draft came from my dissertation, for which Zvi Gitleman, William Zimmerman, and Michael Kennedy were extremely helpful. An IREX/SSRC Fellowship for Soviet Sociological Research funded six months of my fieldwork. One of the direct benefits of the fellowship was that it allowed affiliation and collaboration with probably the leading group of labor sociologists (then affiliated with the Institute of the International Labor Movement) in the Soviet Union and now Russia, and to whom I am deeply indebted: Leonid Gordon, Alla Nazimova, Vladimir Gimpleson, Evgenii Romanovskii, Eduard Klopov, Galina Monusova, Vera Kabalina, and many others. Most especially I am indebted to Viktor Komarovskii, a first-class sociologist of the Russian labor movement, who gave so much of his time to help a young American reseacher. Others who were also helpful during fieldwork excursions include Petr Bizyukov, Yurii Komarov, Elena Kovalyeva, Leonid Lopatin, Vyacheslav Malyarchuk, Anatolii Malykhin, Ilya Shablinskii, Viktor Tolkach, and Viktor Zhadorozhnyi.

Additional fieldwork in the Kuzbass was made possible through work on an expansive project researching the 1993 Russian parliamentary elections, directed by Timothy Colton and Jerry Hough. Further fieldwork in the Donbass came through my affiliation with the project "Working Through Perestroika: The Kuibyshev Miners of Donetsk," funded by the National Council for Soviet and East European Research. The project was directed by Lewis Siegelbaum and Danny Walkowitz; in addition to inviting my collaboration on the project, Lewis has been a good critic, collaborator, and friend.

For help during the writing stage I am very grateful for the support of the Center on East-West Trade, Investment, and Communications at Duke University and especially its director, Jerry Hough, who provided helpful and incisive comments. I would also like to acknowledge the assistance of the Kennan Institute, which provided a short-term grant for the use of resources in Washington, D.C.

A Post-Doctoral Fellowship at Columbia University's Harriman

Institute provided invaluable time for writing and further fieldwork, as well as a critical intellectual environment that helped further many of the ideas presented here. For that I am especially grateful to Jack Snyder, Leonard Bernardo, Alex Motyl, Raj Menon, and Steven Solnick. A Social Science Research Council Post-Doctoral Fellowship provided summer support and a semester off from teaching, which allowed me to make final revisions.

Others who have taken the time to read or discuss all or part of the manuscript at different stages include William Bianco, Michael Burawoy, Paul Christensen, Linda Cook, Walter Connor, Matthew Evangelista, Ellen Gordon, Ellen Hamilton, Herbert Kitschelt, and Anna Temkina. A special thanks to Donald Van Lenten for his careful reading and suggestions on wording. Research assistance was ably provided by Olga Khomenko, Alisa Rotenberg, and Lydia Bryans.

Finally I want to thank Cynthia Van Lenten, my wife and best friend, who made many sacrifices during this long project and whose clear thinking often helped me see the truth I was missing even as it was sitting in front of my face.

Introduction

Well after the disintegration of the Communist Party and the Soviet state—and followed by several years of economic collapse—industrial workers in almost every sector of the former Soviet Union have remained quiescent. Why? Given new opportunities for political expression, the same trade unions, formerly dominated by the Communist Party and largely alienated from their constituency, still hold a virtual monopoly on workers' representation. Why?

As Russia and the other newly independent states confront the daunting task of building democracy and capitalism, few questions can be as significant as those concerning industrial workers. If the countries of the former Soviet bloc are to compete on the world market, they will do so as industrialized economies, giving labor a central position for economic success or failure. Politically, workers are still the predominant social group in these industrial societies; they have the numbers. Recent studies on the political development of Western Europe and Latin America have reconfirmed what political sociologists have long argued: that labor is a central variable in the development of capitalism, democracy, or something else entirely.[1] How are labor's concerns expressed in the political sphere? What effect are privatization and the concomitant growth in unemployment and the threat of the deindustrialization of the economy having on the former Soviet working class? More importantly, how will workers respond?

While such questions are intriguing, what is known about workers in what was the original socialist state remains surprisingly sparse. This work, a comparative case study of two groups of industrial workers at the end of the Soviet Union and the beginning of independent Russia and Ukraine, is intended to shed light not only on where Soviet workers have been, but also on where they are going. It will be argued that, well after the downfall of the Communist Party and the Soviet state, the institutional and ideological legacies of state socialism continue to shape the ongoing economic and political transformations. More broadly, this case provides a useful basis for examining such persistent questions as the relationship of structure and action, how workers and others are able to act collectively to defend their interests, and how those interests come to be defined during a period of dramatic social transformation.

This study began as a backward look at a small question within a much larger event. The larger event was the 1989 Soviet coal miners' strike, the largest industrial strike ever in the Soviet Union. Some four hundred thousand miners in several regions and republics took control of their mines, occupied city squares, and advanced broad economic demands, while the effect of these actions on economic and political reform was being hotly debated in the national and international press. The small question was this: Why, in such centers of strike activity as the cities of Donetsk and Novokuznetsk, did steelworkers stay on the job? The much larger question was not why there was so much labor unrest in the Soviet Union, but rather addressed a more perplexing issue: Why was there so little?

As I began several months of fieldwork to answer these questions, however, the coal miners intervened. They renewed their strike, this time with even more radical goals: they rejected economic demands and sought to lead a general strike aimed at fundamental changes in the structure of the state.

Thus, I was confronted with two closely linked questions. Through what process did the miners evolve, in less than two years, from a "purely economic strike" supporting "perestroika from below," to a "purely political strike" aimed at forcing Gorbachev to resign, transferring power to the republics, and removing the Communist Party from its position of hegemony? More puzzling still, why did the coal miners, working in the country's most heavily subsidized industry, lead a movement not against economic reform but rather pushing for the rapid introduction of the market?

And yet the original small question not only remained, but became more trenchant. Given dire shortages of the most basic consumer goods and the impending painful transition to a market economy, why were there active and even militant workers' movements in some industries and not in others? Why, once again, did the steelworkers remain at the mills?

These questions have become no less compelling over time. Coal miners in both Russia and Ukraine, though increasingly disillusioned with market solutions, remain organized and able to make their anger felt, creating tremendous if somewhat different problems in both independent states. At the same time, long after the downfall of the Communist Party and the Soviet state, and despite high prices, the nonpayment of wages, forced vacations, and threats of bankruptcies, most workers remain unorganized and represented by the former state trade unions workers have long held in disdain.

In short, the task is to uncover the conditions that led to sharp radicalization and self-proclaimed class consciousness in one group and apparent apathy and lack of mobilization in another. This study addresses these questions in part through a "most similar case" study of coal miners on the one hand and steelworkers on the other, two heavy industries quite often located in the same communities, so that many variables can be held constant.[2] Moreover, the two comparisons, between miners and steelworkers and between changes in miners' demands over time, are examined in two very different settings—in Siberian Russia, with newer industry and a stronger market position, and in eastern Ukraine, with exhausted mines and obsolete plants heavily dependent on subsidies. These contrasts of different republics (now different states) and diverging market positions allow for still greater explanatory power.

The study relies in large part on the words of the participants themselves: through primary sources and, more important, through several months of fieldwork in Moscow and the country's two main coal mining regions over several years. The data gathered during fieldwork include extensive interviews with striking miners and other workers, from national leaders down to laborers at the coal face and the blast furnace; observations of meetings, from those coordinating strike activity on a national scale to that of management and the work collective inside a steel plant; and finally materials, from internal documents of the workers' movement to plant newspapers that record the daily conflicts of workers in these industrial communities undergoing transformation. (Such research opportunities, needless to say, have not been possible until now.) Part of the task of this book is to give voice to a group rarely heard and on whose behalf others—whether Party officials or post-Communist intellectuals—usually speak. Further, while concerned ultimately with political questions and outcomes, the approach taken reaches across disciplines, combining political economy, political sociology, and contemporary social history.

Beyond discussing a question fundamental to the fate of Russia and Ukraine—that of labor—this study also engages debates in social theory, in particular questions of the relationship of structure to action. In so doing it examines both the strengths and the limitations of the dominant modes of explanation for social and political action—rational choice and cultural analyses. It does so by arguing that these divergent and seemingly contradictory approaches are best seen, not as opposing paradigms based in different worldviews, but as different analytical tools useful in explaining different kinds of questions.[3]

That being the case, the two main questions posed at the outset are examined through different analytical frameworks. To explain collective action by coal miners but not by steelworkers, the book employs a rational actor approach to argue that the tremendous array of goods and services distributed through the Soviet enterprise has prevented workers' collective action. Further, the level of provision of these goods and services varies between industries and firms and can account for differences in strike activity.

While such an approach provides a parsimonious explanation for workers' collective action in this case, rational actor theory—assuming preferences as given and indifferent to ideology—is silent on the other question that begs explanation: how miners' demands changed so dramatically over time, and in such an unexpected direction. Here cultural factors become salient, in particular the relationship of ideological elements inherited from the Communist era and the alternative envisioned in the liberalism of the West. While declaring themselves anticommunist and pushing for the market, miners continued to use ideological materials from the very system they were condemning—including such notions as exploitation and a labor theory of value. Miner leaders combined elements of old and new values into an ideological framework that led miners to seek control of their enterprises and demand a just wage for their labor, while arguing for a conception of the market quite at odds with that of liberal reformers. Needless to say, these contradictions have not been resolved.

Rather than being an account of the "end of the Soviet Union," this work focuses on a set of institutions and a social group that remain critical to the fate of Russia and Ukraine long after the collapse of the Soviet state: the industrial enterprise, the once-official trade union, and the millions of industrial workers who liberal reformers can only wish would have disappeared along with the Communist Party. This book purports to explain not only what was, but also what is, and how past and present continue to shape what is yet to come.

Thus, this account brings to attention legacies of the Soviet past that have important implications for the outcome of current struggles over democracy and capitalism in Russia and Ukraine. These legacies are both institutional and ideological. The institutional legacies above all concern economic problems, such inefficient state enterprises that often provide the main source of goods and services to their workforce, and former state trade unions, largely detested by their constituencies, that distribute many of these goods and services and thereby retain the position as the main representative of workers.

The ideological legacies concern largely political factors. Miners, while battling explicitly against communism, used many of the cultural concepts inherited from the socialist era, in arguing for example that they were being exploited by the old regime. Yet such notions as exploitation were not jettisoned when market forces began to impinge on mining communities, and miners continue to argue that the new system as well as the old is exploiting them. Yet with the concept of socialism fully discredited in miners' eyes by the Soviet experience, an organized and militant segment of the labor force has been left without the ideological package that has traditionally motivated workers' movements and labor parties in the West—some form of socialism or social democracy. The result is that as the pain from the market transition increases, without an alternative to capitalism or even an alternative within it, workers become increasingly open to extremist appeals.

The book is divided into four parts, which are more thematic than chronological. The first part focuses on theoretical explanations for workers' collective action and radicalization, and the first coal miners' strike of 1989. Part 2 turns to steelworkers in the same communities that did not strike and develops the conception of "mutual dependence" to explain why steelworkers, and some coal miners, have not struck or organized collectively. It also explains why these paternalistic relations have proven resilient even as market pressures have increased. Part 3 returns to the coal miners, to examine their attempts to build a workers' movement, and to explain how they transformed their demands to push for an end to the Soviet Union and for the market. Part 4 focuses on the economic and political difficulties workers face in post-Communist Ukraine and Russia, as miners confront the new regimes they helped bring about and as miners and other workers encounter the dilemmas posed by democratic elections.

The last chapter will draw some conclusions concerning the factors that lead to working-class mobilization and changes in political consciousness, the position of workers in post-Communist societies, and the implications for these societies as they now grapple with the challenges and contradictions inherent in democracy and capitalism.

Part 1.
Theoretical Reflections
and the First Miners' Strike

CHAPTER 1

Workers, Collective Action, and Political Movements

On August 5, 1989, just days after the first coal miners' strike, a trade union conference convened at the Kuibyshev mine, located in the city of Donetsk, to hear the chairman account for union activities since the last conference over two years earlier. He began, as was typical, by reading a report that included the various social benefits provided by the union and the numbers of violations of labor discipline. He was soon cut off. In a scene repeated in mines throughout the country, speaker after speaker rose to denounce the chairman, and those in attendance voted not only to remove him from his position, but to strip him of the title of Honorary Miner of Ukraine. The denunciations moved from the shortcomings of the individual chairman to those of the trade union federation and indeed the political system itself.

Meanwhile, only a few kilometers away, the trade union committee of the Donetsk Metallurgical Plant met to discuss fulfilling the plan. The trade union chair announced that in July (the month of the miners' strike) there had been twenty absences from work, twenty-eight violations of public order, and twenty-two cases of drunkenness. The meeting proceeded without incident. At its conclusion, the results of the latest round of socialist competition were announced: the winning brigades received red banners, a diploma, and a small monetary prize.

How did the coal miners not only strike, but organize themselves, and start marching on a path of increasing radicalization? How did the steelworkers, so close by, not only resist radicalization but even avoid striking at all? Somewhat more abstractly, what determines why some workers mobilize, organize, and strike, while others remain quiescent? And what determines whether the mobilization that occurs is directed toward the radical transformation of existing society or in defense of the status quo?

The present chapter will address this first question—why coal miners but not steelworkers were so active—by reviewing alternative explanations for worker mobilization in certain groups and not in others. It will then examine how previous explanations of the relationship of workers to the

Soviet state might account for the miners' strikes. An alternative perspective will be advanced, one of the "mutual dependence" between the worker and the Soviet enterprise, arising from the unique combination of industrial paternalism and a labor-short economy. Once the position of Soviet workers has been thus defined, it will be examined in connection with the collective action problem as an explanation for the mobilization of one group of workers and not another.

However, in addressing the second question posed—why the miners' demands became so radical and in such an unexpected direction—structural and rational choice analyses, so useful in answering the first question, become insufficient. Once workers have mobilized and organized, the individual level of analysis of rational choice is much less useful. This is all the more the case since the very definition of "interests," assumed as given in structural and rational choice analyses, becomes an object of debate and struggle. The institutions of state socialist societies provide part of the answer to understanding the rapid escalation in the miners' demands. Yet the ideology and cultural concepts generated by those institutions are even more important and outlast many of the institutions themselves. The miners, even as they were denouncing the Soviet system, used the categories of the old state ideology to interpret their situation, and they continue to use these categories to understand the post-Communist world. It will be argued that despite the downfall of the Communist Party and the Soviet state, such cultural legacies will continue to influence Russia and Ukraine for some time to come.

Explaining Strikes

The question of why steelworkers did not join striking coal miners, sometimes almost literally right next door, is a vexing one. Yet a focus on strike activity might seem exceedingly narrow, especially since there are other forms of worker action short of collective walkouts. However, strikes, or at least viable strike threats generated from below, have been reliable indicators in the former Soviet Union of the ability of workers to form independent trade unions and to exercise their voice on vital political and economic questions. Moreover, this difference in strike activity between miners and steelworkers has persisted, beginning with the first miners' strike, now for more than several years.

There has been no shortage of attempts to explain the presence or lack of working-class activism in certain groups, whether in the context of explaining "American exceptionalism" or the overall failure of Marx's prediction that the working class would lead the revolutionary transformation of capitalism into socialism. Explanations for the lack of united action by workers have relied traditionally on either emphasizing intra-class differences of the working class on the one hand or workers' endorsement of society's dominant ideology on the other.[1] Perspectives emphasizing the heterogeneity of the working class will be examined first. Discussions of their ideological incorporation will become relevant when we turn to explanations specific to state socialist societies.

Sources of working-class cleavages discovered elsewhere have been numerous; they include ethnicity, citizenship, the rise of labor aristocracies, the division of new and traditional working classes, and dual or segmented labor markets, among others.[2] Similarly, theories attempting to explain variations in strike activity have focused on differences between work groups, firms, industries, regions, and even nations.[3] The present case, that of mobilization of one group but not another within in the same community, allows many of these factors to be held constant, leading one to look first of all at explanations rooted in industry.

The classic explanation for higher strike activity in certain industries was advanced by Clark Kerr and Abraham Siegel as "The Interindustry Propensity to Strike."[4] In this account, the fact that certain groups of workers—miners in particular—are more strike-prone is explained by reference to the "isolated communities" in which they live, where "miners, sailors, longshoremen, loggers . . . form isolated masses, [are] almost a 'race apart'." In these communities, workers of a particular industry interact largely with themselves, and fail to form the cross-cutting cleavages "of voluntary associations with mixed memberships that characterize the industrial town."[5]

This perspective has met with a good deal of criticism, primarily because of its highly structural nature, whereby workers' behavior is almost mechanically determined; for its assumption that radicalism develops in isolation rather than in interaction with other perspectives and ideas; and because the interindustry propensity to strike has varied greatly over time.[6] Lately, however, this perspective has been given renewed credence, in particular as examinations of the recent British coal strikes emphasize the importance of solidarity inherent in the unique mining communities;[7] the Soviet case would seem to provide another example supporting the thesis of the isolated community. Were this so, we would expect to find that workers' solidarity would be stronger in isolated communities and that miners there would be more radical as opposed to those in multi-industrial towns. In the case of the Soviet coal miners, however, it will be shown that not only does the thesis fail to predict workers' radicalism, but that isolation actually is inversely related to radicalism.

A related approach has focused less on community and more on technology and the organization of work to explain differences in strike activity between industries. This approach, which arose in part from criticisms of the community thesis, argues that stress on community patterns neglects the significance of the workplace and its effect on workers' attitudes; critics adopting this approach stress the more "proximate" influences at the point of production.[8] Thus, the fact that "coal miners around the world are typically the 'aristocracy' of militant labor" is said to derive in no small part from evidence that in mining, "characteristics of the labor process promote unity."[9] These characteristics are said to include the unique experience of working underground; the danger engendering close trust and dependence among miners; the workforce divided into small, tightly knit groups responsible for a single task; and travel time to and from the coal face allowing for communication often unobserved by supervisors.[10]

There can be no doubt that the miners' experience is unique. The solidarity that is part of the miners' everyday work experience can help explain how Soviet coal miners were the first to overcome the problem of collective action to be examined subsequently. And yet such an explanation is not of itself sufficient. As with all workers, the propensity of miners to strike has varied over time.[11] Such a technological approach, taken to its logical extreme, can ignore larger political and economic changes, the position of the industry in the larger economy, and even the influence of wages. The solidarity of Soviet coal miners, it will be shown, cannot be explained outside the context of the economic and physical conditions of the Soviet coal industry. Moreover, while the unique experience of coal miners can help explain why they were the first to exhibit such mass solidarity, steelworkers are also known for toiling in difficult and dangerous conditions, and yet the differences between the two groups' activity—militant on the one hand versus almost nonexistent on the other—have persisted for years.

The political-organizational approach employed by Tilly and his collaborators is rather more useful here. By examining strikes as political acts, one is better able to account for the subsequent radicalization of the coal miners. Moreover, this approach points to a hidden assumption in the other views discussed earlier—that consciousness is translated without problem into collective action.[12] What is necessary, in this perspective, is not simply the desire but the ability to carry out strikes and other collective actions with some chance of success. Thus, the political-organizational approach provides important insights to understanding the two questions examined here, both the mobilization of certain groups and their subsequent radicalization.

Yet beyond these important insights, it is unclear what such a political-organizational model provides. For example, such factors as the "availability of resources" and especially "organizational strength" (the key variables in Shorter and Tilly's study) are of limited usefulness in explaining strikes in a context where the only existing "workers' organizations"—the Communist Party and the state trade unions—actually were instruments of worker domination and the source of problems miners sought to overcome. Moreover, Shorter and Tilly point out that to argue that workers struck because they were angry or concerned about economic issues is trivial; but to argue, as they do, that strikes are political events "is not so much explanation as description, useful as a way of conceptualizing important aspects of the strike process but less helpful as a means of understanding their motivation or determining their possible effect."[13] To understand possible motivation and effect, one needs to turn to the institutional context of the Soviet political economy.

Western Perspectives on Soviet Workers

The totalitarian model was long dominant among Western social scientists as an explanation for relations between the Communist state and society.[14] In the totalitarian view, workers were alienated by fear of the repression that would be invoked if they organized to defend their rights. Consequently, strikes can be explained in this view by the toleration of collective political action under Gorbachev and his successors, which meant that absent the threat of repression, workers could publicly express dissatisfactions stifled for decades.[15] Yet the fact that strike activity and worker organization has been extremely low in most sectors, well after the downfall of the Communist Party and the Soviet state, suggests the need for another explanation.

In response to the totalitarian view, an alternative approach explained the combination of continued social peace with the decline in overt repression in the post-Stalin period by a tacit "social contract" between the regime and society, especially industrial workers. In this view workers were given full employment, rising wages, and a wide array of social services in exchange for their political consent and compliance.[16] The legitimacy of the Soviet state rested on a social base of blue-collar support, but this legitimacy was contingent on the state's ability to deliver the goods.

Relying on this analytical framework, both Soviet intellectuals and Western Sovietologists of the Gorbachev era saw workers as one of the main obstacles to reform, since perestroika promised to break the guarantees of the old contract, though Soviet elites were constrained by the fear of worker unrest.[17] This presents a compelling explanation for the dilemma of perestroika: the problem was not simply to modernize an outmoded economy, but to transform a system that maintained social peace by a means costly to the very economic growth on which it relied. In this view, strikes could be explained by workers' perceptions either that a decline in living standards signaled a breach of the contract or that Gorbachev himself was preparing to break the contract through the introduction of a market economy.[18]

There are several problems with such a conception, however.[19] First, there is no theoretical construct to explain why workers were so powerful that they maintained a veto over the fate of perestroika, particularly since workers were, and remain, largely unorganized, while even organized labor movements in the West provide ever less restraint to state policies.[20]

Further, by focusing on the macro level, the social contract thesis largely accepts the totalitarian view of society as divided between elites and masses, with the latter able only to either acquiesce or "rise up" over the level of the state's material outputs. In so doing, it misses how the Soviet welfare state was administered—largely through the industrial enterprise—and the conflict that the distribution of these goods and services generated, even during periods of economic prosperity.

Still more problematic for the thesis is the fact that by now virtually all the legs of any social contract have been kicked out in most every post-Communist society—prices have risen astronomically, social services have all but collapsed, and the notion of guaranteed employment has suffered a frontal assault—and yet workers in most every sector show little sign of activity, let alone outright unrest.[21]

One further problem has been the implicit assumption—shared by much of mainstream Sovietology—that Soviet industrial workers were conservative and supported the status quo. While there can be no doubt that workers in the former Soviet Union stand to lose a great deal in the face of rising prices, unemployment, and plant shutdowns and may well organize explicitly to halt the further introduction of market reforms, a significant segment of the Soviet working class, the coal miners, placed themselves at the very forefront of those demanding radical political change and, surprisingly, market reform. The strong attack these mobilized workers mounted against the status quo ante raises important questions as to how much Soviet workers actually were "incorporated" into the dominant value system or willfully accepted a "social contract" with the Soviet state.[22]

The social contract argument has been grounded on the premise that with the lessening of overt repression, "social peace" signifies voluntary compliance and legitimacy. This premise has been caused by two shortcomings: (1) an overly mechanical view of how grievances and consciousness lead to collective action, missing obstacles facing workers and hidden sources of conflict, and (2) a simplistic view of how preferences and interests are formed, missing the influence of ideologies, both old and new. These shortcomings correspond to the two questions posed at the outset: why steelworkers (and most other workers) did not strike along with the miners and why the miners transformed their demands in such a radical and unexpected direction.

Two alternative views are more directly helpful. One might be labeled "workers' control," the other "paternalism." In examples of the former view, Burawoy and Stark, using a micro-level approach, both found sources of conflict within the enterprise despite the lack of strikes or other collective action.[23] They also built on Kornai's insights into the "shortage economy," whereby the economic mechanism in state socialist societies that was able to create stunning rates of growth eventually produced widespread shortages that became a brake on further growth.[24] The continual shortage of the factors of production, including labor, created uncertainty in the labor process and in turn led management to cede control to core production workers. The labor shortage also removed the sanction of firing workers for breaking work rules or lowering productivity, furthering workers' control over the production process.

In this conception it is not elite preferences but the economic system that, by creating labor and other shortages, has given workers autonomy. If, in a capitalist economy, workers are atomized through labor market competition where they face the continual threat of unemployment, in state socialist societies the situation has been quite different. In Hirschman's terms, while workers in these societies have traditionally been denied "voice," they have used the possibilities of individual "exit," leaving jobs in a labor-short economy to find a better deal for themselves elsewhere.[25] The concept of "exit" can be broadened to include not only labor turnover, which may create increased demand for labor, but also slacking, slowdowns, absenteeism, and the "withdrawal of efficiency."[26]

Mutual Dependence

Yet if workers hold such power resources, why have there not been more examples of collective action among workers in these societies, especially when "voice" became a real possibility? Whatever the benefits to be had through individual exit, it is undoubtedly in the collective interest of workers to combine together, and this interest would seem to increase during periods of economic decline. It will be argued here that the worker in state socialist society has been in a position of dependence, not simply as an individual dependent on the state, but as a working person on the place of work—in particular the industrial enterprise—as the provider of one's basic life needs.[27] If a worker in capitalist society receives a wage packet and health benefits, a worker in state socialist society received that and also housing, access to the enterprise hospital, to day care and other forms of education for one's children, often employment for one's spouse, trips to rest homes and vacation centers, and consumer goods that can range from cars to cabbage. Such a set of ties can be a powerful disincentive to collective action, particularly when the distribution of these goods and services takes place largely at the discretion of management and alternatives are few.[28]

This depiction of enterprise paternalism is not entirely new. In Andrew Walder's account of Chinese industrial relations, there are social and economic dependence on the enterprise, political dependence on management, and personal dependence on one's superiors. Yet Walder was not ultimately successful in extending his "neo-traditionalism" as "generic features of modern communism,"[29] since unlike the Soviet Union and Eastern Europe, China remains an overwhelmingly peasant society, with the implication that workers have not faced excess demand for their labor, but rather considerable unemployment. That perhaps explains Walder's rigid model of domination, where there is little chance for subordinates to escape their plight other than by accommodating themselves to the system. (More recently Walder has revised his argument along the lines suggested here, arguing that the lifetime tenure of Chinese workers in state enterprises makes management dependent on them, hence managers must provide a high level of benefits in order to maintain productivity.)[30]

Indeed, in order to make sense of the position of workers in Soviet (and now post-Soviet) society, one needs a synthesis of the workers' control and paternalism perspectives.[31] In the Soviet Union this dependence has not simply been top-down, but two-way, or "mutual"—the enterprise on the worker in an economy that has created shortages of all inputs, including labor, and workers on the enterprise in that virtually all of their life needs are met through the workplace. Workers have often used the taut labor market to obtain a better packet of enterprise benefits elsewhere,[32] leading managers to acquire better goods and services in order to retain current workers and attract others. Yet turnover also occurs most frequently among young (and single) workers, tied in part to the facts that one's spouse and children also become dependent on the enterprise, that many seniority rules have been put in place to discourage turnover, and that queues for housing extend for several years at least. Moreover, the goods and services at the disposal of the enterprise are distributed very unevenly in order to retain those skilled workers most needed for production.[33]

Workers, I argue, are caught in a collective action problem:[34] the selective incentives that enterprise managers have used to prevent workers from acting individually and seeking work elsewhere can also be used to prevent workers from acting collectively. Conversely, as Burawoy has argued, "The more independent the reproduction of labor power is from enterprise control, the greater is the ability to resist managerial offensives."[35] While workers everywhere face the problem of collective action,[36] workers in Soviet enterprises have run the risk that an unsuccessful strike would likely deprive the initiators not only of wages, but of housing, day care, summer vacations, and the rest. (Indeed, the stakes are quite high on both sides. While the miners clearly gained through their strikes, many managers did not lose profits, but rather their jobs, as the miners removed the old bosses and elected their own.)

How were the miners able to overcome this dilemma? The distribution of these goods and services is also highly uneven between industries, depending (initially) on the preferences of planners and (later) on the ability of management to barter its product. In some industries and enterprises workers have been better provided for, while in others, such as coal mining, workers have had less to lose. Hence, the variation in the level of this enterprise dependence between industries, and even firms, as we shall see, can account for much of the variations in strike activity.

From Mobilization to Radicalization

The preceding discussion suggests a parsimonious explanation—management's use of enterprise goods and services as selective incentives to prevent workers from acting collectively—which can help answer our first question—why did steelworkers not join the miners, often right next door, in striking? But what of the second question—why did the miners transform their demands, in less than two years, from economic concerns and support for perestroika from below to political demands aimed at bringing down the Soviet system? Moreover, why did the miners, in the country's most heavily subsidized industry, demand the rapid introduction of the market?

The rational actor approach used to answer the first question is less helpful in answering the second, because it employs an individual level of analysis and ignores the impact of cultural factors. We will examine each of these points in turn.

The individual level of analysis, or *methodological individualism,* is justified in the first case precisely because it is the position in which the subjects find themselves prior to acting collectively. In the Soviet Union, this isolation, often referred to as *atomization* in a society almost devoid of independent social organizations, was enforced over the years through harsh penalties for collective action and deepened by the individual strategies workers used in a labor-short economy.

Yet the individual level of analysis is insufficient even before mobilization. Workers share a common predicament that provides incentives for organizing. Further, the decision to act collectively is rarely made in isolation, but in an interactive process with others, with whom the individual will have continued contact as more-or-less permanent work partners. Yet while this interaction is important to a degree before, it is after the decision to act collectively is made and carried out successfully that the interactive group process predominates, as workers build their own organizations and learn they can overcome the demands of their bosses with a degree of impunity. For this reason, the individual level of analysis cannot account for the dramatic radicalization of the Soviet coal miners once they mobilized.

One possible explanation for the radicalization of the miners' movement is provided by resource mobilization theory, long the dominant perspective (at least in the United States) for analyzing social movements.[37] As the name suggests, the theory is most persuasive in explaining the mobilization process, and the preceding argument on the mobilization of the coal miners has borrowed several key points from resource mobilization perspectives: the assumption that conflict and grievances existed long before protest behavior and that the ability to overcome obstacles to collective action is central to understanding the generation of strike activity.

Yet the emphasis in resource mobilization theory on the role of existing organizations presents a problem in the present context.[38] First, there were no existing organizations on which the miners could rely prior to mobilizing, though some did spring up almost immediately thereafter. Second, while the miners engaged in considerable organization building after their first strike, and the role of these organizations and worker-leaders was important, it will be shown that formal organizations were by no means the central determinants of the miners' actions.

There is a further problem in resource mobilization theory, one that it shares with both rational choice and structural Marxist perspectives.[39] Within these traditions, the interests of social actors are nonproblematic: interests are objective and clear and can be straightforwardly inferred by outside observers based on incentive structures.[40] With such a direct relationship between objective conditions and individual behavior, there is no mediating process by which people attribute meaning to events and interpret situations.[41] While such a perspective can explain how a movement develops and whether it in some sense succeeds, it is indifferent to the content or the ideology of the protest. This is no small issue for the Soviet coal miners' movement. While it is perhaps not too hard to explain why the miners began raising political demands (especially in the context of the paralysis of the state), it is necessary to explain why the miners did not mobilize in the conservative direction that so many had predicted. Why did the miners' perception of their interests differ so remarkably from the material interests that both rationalists and structural Marxists see as paramount? How, after all, did the Soviet miners, in conditions of full employment and subsidized prices, come to demand the dismantling of the Soviet state? Furthermore, why did workers in the single most subsidized industry demand the introduction of a market system? The argument to be made here is that cultural factors, in particular the ideological frameworks that miners constructed in order to make sense of their situation, are central to the explanation.

Confronting Culture

In making a case for the importance of cultural and ideological factors in understanding the miners' trajectory, it would be useful to discuss how this argument differs from previous treatments of culture in politics. In political science, the "political culture" concept long dominated the field, whereby a nation's political culture compromised its fundamental beliefs and values concerning political processes and institutions.[42] Following in the wake of Parsons, this approach argued that culture was determined by end values, around which a given society cohered. The research agenda of this approach typically focused on measuring a rather narrow group of attitudes such as political efficacy, political trust, and support of competitive elections and a multiparty system.[43]

The political culture approach was once the bedrock of area studies, in particular studies of comparative communism.[44] The argument that distinct value systems explained the behavior of different societies appealed to area specialists who could refer to their unique understanding as a means of making sense of particular societies. This argument was all the more persuasive in the case of Communist societies, since political realities often prevented access to data that might offer alternative explanations. Such arguments stressed continuity above all—such as in explaining the Soviet dictatorship by underscoring autocratic traditions in Russian history.[45]

While the political culture approach was heavily criticized, the alternatives tended to push cultural factors to the periphery. Modernization theory, for one, argued that as a society achieved higher levels of industrialization, education, and technology, cultural differences would become less salient. Modern industrial societies would converge, leading to modern values or a world ideology. While this theory has been roundly criticized over the years, it has recently enjoyed a resurgence, especially with the fall of communism.[46] In this conception, the Soviet experience was a long detour on the road to liberalism, since given the relatively high levels of education and industrialization in Russia, one could predict with some confidence that they will embrace democratic and capitalist values.[47]

Proponents of the various "new institutionalisms" would claim that such arguments for a post-Communist convergence overlook the importance of institutional constraints, such as path dependence, in arguing that future options are dependent on previous choices.[48] Yet most institutional approaches, while specifying the conditions and constraints in which people maximize their interests, elude discussion of how institutions shape ideas and perceptions of interests.[49]

Another avenue of explanation for the transformation in the miners' demands is suggested by the term *moral economy*. In this theoretical tradition, collective action is a response to violations of norms and standards.[50] This argument has been most forcefully applied to agrarian societies and peasant rebellions, as well as craftsmen and artisans facing the onset of large-scale commodity production. While such an argument can help make sense of the ideological underpinning of the miners' protest, the moral economy approach falls short of the mark in this case.

We have already questioned whether anger or moral outrage is a sufficient condition for collective protest. Most telling, however, was the direction of the miners' demands. In the moral economy approach, "[r]ather than reflecting some emerging new consciousness, then, protests under a moral economy aim at resurrecting the status quo ante. The goal is not to negotiate and redefine the terms of exploitation but to reinstate them after they have been abandoned."[51] Thus, revolutionary movements are often led by "reactionary radicals," such as peasants or artisans, who use traditional cultural values to defend themselves against impending change. Industrial workers, on the other hand, most typically demand reform, not radical change.[52]

Such was not the case with the Soviet coal miners, nor with other workers' movements in Communist societies, especially Poland's Solidarity.[53] Here workers did not call for a return to the status quo ante; on the contrary, they demanded the fundamental transformation of a system they perceived as profoundly unjust. This sense of injustice, it will be argued, was in part a product of traditional cultural values, as workers appropriated the language and symbols of the dominant (Communist) ideology to argue that the system was exploitative. At the same time, the miners took hold of the language and symbols of liberal reformers to argue in favor of democracy and markets, while redefining these concepts in order to meet their own needs and desires.[54]

To make sense of this experience, an alternative approach to culture is needed, one that would incorporate several elements. First, culture can be viewed—rather than as end values in a little-changing political culture—as "points of concern" for a particular society: within a given cultural milieu, certain issues become sources of debate or even of great conflict, while other issues are left silent. In this way culture can frame debates and set agendas.[55]

Second, as Ann Swidler has argued, culture can be seen as a "tool kit" of habits, skills, styles, or worldviews, from which people construct "strategies for action." Such strategies—persistent ways of ordering action through time—are not determined by cultural values, but their choice is greatly influenced by available cultural habits and styles.

Third, the importance of cultural factors varies greatly over time. During "unsettled periods" of social transformation, when old institutions disappear and standard practices become untenable, bursts of ideological activism occur as competing ways of organizing action compete for domination.[56] Thus, while revolutionary transformations are mostly set into action by material and social forces, leading to collapse of the state, ideological struggles come to the fore once the state has lost the initiative and contending forces compete to build a winning coalition. Ideological innovation is high during this period, but competing ideologies are crafted from the available materials within a given cultural setting.[57]

Taken together, these elements suggest the recent discussion in the social movement literature of collective action frames—interpretive schemata for understanding and acting in the world.[58] The construction of frames, undertaken by movement leaders, involves "inscribing grievances in overall frames that identify an injustice, attribute responsibilities to others and propose solutions."[59] Yet collective action frames are distinct from formal ideologies in that they are quite flexible and adaptable to a given situation. Further, in constructing frames, movement leaders are constrained by existing cultural meanings, because a frame must resonate with a target population to be potent. This construction involves frame alignment—placing a movement's frame at the intersection between existing cultural meanings and attempts to transform traditional meanings and institutions. Thus, movement organizers are both "consumers of existing cultural meanings and producers of new ones"; in Tarrow's vivid metaphor, "the symbols of revolt are not drawn off the peg from a cultural closet and arrayed ready-made before the public. Nor are new meanings fabricated out of whole cloth. The costumes of revolt are woven from a blend of inherited and invented fibers. . . ."[60] Such a view of culture does not appeal to unchanging end values, nor does it detach culture from institutions and power relations, as does much poststructuralist theory.

Rather, a modest argument can be made for the intervening influence—at times critical—of cultural variables between structure and action.

Institutions do indeed help shape preferences and the vision of alternatives. The institutions of the Soviet political economy help explain the rapid politicization of the miners' movement. The miners' radicalization— the escalation of both demands and the level at which they were directed— can at least partly be explained by their reaction to the "fusion" of the state socialist political economy: the fusion of politics with economics and the fusion of "production politics" with state politics. This fusion means that the state is perceived by workers as a visible presence at the workplace both as "oppressor"—as the instrument of domination—and as "exploiter"—in the sense of distributor and redistributor of the product in the absence of a market.[61] Likewise, the fusion of politics and economics makes the state fully culpable for economic conditions on both the micro and the macro levels. In capitalism, workers' concerns generally are isolated within the firm and within the limits of the firm's survival, since without it they will lose their jobs; in state socialism, however, conflicts involving workers are almost immediately directed against the state. Thus, the very visible hand of the state is squeezing the worker at the point of production and is responsible for distributing that product throughout society.

While such institutional arrangements of the Soviet political economy help explain why the miners became so rapidly politicized, they help only partially in answering another intriguing question: Why were workers in the country's single most heavily subsidized industry pushing for the market? It will be argued that the impact of institutions in shaping interests and worldviews of social actors can outlast the institutions themselves.[62] Even the experience of past institutions can set agendas, so that certain alternatives are sought more quickly, while others are hardly considered.

In other interpretations of the Soviet miners' movement, workers allied themselves with liberal reformers and pushed for market reform because they were duped by intellectuals.[63] Here we find the familiar appeal to false consciousness to explain why workers fail to act in their "real" interests, rather than an attempt to understand the concerns of real people in historical situations.[64] One must ask: Why, not only in the Soviet Union but in Poland as well, did such strong workers' movements not only attack state socialism but also ally with liberals to embark on an economic course so seemingly counter to their interests? Are workers in these contexts simply myopic and incapable on their own of seeing where their true interests lie, thus proving Lenin correct after all?[65]

It will be argued in subsequent chapters that, even as they were attacking the Soviet system, the miners were interpreting their position through the once-dominant ideology in arguing that they were being exploited by a parasitic state. Miners, as they saw it, were not getting justly paid for their labor. With this belief, they rejected the only social system they had ever experienced—and indeed rejected "socialism" in any form. Having thus narrowed the list of alternatives, the miners soon embraced the new utopia of the market offered by liberal intellectuals. But for the miners, and for most Soviet citizens, the idea of the market arrived well before market institutions themselves.[66] How does one comprehend something before experiencing it? To do so, one takes shortcuts—in coming to terms with and indeed creating the idea of the market as an alternative, miner-activists reached into their cultural tool kits and pulled out mental templates that created a shortcut to understanding a market economy. In so doing they grafted their own notions of utopia onto that proposed by liberals. They had rejected socialism, but built concepts of the market on the socialist ideals that communism failed to bring to life.

While they called for the rapid introduction of the market, miners envisioned a just payment for their labor power as being based not on its market value, but rather on a materialist-based labor theory of value. As miners, they were producing a material good and deserved a high wage, while workers in the service and trade sectors were producing nothing and thus did not.

Bosses, of course, also produced nothing, and given the state's role in the economy, it was not difficult for the miners to see a straight line extending from their foreman up to state elites in Moscow. The problem, as they soon saw it, was that people were not getting paid according to their labor—those that worked hard and produced something of material value were being cheated, while those who redistributed this wealth were enriching themselves without real work. Over time, as miners from different regions discussed these ideas in their various forums, they began to envision the essence of the Soviet system as the ability of self-appointed elites to distribute and redistribute the wealth of others. One way to break this system and end the exploitation it caused was to join with reform-minded intellectuals in pushing for the market. But the miners had quite a different conception of the "market" than did their liberal allies: For the miners the market meant distribution according to labor—Lenin's definition of socialism rather than the traditional definition of capitalism. Further, the miners' vision of the market also included workers' ownership and control of their enterprises. In this way the miners had appropriated elements of both the once dominant ideology—Marxism-Leninism—and the newly emerging ideology—liberalism—and elaborated and expanded on those elements to craft an ideology of their own.

While this ideology proved powerful—among other things, it led the miners to call a general strike aimed at Gorbachev's ouster—it was beset by fatal contradictions.[67] One contradiction lay between the desire for the independence afforded by the market and with the understanding that most mines were heavily dependent on state subsidies for survival. While the relatively more profitable Kuzbass led the way in calling for the market, the more heavily subsidized Donbass soon followed and was ultimately no less strong in calling for independence.

A further contradiction lay between the miners' use of class concepts to interpret their situation and their inability to organize these notions within a viable ideological framework. If the miners used the cultural concepts from the Soviet era to interpret their situation, they did so without acknowledging them, for they explicitly rejected the Soviet system. This left them without a name around which to organize their thinking: The Soviet state had already appropriated the traditional ideology used by workers' movements to create solidarity and the concept of an alternative future—*socialism* in any sense of the term. Even the idea of social democracy was suspect. The lack of an ideological alternative led miners to embrace a liberalism that threatened to destroy their livelihood.

But first, let us start at the beginning, with the first coal miners' strike. Only with an examination of this first strike can we start to address the two issues raised at the outset: the failure of other workers to join the miners and the radical trajectory of the miners' demands.

CHAPTER 2

The 1989 Miners' Strike

The July 1989 mass strike by Soviet coal miners changed the tenor of perestroika, because the largest social group in society, the working class, had
joined a struggle that had hitherto been confined to the intelligentsia,
national independence movements, and conservatives in the state and
Party apparatus. Involving four hundred thousand miners, the action presented the Soviet state with a challenge—the mass industrial strike—that it
had not seen in more than sixty years. Not only did the miners push "perestroika from below," as some have argued, but they were to do so in a
way that went far beyond the reformers' control.[1]

What follows in this chapter is an account of the first miners' strike,
taken from original sources and both Soviet and Western reports. That
account will be followed by an analysis of the causes of the strike and of
various explanations of why the strike followed the course it did. Finally,
the demands of the strikers will be examined in detail, since their non-
fulfillment was to drive the miners to search for new allies and ever more
radical measures.

Precedents to the Strike

The strike was not a new phenomenon in Soviet society, even before perestroika.[2] With the lessening of the threat of coercion and the increased
pressure on enterprises through the first attempts at economic reform,
strikes increased on an unprecedented scale. Analysis of strikes reported in
the central press from the second half of 1987 to the first half of 1989
shows that most strikes were small, usually involving less than a full enterprise, lasted one to three days, concerned pay and conditions of work, and
despite the fact that "public organizations" (i.e., Party and trade union
committees) sided with the management, the outcome frequently was one
of compromise or concessions from management and rarely involved concessions from workers or sanctions against them.[3]

Strikes had not been unknown in the coal industry, either, especially
in the first half of 1989. In fact, were it not for all the background noise of
social conflict throughout society, it is hard to see how the warning signals

could have been missed. According to a secretary of the central committee of the official miners' trade union, there were a number of incidents of strikes at mines in March and April of 1989 in various regions, which the official linked to the introduction of self-financing (*khozraschet*) in the coal industry from January 1989. While there had been strikes before, "the mines stopped for a rather long period. This was new for us."[4] In one case in the Kuzbass, a major coal mining region in Siberia, two sections of a mine refused to come up on the surface after a shift until their demands were fulfilled. The director threatened to bring them up with the help of the police and mine rescue workers, which led the miners to escalate their previously narrow demands to include the removal of the director and his chief engineer. Earlier in the Kuzbass, where the July strikes were to originate, the regional Party committee (*obkom*) denounced "group refusals of workers from work" (the word *strike* apparently still was difficult to pronounce) in Kemerovo, Novokuznetsk, and three other cities in the region.[5]

Even in the mine where the July strike began, the signs of conflict were long evident. In December 1988 three sections of the Shevyakova mine in Mezhdurechensk sent a letter to the national television program "Searchlight of Perestroika," raising the issues of food supply problems and additional pay for evening and night work and demanding that the mine be awarded the status of state enterprise, giving it greater independence. The complaint was routed from national television to the central committee of the trade union, from there to the territorial trade union committee, and then to the mine, where a commission officially "closed the complaint," solving nothing. The miners then formulated eight clear demands, which they sent to the central committee of the trade union, the city committee of the Party, and the director of the mine, with an ultimatum: if their demands were not answered by July 10, they would strike.[6]

The July Strike

What was different this time was that rather than remaining contained within a shop, factory, or mine, the strike began to spread. When eighty miners from the night shift of the Shevyakova mine refused to give up their lights after their shift, they were joined by workers from the first and second shifts, 344 workers in all. They were soon followed by others. By the next day, all the enterprises of the coal industry were on strike in Mezhdurechensk, and several thousand miners occupied the city square, awaiting the arrival of the minister of the coal industry. The minister soon arrived.[7]

The strike continued to spread quickly. By the third day practically the entire city of Mezhdurechensk was shut down, and miners in other cities began to strike. Within four days, all the mines were on strike in several cities, and within a week 166 enterprises had closed down in the Kuzbass, with 181,000 workers on strike, while 5,000 miners gathered for a demonstration in Makeevka, a city in the Donbass mining region of Ukraine. When, on the ninth day, the strike ended in the Kuzbass, it began in earnest in the Donbass. In all 400,000 were to strike, in the Kuzbass, Donbass, in Vorkuta, Karaganda, indeed in virtually every mining region in the country from L'vov in Western Ukraine to Sakhalin in the Far East.

The Strike Committees

The miners in Mezhdurechensk did not expect this outbreak of solidarity. Indeed, they concluded their own agreement with Minister Shchadov and within four days of the beginning of the strike published an appeal to workers of the Kuzbass, saying their basic demands had been met, that the Mezhdurechensk workers were returning to work the next day, and that other strikers should do likewise "or further continuation of the strike might lead to an uncontrollable situation and unforeseeable consequences."[8]

Yet the strike grew. And despite the total lack of preparation, the miners quickly organized themselves, and quite well at that. The July strike was distinguished from previous conflicts not only by its size but also by the appearance of strike committees. Such committees formed almost immediately, everywhere the strike hit, and in practically every case were elected democratically. As one strike leader from Novokuznetsk, a city not far from the original strike, recalled, "When our people went to Mezhdurechensk and returned, and told what was happening there, it had already begun here. But once the strike began strike committees were already in action at the mines, and immediately we elected a borough strike committee, which has now become the city strike committee."[9] A roughly similar process took place in other towns and cities: representatives were elected from each section of a mine, and from this group representatives were delegated to a city strike committee and from there to a regional committee. Within seven days of the beginning of the strike in the Kuzbass, 227 representatives of city strike committees met to form a regional strike committee, which went on to formulate a joint packet of demands.[10]

These committees were composed overwhelmingly of manual workers. In the Kuzbass 82 percent of strike committee members were manual workers, and in the Donbass the number appears to have been similar.[11] They were also young, with the average age in the mid-thirties, and a significant number—anywhere from one-quarter to one-half—were Communist Party members. Yet these were "almost exclusively rank-and-file members or low-level activists."[12]

The miners displayed their organizational skills throughout the strike. From the very first day, the strike committee in Mezhdurechensk maintained order by forbidding the sale of alcohol in the city, and workers together with the local militia patrolled the streets. This scenario was repeated throughout the Kuzbass and the Donbass, as black marketers with alcohol were apprehended, drunks were carted off, communal services and schools, hospitals, and bakeries were kept open, and maintenance details were kept up at mines to prevent cave-ins and explosions.[13]

In many of the cities, miners displayed the same amount of discipline that they would be expected to show at the workplace. In Prokop'evsk, for example, miners showed up for their shift at the mine, dressed in their work clothes, received their helmets and lanterns, and went to the city square, where they spelled their comrades from the previous shift. In the city of Donetsk, the strike began in one mine as miners followed the example of the Kuzbass, marching in their work clothes four abreast for 8 kilometers to the square in front of the regional Party headquarters.[14]

Miners in most cities occupied the city square, often in front of the local Communist Party headquarters and frequently the site of official holiday celebrations. The work clothes, helmets, and lanterns were intended as a sign that they considered the strike, too, to be work. While the choice of venue and attire was symbolic, the demonstrations themselves were functional. It was there that the miners, not trusting mass media, could receive information on how many mines were out and how the negotiations were progressing. There they could also discuss new demands. More important, through these demonstrations the miners were able to reinforce their sense of solidarity.[15]

The miners' considerable self-organization and discipline reflected, in no small part, their fear. Their action was unprecedented, and they were well aware of smaller strikes, in mines and elsewhere, that had been brutally repressed. "It was terrifying," striker Yurii Komarov recalled later with a smile, "absolutely terrifying," suggesting both awe and fear, and many other participants used similar language. The miners policed themselves during the strike largely to avoid giving authorities any pretense for repressive action.[16]

The concern the miners showed for maintaining control during the strike extended to the scope of the strike itself. Strike leaders took pains to characterize their strike as purely economic. Thus, the deputy chair of the regional strike committee of the Kuzbass would state, "Ours is a purely economic strike, we haven't advanced any political demands," while a leader of the Makeevka strike committee claimed "our demands are not political but socioeconomic," and the Donbass miners generally, it was said, did not advance political demands "in principle."[17]

Moreover, the miners sought to keep the strike contained to the mining industry. On the third day of the strike in Mezhdurechensk, a railroad worker took to the podium to announce, "I want you to know: we can shut down not only a station, but the entire rail line. We can do it. Should we do it?" The square of miners responded unanimously, "Don't do it (*ne nado*)."[18]

There were exceptions. For example, bus drivers struck in the town of Miski, as did some bus lines in the city of Novokuznetsk.[19] In Prokop'evsk and Mezhdurechensk, almost the entire city was said to have struck, but the mining industry was overwhelmingly the dominant employer in these towns.[20] Thus in Prokop'evsk, "when workers of many other enterprises wanted to join the strike, the electro-mechanical factory and the plant 'Eloktromashina' were allowed to strike, but the bus drivers, a house construction concern and others were told to express their solidarity by other means." They came to the square in their free time, included their demands with those of the miners, and contributed money to the strike fund.[21] In Kemerovo, the administrative center of the Kuzbass and a city with few mines, there were more sympathizers than strikers on the city square, though people from other enterprises carried signs of solidarity. When the city strike committee learned that the bus drivers were planning to join the strike, they considered this a serious affair, since it "would seriously violate the life rhythm of the city." Together with the chair of the city Soviet, members of the strike committee went to talk to the drivers, and the buses were soon back on the streets.[22] In Novokuznetsk, a city of more than six hundred thousand people with eighty thousand metallurgical workers, among others, the leader of the city strike committee explained, "We decided to do it this way: ours is a big city, and not only miners live here, and there is no reason to muddy the waters with demonstrations. So we will organize a sit-down strike and not leave the mines."[23]

Thus, the demonstrations that did take place in Novokuznetsk in conjunction with the strike were not of miners, but of *neformalnie*—small parties and other radicals hoping to use the strike to promote political change. To such demonstrators the miners in Novokuznetsk, as elsewhere, gave a universal rebuff. People representing various interests arrived from around the country. As one observer noted, these intellectuals "wanted to help the strikers formulate political demands, and unite with them in the struggle for democracy. But they were requested not to interfere. The strike committees quickly sent packing those who distributed political pamphlets or gave speeches."[24] One speaker addressing the miners, giving a rather standard criticism of communism, was heard without comment until he identified himself as a member of the Democratic Union, a new political party, at which point he was shouted and whistled off the podium. Said a member of the strike committee, "We protest this speech. Miners, let's not become toys in the hands of such people!"[25]

Undoubtedly, such rejection had a class character. Indeed, as Friedgut and Sieglebaum noted, "perhaps one of the strike's most remarkable aspects was the absence of any influence by the intelligentsia."[26] Thus, while members of the Democratic Union were being shouted down, a "worker-neformalnyi" from the union Independence in Leningrad had more luck. The miners "broke bread with him, read his leaflets, and then discussed how 'workers' democracy' was better than 'workers' dictatorship,' and how workers must strike competently."[27]

Despite all the attempts by the miners to keep their strike confined to economic issues—the characterization of the strike as strictly economic, the containment of the strike to enterprises within the coal industry, the rejection of interference of political groups of any stripe—the strike was political in many ways. Thus, one could argue that "from the outset the demands . . . were a mixture of mundane economics and high politics" with "no clear barriers separating economic from political issues. . . ."[28] While the demands of the strike will be discussed in detail subsequently, the political nature of the strike was manifested almost immediately in the authority gained by the strike committees in running their communities. In Mezhdurechensk it was reported that "for a week now, the strike committee had been in command of the city," and that its chair, a mine foreman, was giving orders to the city's enterprise directors.[29] Elsewhere, it was noted that "the strike committees, in essence, became the authority in the towns. They were occupied with questions of trade, transportation, maintaining order. From morning to night people who for a long time had been unable to get help or support from any other organizations came to the committees. And their members looked into each problem, asked specialists, and helped where they could with medical treatment, repairs, job placement. . . ."[30] In Kemerovo, "the strike committee found itself besieged by citizens who assumed that at last they had found an institution to help them. Petitioners lined up all day for a stamp and a signature to enable them to get a bank loan; for advice about what to do when the person renting them a room wanted to terminate the lease; and to discuss a host of everyday problems that fell far beyond the responsibilities the strike committees ever intended to undertake."[31]

Indeed, the strike committees did not wish to wear much longer the mantle of authority that had been thrust upon them. In the words of a member of the Novokuznetsk strike committee, this dual power is "a temporary, extreme measure. Power should be returned to the Soviets, not the present ones, which have solved nothing, but new ones, which might have some of us elected to them. Look at our guys, how they are working—the city Soviets should work so hard!"[32]

The position of the traditional institutions of authority toward the strike was at best ambivalent and certainly confused. The central authorities' initial reaction was sharply against, and they entertained the notion of sending in strikebreakers and even tanks; Party workers and activists were told that participation in the strike was incompatible with Party membership. Yet rank-and-file members were demanding that their Party committees not oppose the strike; not surprisingly, "the result was confusion and paralysis in many of the local Party organs, preventing them from engaging in any constructive communications with the strike committees." The Party committees, normally the dominant presence in these towns, were hardly noticeable.[33]

The record of mine directors during the strike was not much different. Many were judged quite harshly by their subordinates, as we shall see, but there were some exceptions. Mikhail Naidov, a former mine director in Mezhdurechensk (and former city Party committee secretary), who was quite popular with the workers, was called upon to return to the city by the miners when the strike began. At the Zasiad'ko mine in Donetsk another popular director, Efim Zviagilskii, was informed that the miners intended to walk out, agreed with their decision, but advised them to wait until another mine had struck, rather then being the first to go out. Also in Donetsk, the director of the Skonchinskogo mine argued that "until the last possible moment I tried to persuade my miners not to strike," but when they voted to do so anyway, he led a column of the marching strikers onto the city square.[34]

The spontaneous organization displayed by the strike committees throughout the strike contrasts sharply with the conduct of the state trade union. The experience of the city of Prokop'evsk seems typical. "The miners' trade union committees, who were reminded by the strike committees that it was their duty to defend the interests of workers, remained in a state of confusion for days, waiting for orders from the territorial committee." A representative of the territorial trade union committee seemed to have disappeared for the first three days of the strike, until he was spotted by a reporter waiting in line at a store for cream. He claimed to be disoriented and unable to react to the events. One mine trade union chair, not waiting for an order but on his own initiative preparing food for the strikers, was made a member of the strike committee, though he appears to be an exception. After receiving orders from above, other trade union committees also began bringing food to the strikers on the square.[35]

In Donetsk, one trade union secretary gave a frank account of the trade union's behavior after he was dressed down by the miners: "Yes the strike is over. The train has pulled out of the station and we are left standing on the platform. Our trade union officials turned out to be totally unprepared for any such extreme situation. The people launched their attack and marched right by us, and we were left dragging soup kitchens after them."[36] If any further evidence was needed that these were state rather than workers' trade unions, it was given to the miners when the official trade union negotiated and signed the agreement that settled the strike, but on the side of the government rather than that of the workers.

Control in the Enterprise

The miners, for their part, not only denounced their superiors, but sought to remove them. An avenue had been provided by the Law on the State Enterprise, an attempt at decentralizing economic decision making as well as institutionalizing a degree of self-management for workers. One institution greatly expanded by the law was the Council of the Labor Collective, a body to be elected by the entire workforce, which would participate in enterprise decision making. The Soviet Trudogo Kollektiva (STK) in practice remained under the command of the administration, which controlled the meetings at which candidates for this position were elected. Thus, in a strike at the beginning of April in Kemerovo, a Soviet journalist found that miners expected no help from the STK or its chair because, in their words, "it's not known who elected them." When, before the July strike, the future strike leader Yuri Boldyrev appealed to his STK for help after running afoul of the mine's directors and Party committee when he proposed radical changes in the running of the mine, he heard the comment, "Let's get rid of him now, otherwise we'll have ten like him next year." Much like the trade union committees that were also supposed to defend the interest of workers, it was said that during the strike the STKs "simply didn't exist."[37]

Yet when the strike committees were looking for ways to institutionalize their newfound power, the STK was one place they turned. Rather than dealing with the old council, they demanded that it be reelected. In Boldyrev's mine in the Donbass, for instance, only two of the sixty-two members of the old STK were reelected to the new council, and twenty-three of the new members were from the strike committee. It was reported that chairs of the STKs were replaced in most of the Donbass mines.[38]

But the STK was not the only innovation of the Law on the State Enterprise that the strikers were to seize upon. According to the law, all management within the enterprise, from the foreman to the director, must be elected by the work collective. Once again, these elections were not everywhere genuine, especially since they were organized by the STK, itself often under the control of administration. This too was to change with the strike. Directors were dismissed, sometimes along with their entire administration. At other mines, directors were given votes of confidence, while others in the administration were voted down. One-third of the mine directors in Donetsk were dismissed by their labor collectives, and it is likely that the number was much the same elsewhere. Many directors were said to have resigned rather than continue to work under such pressure.[39]

The same fate befell the old trade union committees. In the words of one Prokop'evsk miner, "This strike has shown how idle the trade union is. . . . The workers at our factory have decided to reelect the entire union committee because they couldn't care less what happens to us." At a joint meeting of two mines in Donetsk, three hundred delegates sat all day interrogating new candidates for the trade union committee; in a nearby mine, only four of the thirty-five members of the old trade union committees were reelected. In general, it was said "the do-nothing 'office intelligentsia,' the illusory role of regulated self-management, the dependence of the trade unions all became clear during these days. The strikers said: 'We must reelect the mine's trade union committees and STKs or put the strike committees in their place.'" The miners hedged their bets and did both. If before they were working under a director, a Party committee, a state trade union, and a sham workers' council, in many places the mine was now controlled by a strike committee, a revived trade union, and a now genuine workers' council, with a director held accountable by the workforce and a Party committee effectively rendered impotent.[40]

Explaining the Strike

Why did the strike spread to disparate regions and republics of the Soviet Union along industrial lines, rather than within the community or region in which it began? After all, the economic downturn affected more than one industry, and the problem of empty store shelves, such a sharp object of complaint, would seem to affect those workers in one region equally hard.

We will examine later why workers in the steel industry, quite often located in large numbers in the very same communities as the coal miners, seemed to be "in another world" at the time of the strike. Here it is necessary to analyze the first side of this question, namely, why were coal miners the first to strike in such great numbers in the Soviet Union?

Various explanations and theories have been advanced to explain the militancy of coal miners throughout the world. As we have seen in the first chapter, the classic explanation of the "interindustry propensity to strike" has been that of the "isolated mass," those workers who are often physically and socially cut off from the rest of society, unable to form the sort of crosscutting cleavages that might mitigate working-class radicalism.[41] From this explanation, one would predict that the miners' strike would begin, solidarity would be most strong, and the demands would be most radical in smaller mining towns rather than in bigger cities, which have many industries and a population of various backgrounds and classes.

Soviet coal mines typically are located in one of three arrangements: mines within large industrial cities, such as Donetsk or Novokuznetsk; smaller cities like Mezhdurechensk or Prokop'evsk, where there is some other industry, but mining predominates; and a mine or mines at the center of a community or settlement (*poselok*), typically quite isolated from other communities or industries. At first glance, the Soviet case would seem to give support to the isolated mass thesis, in that the July strike began, if not in a small settlement, then in a city of just over one hundred thousand where the coal industry is the dominant employer.

On further inspection, however, the thesis is not supported by this case: the radicalism of the Soviet coal miners was inversely related to their isolation, whether physical or social. While the July strike first began in a coal mining city, the demands were less radical there than elsewhere, becoming political only after several days and contact with other cities. Thus, in a large industrial city like Novokuznetsk, strike leaders could proudly argue that their demands were much broader than those of Mezhdurechensk.[42] Moreover, the miners of Mezhdurechensk were least concerned with the problems of solidarity and coal miners in general; in fact, the city strike committee called on other miners to return to work once it had reached an agreement that satisfied their local problems.

Nor are examples of the inverse relationship of "isolationism" and "radicalism" confined to Mezhdurechensk and the 1989 strike. As we shall see, the smaller mining towns and settlements were to have significant problems in maintaining their workers' committees between the various coal mine strikes. Indeed, during extended research in each of the two major coal mining regions, the author was to repeatedly hear that the large multi-industrial towns were clearly more radical, better organized and more strike-prone than the coal mining towns and settlements. Two reasons were generally given.

First, the smaller mine settlements were the least likely to join the strikes, since these mining enterprises were often interconnected with collective or state farms and through barter arrangements were able to feed themselves well at a time when such basic consumer goods as farm products were in high demand. It was not simply that miners in such settlements were well fed and therefore satisfied, but that by striking they would have violated their barter agreement and the farms would have provided their goods to a new partner.[43]

Second, and not surprisingly, the larger cities provided much greater access to information, especially when the strikers felt that the official media could not be trusted. These cities often became the regional headquarters for the strike movement, collecting information from throughout the region and receiving and exchanging information from other striking regions as well. Further, workers gathered daily on city squares for updated reports and news of any progress in negotiations.

Another reason that the isolated mass thesis seems wrong in this case is the presence of one of the conditions that is supposed to prevent worker radicalism: contact with other groups and classes. While many of the ideas the miners put forth arose from within their own ranks, particularly during the 1989 strike, exposure to intellectual critiques and condemnations of communism and expressions of alternative political and economic arrangements clearly had an impact. Those living in cities where there were not only mines, but hospitals, newspapers, research institutes, and universities had greater access to such views.

A more compelling form of explanation has focused on the labor process as the causal factor explaining the presence or lack of working-class consciousness in various industrial settings. Thus, the coal miners' reputation as the "aristocracy of militant labor" is said to be due in no small part to the fact that in mining, "characteristics of the labor process promote unity."[44]

There can be no doubt that the coal miners' experience is unique. Yet if the uniqueness of the labor process can help explain why miners showed such unity in their strike, it is not sufficient to explain why others in the same communities, such as steelworkers, who were also engaged in rough, dirty, and dangerous work, did not join the strike, if not in July of 1989 then in the years hence.

Furthermore, the labor process cannot account for those who did join the strike. With some exceptions, the strike was not confined to underground mines but rather to enterprises of the coal industry as a whole. Thus, not only did such natural allies in other industries as steel remain outside the strike, but the strike was joined by enterprises within the coal industry with very different work regimes, namely open-face mines and coal enrichment plants.[45] In the city of Mezhdurechensk, for example, strikers on the city square were not pacified when Minister Shchadov agreed to place the city's underground mines under local control, but demanded that the open-face mines be included as well or no deal. The minister eventually relented.[46] Therefore, to explain the course of the strike, we need to look at the condition of the Soviet coal industry and the structure of the Soviet economy itself.

The Soviet Coal Industry

As far back as the late 1950s "a brake was applied to the development of the coal industry" as planners in Moscow decided to place greater emphasis on oil and gas in the energy balance at the expense of coal. As a result, not enough funds were assigned for the reconstruction of coal mines.[47] From this situation, a whole series of problems emerged, not least of which was the extremely hazardous conditions under which Soviet miners were forced to work.

Mining everywhere is a dangerous occupation; miners face not only the possibility of fatal accidents, but also the threat of crippling injuries and black lung disease. Yet the problem of accidents is particularly acute in the Soviet coal mines.[48] Whereas miners in the United States fought long and hard to improve safety standards for the industry, the same could not be said for Soviet miners. At the time of the first strike, coal mining accidents were fifteen to twenty times more likely in the Soviet mines than in the West, placing Soviet miners on a par with those in South Africa. As one source put it, some fifteen thousand Soviet troops died during the ten years of the Afghan war; during the same period, ten thousand Soviet miners died on the job. The losses, as the miners expressed it, added up to roughly one life lost for every million tons of coal extracted.[49]

Such a record of accidents is merely the most shocking example of generally appalling working conditions. While mines in the West usually are fully mechanized, Soviet miners used jackhammers and, occasionally, picks. Highly skilled miners often were compelled by the lack of proper equipment or materials to perform backbreaking manual labor. Thus one of the conflicts that led up to the July strike was said to have arisen when shaft workers of a particularly high skill rating were forced to drag heavy beams hundreds of meters.[50]

Not only work conditions were affected by the state of the coal industry, but social conditions were as well. If in capitalist economies, communities are directly affected by the health of a local industry—principally through the level of employment and the amount of money workers have to spend on other goods and services—in a state socialist society this relationship was even more direct. The ministry itself, through the enterprise, provided much of the social infrastructure, including housing. Thus the chair of the Mezhdurechensk strike committee characterized the city's social conditions as follows: "numerous families living in dormitories, overcrowded buses, a shortage of day-care spaces, schools that work in three shifts . . . , lines at the polyclinic as long as lines for imported shoes; only two cafeterias accessible to the general public, one cinema, no sports or youth center." This in a city of 107,000 that, he added, provided the country with thirty-one million tons of coal a year. In the Kuzbass at the time of the strike, two hundred thousand miners and their family members either did not have housing or lived in dilapidated or substandard housing. Much substandard housing consists simply of barracks. Elsewhere, conditions are even worse. In Vorkuta and Inta in the north, miners, despite arctic temperatures, live in barracks built for use in Stalin's gulags.[51]

Such abhorrent conditions would seem to reflect yet another case of a declining industry. Coal, this argument would go, so essential to industrialization, becomes less important as industries become more efficient in their use of energy, as alternatives such as oil, gas, and nuclear energy become less costly, and as society approaches postindustrial status. Thus, the coal strikes may be seen as a social reaction to the inevitable dislocations of a modernizing society.

Yet the rise and fall of industries in state socialist societies did not reflect the invisible hand of the market but rather the deliberate choices of planners. Did the status of the Soviet coal industry somehow reflect, through planners' decisions, the declining value of coal versus other sources of energy and thus the need to drastically reduce the amount of coal extracted? While the decision to shift the energy balance to oil and gas made in the late 1950s greatly affected conditions in the coal industry, coal does not easily fit the profile of a declining industry.

Ironically, the importance of coal in the Soviet energy balance rose quite some time before the strike, with the oil shocks of the 1970s. As a heavy consumer of oil and gas, the Soviet Union was compelled by the increase in world prices (and the amount of hard currency to be earned) to increase its reliance on nuclear energy and coal. Indeed, according to one observer, "Expanded coal use underpins the Soviet Long-Term Energy Program; planners are counting on coal, in conjunction with nuclear power, to provide nearly all new energy output once gas production levels off in the mid 1990s." Because of the reserves of coal and "dwindling high quality reserves of oil and eventually of gas, [the Soviet Union] is likely to continue to emphasize coal in its long term energy plans." The Chernobyl nuclear disaster further underscored the importance of coal for Soviet energy needs. While investment had favored oil and gas, investment in the coal industry continued to grow as well. Thus, just before the 1989 strike, one could argue that "in recent years the attitude toward the development of the coal industry has changed for the better."[52]

The situation in the Soviet coal industry is complex, however. From 1980 to 1986, labor productivity in underground mines decreased by 9.1

percent, and production decreased by 3.3 percent. Output increased from 1986 to 1988, but largely through additional labor inputs. Hence "coal production at most of the major basins that rely on underground mining is now essentially stagnant." This statement is particularly true of the Donbass, which has been mined for two centuries. The easily exploitable coal has been exhausted, the shafts have been sunk deeper and deeper, some more than one hundred meters, and the remaining seams have become thinner and thinner. Moreover, concentrations of methane gas make these mines even more dangerous. The cost of extracting one ton of coal was one-third again as high in the Donbass as it was in the mines of the Kuzbass, the other major basin. The Kuzbass is not without problems of its own, with many of the mines there in need of reconstruction.

The problems in the Soviet coal industry were only to deepen with the first attempts at economic reform. One important step was the introduction of full *khozraschet,* or self-financing, intended to increase management's concern with profits and losses. Yet this step was not accompanied by reform in prices, which gave the reform a perverse effect, most particularly in the coal industry. The price a mine received for one ton of coal extracted—the official wholesale price—was roughly one-half the cost of extraction. While the cost of extracting Soviet coal was often high, the wholesale price in no way reflected demand. This situation made coal the only "planned-loss" industry in the country. Since the wholesale price of coal was administratively set at such a low level, it was nearly impossible to untangle the exact cost of extraction and the amount of subsidies or profits if the price of coal were more closely to reflect its market value. Yet the Soviet economy has been well known for its concern with gross output and plan targets rather than profits and losses calculated by market prices. Thus, when Shchadov was named coal minister a short time before the July strike began, he was able to speak of the healthy financial picture of the industry and, indeed, of "above-plan profits" of 380 million rubles in 1988.[53]

Given such a financial situation, it is not hard to understand that the introduction of self-financing would lead to problems in the coal industry. The idea that each enterprise should earn its own keep did not make much sense in an industry where most enterprises operated at a loss. Indeed, the change, which occurred at the first of the year in 1989, has been said to account for the wave of strikes in individual mines in March and April of that year.[54] The version of self-financing introduced was also intended to tie wages and bonuses more directly to above-plan profits. This type of self-financing, together with a bureaucratized wage system that linked bonuses to plan fulfillment, meant that missing the plan by 10 percent could lead to a 50 percent drop in pay.[55]

The sad state of the Soviet coal industry and the resulting conditions of work and life take one a long way toward understanding why the miners were the first Soviet workers to strike on such a massive scale. But why did the strike not spread elsewhere? If we look at this question from the perspective of the miners, rather than other workers, we can begin to reach some conclusions. First, as we have seen, the miners consciously decided to keep the strike contained to the coal industry. This decision may have been due in part to fear of public outcry, or worse, should basic social services be shut down. Yet it clearly reflects the notion that this was a miners' strike, concerning the mining industry, and thus open-face miners and enrichment plant workers were seen as natural allies in a way that other manual workers were not. In this way, confronting the minister of the coal industry until he granted local control over open-face as well as underground mines was seen as a matter of principle, while miners demonstrating openly in a city with many other kinds of workers would have been unnecessarily "muddying the waters."

If the unique labor process of coal mining and the specific conditions of the Soviet coal industry are sufficient to explain why miners were the first to walk out on such large scale, it is the specific institutions of state socialist economies that can best account for the spread of the strike.[56] The ministerial structure of the command economy explains how decisions were made to allocate investment funds, first to oil and gas rather than coal, and then into unproved strip mining technologies, all at the expense of underground mines. Further, these institutions place the Soviet worker, through the enterprise, in direct dependence on the ministry, not only for wages, health care, and other benefits, but for the allocation of housing, food, basic consumer goods, and more. The strikers addressed their appeals to the coal ministry, backed up by the government, a ministry they understood to be both the cause of their misfortune and their potential savior. It was for this reason, and not some abstract notion of occupational solidarity, that the Donbass miners began their strike only after the ministry and the government had promised so much to the miners of the Kuzbass. For workers from other industries to join the strike or for radicals representing new political parties to interfere would have been a hindrance to the goal of raising the wretched standard of living of Soviet coal miners.

From Economics to Politics

The miners' demands deserve separate discussion, since they explain not only the miners' understanding of the causes of their strike, but also because the demands went unfulfilled, so they account for the fact that the

strike was the beginning of a social movement rather than a one-time phenomenon.

There is no question that at base the miners' demands were economic.
For instance, *Izvestia* published a survey of Donetsk miners, who cited the
lack of consumer goods and low pay as the top grievances, mentioned by
86 percent and 79 percent of respondents, respectively, together with
insufficient vacation time (62 percent), inadequate pensions (50 percent),
high prices (41 percent), and poor housing (41 percent).[57] The most common refrain heard throughout the strike, indeed for some time thereafter,
was "We can't live like this" (*tak zhit' nel'zya*).

The strong concern with wages is interesting, since miners were rather
well paid by Soviet standards, at almost twice the income of the average
Soviet industrial worker. Their pensions began earlier and were higher as
well. Yet, unlike in capitalist society, a high wage in Soviet society did not
directly translate into a high standard of living, particularly during a time
of consumer goods shortages. The fact that the living standard of the
Soviet worker was directly tied to the enterprise and all the services it
offered, while the enterprise in turn was dependent on the ministry, is
significant. In this way, even the most basic economic demands became
political.

There is no clear boundary in state socialist societies between the
political and the economic, or between political figures in the "public
sphere" and private entrepreneurs with whom a workforce must negotiate.
Thus, to make basic economic demands is to risk continual escalation,
bringing one's demands ever higher in search of a solution.

For example, the strike committee chair of the Kalinin mine defended
the strike against journalists who propagated the official line that "the
demands are just, but this is not the method" by pointing to one demand—
additional pay for evening and night shifts—that had long ago been
decreed by the government. "I would like to ask these writers, maybe they
know, under what box of which bureaucrat has the government decree on
paying miners for the night shift been lying for so many years. This
bureaucrat desk-boss was not fulfilling the government decree, with
impunity. So how do you wish us to fight with him? To beg and plead?"[58]
Here a most basic economic grievance, additional pay for a night shift,
was directed not to a private owner, not even to a corporate headquarters,
but to a faceless bureaucrat somewhere in the giant state hierarchy. Where
is he? Who knows? Not at the very top—they enacted the decree, after all.
But somewhere, probably in Moscow. And so, with simple grievances the
miners took their first steps up the hierarchical ladder, in search of the
enemy.

Furthermore, the economic demands became political through a sense not simply of injustice, but of exploitation in a way that Marx would have described it. The miners felt alienated from the means of production, that the fruits of their labor were taken from them with only just enough returned so they might continue to work, and that much of their labor fed an army of managers and clerks who were not necessary for production.[59]

This sense of exploitation was expressed through the many specific grievances against the organization of work within the enterprise, and the weapons that management used to enforce that organizational structure, or what has been called elsewhere "the politics of production."[60] The miners complained of the arbitrary use of power by their superiors, particularly their power to distribute bonuses and punishments and allocate personnel as they saw fit. This included the system of *podsnezhniki,* or "snowdrops," people who were paid out of the mine's wage fund but "in fact were used as 'house serfs' to work for the bosses—repairing their houses or even tending their gardens, opening and closing their dachas in accordance with the season, and even doing work for visiting inspectors, as a way of insuring favorable reports on the mine."[61] The *podsnezhniki* were also given minor positions in the mine's administration, where they could attend meetings of various organizations and push the administration's viewpoint. Moreover, not only blatant corruption but also the simple privileges of management drew the miners' ire. The saunas, summer vacations, cars, and houses of the bosses were strongly resented, since miners had to wait in lines for such things, often for many years, only to receive them from the very same bosses.[62]

Thus, when the miners gained control of the workers' councils and other organizations within the mines, they often shifted the power to assign rewards and punishments from the hands of the administration to those of elected worker representatives.[63] They put the bosses' saunas under the control of the medical clinic, demanded that the pay of every mine employee up to the director be posted openly every month, and dictated that all *podsnezhniki* be removed from the mine's payroll. The miners also demanded that the mine's bureaucracy be cut: in one case a workers' council required that within twenty days the mine director submit to the council a plan for cutting the managerial apparatus by 30 percent by combining jobs, and if he failed to do it, the council would do it for him.[64] If only at the level of the enterprise, such demands were clearly political.

Interpreting the Demands

There have been various attempts to interpret the first Soviet miners' strike, often with sharply conflicting views. Some observers have characterized the strike as a push for radical change and "perestroika from below";[65] others have argued that it was due chiefly to the dislocations caused by the first steps toward the market; still others that any political demands were the result of influence by mine managers and the government.[66]

There is plenty of evidence to support each of these views. The miners consciously sought to keep their actions and their language within the bounds of perestroika, though arguably they were motivated not only by a desire to make the promises of perestroika real, but also to avoid provoking the coercive powers of the state. In the aftermath, on the other hand, local and central authorities actively portrayed the strike as a support for reform and tried to play down the challenges it presented. Miners in many areas protested strongly against medical and service cooperatives, the strongest representatives of the burgeoning market economy, while the introduction of self-financing certainly caused conflict in the coal industry.

The difference between these positions hinges on the demands of enterprise independence. Proponents of the reform thesis have pointed to the demands for independence as evidence that the miners supported the general direction of reform and wished to accelerate it. Others have argued that calls for independence were not among the original demands, that they originated outside the working class and were a means for mine management to press "their own aspirations for greater independence from the Ministry and from government on the basis of financial autonomy and higher coal prices."[67] Since the problem of enterprise independence continued to be central to the miners' struggle and to the crucial question of their support for market reform, it is worth examining the origin of this demand in some detail.

As stated earlier, the miners were beset by strong economic grievances, a sense of exploitation, and a dependence on the enterprise to satisfy almost all their basic needs. This situation left the disgruntled miners with two alternative courses of action: either to demand that the state distribute greater resources for the miners' working and living conditions (as they saw it, a share that would more closely reflect the amount of effort they were expending and the wealth they were producing) or to seek greater independence from the state by having more control over the enterprise and its resources. In fact, the miners did both.

As a result, there were many straightforward bread-and-butter demands. The agreement reached in the Kuzbass not only included such workplace reforms as additional pay for evening and night shifts plus increased vacation and pension benefits, but also encompassed a shopping list of consumer goods to be delivered to the region: for example, specific quantities of meat, butter, shoes, and televisions.[68] Demands of this sort would appear to strengthen the dependence of the miners on the state.

At the same time, demands for independence arose quite early, and the reason is not hard to find. The miners' sense of exploitation was fueled in no small part by the wholesale price of coal, that is, the amount the government paid the enterprise for the coal the miners produced. This amount they understood, quite rightly, to be well below the world market price.[69] Thus the miners argued that self-financing was not a problem in and of itself, but was impossible to achieve given the artificially low price for coal. The miners asked that they be allowed to sell above-plan coal to any consumers they could find, including foreign buyers, at market prices. A miner from Stakhanov proposed this arrangement to the Supreme Soviet on July 6, before the strike began. "We should have this money," he said, "not for ourselves, not to buy such things as VCRs, but to solve basic social problems, such as housing, hospitals and the like."[70] It was not the first time a proposal of this sort had been made, and whether it was first articulated by a coal-face cutter or a reform economist is irrelevant: such proposals resonated among the miners.[71]

Further, while some have argued that the Mezhdurechensk miners had not included enterprise autonomy in their original list of demands, it clearly was of concern to them from the outset. Thus, among the original demands of the Shevyakova mine in Mezhdurechensk where the mass strike began was the insistence that their mine be given the status of "state enterprise," which in the coal industry had been reserved for "production associations" that control several mines and are the next level up the economic hierarchy from the individual mine. This seemingly insignificant step would give the mine the greater decision-making authority it was intended to have in the 1987 Law on the State Enterprise, including the right to market above-plan coal. Without it, a mine director, though typically in charge of a workforce of over a thousand miners, could not approve an expenditure of more than 100 rubles without permission from a higher authority.[72]

This demand was to escalate to the level of the community when the strike seized the entire town of Mezhdurechensk. The mines of this town were subordinate to a production association in Novokuznetsk, while the open-face mines were under a separate production association in Kemerovo. The miners often suspected that part of what was earned by them went to support poorly working enterprises in other cities (and here we see the sense of exploitation on another level); they long wanted their own production association, to be located in their own town, which could give more resources to the needs of the city. When the minister arrived and began to negotiate night and day with the miners, this point became crucial, and it was here that he was confronted on the question of the open-face mines. "Give us what's most important—status!" shouted one miner to the minister, referring to the status of "state enterprise." "Let us manage ourselves independently, then we ourselves can solve our problems."[73]

Another miner, addressing his colleagues on the square in Prokop'evsk, was to articulate how economic grievances were connected to a sense of exploitation, and in turn to a demand for independence. "The basic demand of the workers is the raising of our standard of living. If someone from Prokop'evsk earns his own money, why should he give it to someone else? Every worker feeds five to seven workers in the managerial apparatus. All profits should remain here . . . . We shouldn't give it to the common pot, they won't ladle anything out for us, it's empty. I see only one outcome—we need full *khozraschet,* and this will give us better pay, health care and social services."[74]

Given such concerns, it is not surprising that when the representatives of the regional strike committee of the Kuzbass were to meet, questions of economic independence, along with increasing the wholesale price of coal, the right to sell above-plan coal abroad, and the distribution of profits, were put at the top of the agenda. Included in the discussions that took place among the regional strike committees was the right of the labor collective to determine the form of property of the enterprise, "whether state, lease-holding, or cooperative," and the amount of profit that should be given to Moscow and the local governments (proposals ranged from 40 percent to the state to 100 percent to the enterprise).[75]

Hence, far from being somehow alien to the Soviet coal miners, the question of enterprise independence seemed quite natural to them. But if it could have been argued that the miners supported "perestroika from below" through their strike, they were soon to push beyond it. As we have seen, despite the miners' claims to the contrary, this was not a purely economic strike any more than future strikes were to be purely political. Rather, it was a strike on the level of the enterprise and community over which the miners wanted some control. Their initial reaction to this spontaneous mass action was to appeal to the state to strengthen its ties to these enterprises and communities and, at the same time, to pull away from it. When this contradictory approach was to fail, the miners were to seek other, more radical strategies.

In the words of one observer, the strike "permanently altered the course of Gorbachev's reform strategy."[76] More specifically, the strike had two crucial consequences. Politically, the success of the strike demonstrated that mass collective actions would not be suppressed by the coercive powers of the state.[77] Economically, the strike made clear to Gorbachev and his advisers that labor unrest could easily be the result of the painful changes promised by perestroika, thus increasing even further the difficulties of economic reforms and the willingness to implement them.

But if these were the lessons of the July miners' strike, they seemed to have been lost on other workers. The miners established that strikes were not only permissible, but also brought concessions. Beyond their first strike, the miners were to organize independent trade unions and worker organizations, direct political demands at the Soviet state, and strike again. And yet workers in most every other industry remained silent. If the miners first struck to gain a level of control over their enterprises and communities, what about workers in different industries within the same communities? What of the steelworkers, right next door?

Part 2.
Cold Steel: Soviet Workers and Mutual Dependence

CHAPTER 3

Steelworkers and Mutual Dependence

We turn to one of the main questions posed at the outset, namely, why
other workers did not join the nationwide miners' strikes, particularly
why not the steelworkers working and living, often quite literally, right
next door. If the miners' actions did not continue beyond the first strike in
the summer of 1989, the problem would not be so intractable; it is not
only a question of explaining why the miners were the first to strike on
such a large scale, but why they were not joined by others in the years following. For if the miners initially demanded improvements in their own
immediate material position, they gradually began demanding broad
political changes affecting the entire Soviet Union. And if they had asked
others to remain at work during the first strike, they later tried to lead a
general strike. Moreover, these changes occurred against a backdrop of
great political fragmentation and increasing economic hardship; however, there was little evidence of unrest among steelworkers or other
industrial workers.

Even in 1989, before the miners walked out, there was reason to question why steelworkers were remaining so seemingly acquiescent. As one
American observer, who closely followed events in the city encompassing
one of the world's largest steel mills, recalls:

> During my 1989 trip to Magnitogorsk I expected the steel plant to
> burst into flames at any moment, given the palpable atmosphere of
> social tension and the sheer number of workers. Nothing of the sort
> occurred. Even when huge strikes broke out in coal-mining regions of
> the Ukraine and western Siberia in July 1989, workers in Magnito-
> gorsk remained docile, engaging in neither work stoppages nor orga-
> nizational activity. . . .[1]

If such could be said of Magnitogorsk, at least a thousand kilometers from
the nearest strike activity, what of steel towns in the heart of the coal mining regions? And if not during the first strike in 1989, why not later?

The following two chapters will answer this question through micro-
level case studies of two steel plants located in the center of the two main

coal mining regions. First, after looking at the background of Soviet enterprise communities, the two case studies will be examined. In the next chapter we will turn to competing theoretical explanations. It will be argued that the concept of "mutual dependence" developed earlier can account for much of the variation in strike activity between industries. Finally, counterexamples—coal mines that did not strike—will be examined to give greater confirmation to the mutual dependence thesis.

In the Soviet Union, industrial enterprises, rather than local governments, controlled many, often most, of the social and consumer services for the urban population. While in some cases this setup merely extended the company town arrangements of the tsarist regime, Stalin's industrialization drive built entire cities within a few years where only villages had previously existed. Planners chose spots on the map as sites for industrial conglomerates because of their geographical characteristics, with little thought to how people might actually live there. Production came first; "social problems," in the Soviet euphemism, were an afterthought.

Responsibility both for the building of new factories and for investment in urban infrastructure was placed in the hands of industrial ministries.[2] That left enterprises and their ministries in Moscow in charge of virtually all of the life needs of the labor force. More than one thousand cities have been built in the Soviet Union since the 1917 revolution, most of which "have been born and raised as Soviet-style company towns, in the shadow of one industrial establishment or with several establishments dividing responsibility or competing for control." These enterprises provided "housing and whatever meager services" there were.[3] In 1971, enterprise housing still accounted for two-thirds of all of urban housing; by the mid-1970s, industrial ministries continued to account for 70 percent of appropriations for housing construction, 65 percent for construction of kindergartens and day-care centers, 30 percent for construction of hospitals and clinics.[4]

As a result, differences between plants determined the living conditions of workers much more than in the West, and the life of the Soviet worker centered around the enterprise much more so than the community. This situation was all the more so given the much higher percentage of Soviet workers employed in large enterprises: in 1973, 54.6 percent of Soviet enterprises were quite small, with up to two hundred workers, but they employed only 8.9 percent of the labor force.[5]

Housing was often the crucial consideration for workers, especially for those in areas such as Siberia and the Far North, where the supply was limited and conditions were often dreadful. New employees, wherever the enterprise, were typically housed in workers' dormitories for several years as they waited for enterprise housing. The differences between plants and between sectors in the provision of housing was astonishing—those employed in heavy industry were eighteen to twenty times more likely to get housing than those, primarily women, working in light industry.[6] In a labor-short economy these differences contributed greatly to labor turnover, which was not only due to differentials in pay, but "can best be described by an increasing structural differentiation (or sometimes polarization) of various enterprises and their socio-economic and cultural services."[7]

Before turning to the case studies, it might be useful to briefly restate the argument for mutual dependence. In conditions of shortage for all factors of production, including labor, as well as for basic necessities and consumer goods, the worker and the industrial enterprise became mutually dependent: the enterprise on the providers of scarce labor and the laborers on the provision of virtually all one's needs through the enterprise. Moreover, since not all labor is equally valuable nor equally scarce, it is in the enterprise manager's interest to distribute scarce resources differentially, rewarding some considerably more than others.[8] Hence, collective action on the part of the workforce is inhibited in two ways: first, through its dependence on the enterprise for the provision of essential goods and services, and second, through intraclass divisions created by the administration's distribution of those goods and services.

The two steel plants examined here are located in the two "epicenters" of the miners' strikes. It was hoped that by being so closely located to the miners' conflict, the "fault lines" of labor conflict within the plants would be more readily revealed. The plants are also located in two very different regions, the Donbass and the Kuzbass, which during the course of events examined here became part of different sovereign states.

The plants themselves are quite different as well. The Donetsk Metallurgical Factory (hereafter referred to by its Russian name, Donetskii) was established by John Hughes, a Welsh entrepreneur, in the late 1860s. The surrounding area was semiarid and largely unpopulated; the mining and mill town that rose along with the plant was named Iuzovka after its founder.[9] The Donetsk plant, like the other old plants in Ukraine, was rebuilt and enlarged during the Soviet era. By 1989 its workforce numbered more than 17,000, quite large by world standards, though not so in the Soviet Union.[10] As in many plants in Ukraine and Russia, open-hearth furnace production remains dominant at Donetskii; whereas in 1985 only 7 percent of U.S. steel was produced in open-hearth furnaces, and none in Japan and West Germany, the Soviet Union continued to rely on open-hearth furnaces for more than 50 percent of its steel production.[11]

The history of the second plant, the West Siberian Metallurgical Complex, is entirely different. Whereas blast furnaces have been fired at Donetskii for more than 120 years, West Siberian was constructed in the 1960s and 1970s, ranking it among a handful of "cutting edge" plants in the Soviet steel industry.[12] Steel at the complex is manufactured mainly in oxygen converters rather than through open-hearth casting. Overall, the plant enjoys a much higher level of mechanization of labor-intensive processes than most others in the former Soviet Union. With the Kuznetsk plant, built during the first five-year plans and located thirty kilometers away, it forms the largest steel-producing center east of the Urals, producing 90 percent of all steel in Siberia.[13] In 1991, the West Siberian Complex alone employed more than thirty-two thousand workers.

In their contrasts the two steel mills mirror the coal mining regions in which they are located. The history of coal mining and steelmaking is closely intertwined in the Donbass,[14] and time has taken its toll on both industries. The dwindling supply of high-quality coking coal in the Donbass, the reason for the steel industry's existence in the area, has forced Ukrainian plants to import coal from Siberia and elsewhere. The increasingly difficult situation in both industries has important implications for market reform in the region, a point not lost on the Donbass miners, as we have seen, and steelworkers, as we will see subsequently.

Similarly, the relative strengths of the West Siberian plant mirror the strengths of the Kuzbass coal industry: because the plant is one of the most modern plants in the industry, both management and workers perceive it to be in a strong position to compete under market conditions. Moreover, the harsh Siberian climate, its isolation and long distance from Moscow, and its very profitability have had strong effects on the political outlook of the workforce, as will be shown subsequently, just as was the case with the Kuzbass miners.

These strong contrasts—between size, age, technology, market position, region, and ultimately different states—should add strength to the conclusions drawn about the differences between steelworkers and coal miners.

The following case studies will be based in part on in-depth interviews with steelworkers in both regions, both worker-activists and workers met at random. However, since steelworkers did not strike and did not form their own independent organizations, opportunities for interviews were more limited than with miners. Therefore, the case studies will be largely based on a close reading of plant newspapers (*mnogotirazhniki*) during the two-year period surrounding the miners' strikes. Historically, these plant newspapers have been organs for the plant administration and the Communist Party and trade union committees, and as such have been of limited use to the researcher. Yet, as will be shown, the miners' strikes had a strong effect on these plants and, along with the greater political changes developing throughout the Soviet Union and its successor states, helped make the papers real forums for debate and even objects of conflict between management and the workforce. Further, a study of the record provided by these plant newspapers gives a unique opportunity for the micro-level study of large state enterprises in a vital sector of the economy during the transition from Soviet socialism to a destination as yet unknown.

The Soviet economy has been characterized as "a coal and steel economy,"[15] and the two industries remain closely linked in the former Soviet republics, as in the height of the industrial revolution. As with all Soviet industries, the steel industry consumed a large amount of raw materials, including one-quarter of all coal consumed each year in the Soviet Union.[16] Not only does the steel industry remain dependent on a constant supply of coal to maintain output; in addition, since the shutdown of a blast furnace due to lack of coking coal can have disastrous consequences, the coal strikes became a source of considerable concern within the steel plants.

In fact, the response to the miners' strikes from steel enterprises and their representatives was sharply critical and usually contained urgent demands for coal. Within a week after the first strike began, the regional newspaper, *Kuzbass,* reported that the strike committees had begun to receive telegrams from "dozens" of steel enterprises, appealing for the miners to return to work.[17] In an interesting twist on working-class rhetoric, they appealed to "working-class solidarity" in asking the miners to stop the strike. A telegram from the Zaporozhstal' Works said, "in the hope of proletarian solidarity, which has always been the basis of work and life of miners and steelworkers . . . we ask you to stop the strike and return to work, because otherwise the consequences will be workers left without pay, . . . the social program will not be fulfilled, which is directed above all at raising the living standards of workers" at the plant. And the STK of the Donetskii plant wrote to ask the miners to return to work because "the working class of steelworkers" would otherwise lose their pay.[18]

In early October, *Pravda* published an open letter from four Peoples' Deputies from the metallurgical industry, in which they told the miners,

> The labor of steelworkers is not easy either, and we understand better than others your desire for social protection and for justice. But we cannot agree with your chosen methods for obtaining these goals.

What has your general strike brought? Production and the economic bases of the coal industry have been undermined. An increasingly threatening situation now exists in the metallurgical industry.[19]

Such rhetoric was to continue throughout the period under examination. More than a year after the strike, metallurgical and coking plants were still blaming their own shortfalls on the strike.[20] When the nationwide strike in the coal industry was renewed in March 1991, there was a surge of reports in the central press about steelworkers' appeals to miners to return to work and about steel enterprises on the brink of being shut down.[21] Metallurgical plants sent personal representatives to the miners' strike committees to plead with them to supply their particular plants with coal.[22] The two steel plants examined in this chapter were each featured in front-page photographs in the central press during the strike as examples of workers continuing production despite the shortage of coal and the threat of a general strike.[23] These accounts suggest the paradox of miners choosing to stop production (and to accept the resulting sacrifices), while steelworkers were struggling to continue to work at all costs. At a lower level of analysis, however, the situation becomes more complex.

The First Strike

Only two days after the July 1989 strike reached the Donbass, workers in Donetskii's open-hearth shop, the oldest and most troubled shop in the plant, gathered for the elections of a new shop head, as stipulated under the Law on the State Enterprise. "But the discussion was not limited to elections alone," reported a plant correspondent. "The hot breath of the [coal] strike was felt in the steelworkers' speeches." Working with antiquated equipment, the shop was short of the plan from the beginning of the year by twenty-six thousand tons of steel. The "cadre problem"—the shortage of skilled workers—was a major concern, "and the problem of raw materials doesn't help either. From all this we get low pay, and then [more] people leave the shop" for work elsewhere. The discussion touched on "all this, and not only this." But the collective of the shop, "taking into account the specifics of production and the economic position of the country at present, declined to strike. Nevertheless, the steelworkers advanced a series of problems, demanding urgent solution." Throughout the miners' strike, "meetings were held in various shops several times" where "passions boiled."[24]

A general meeting of the plant held shortly after the miners' strike ended was said to be "sharply distinguished from previous" meetings, since a microphone was placed in the hall and "all felt equal participants in the dialogue." Some in the hall compared it to a session of the Supreme Soviet, whose televised proceedings coincided with the coal miners' strike. Yet despite "heated arguments" on many points, the plant's director remained in control of the meeting. He informed those gathered that the Ministry of Ferrous Metallurgy had already formed a commission to look into the problems of steel enterprises and that the plant's STK was "collecting information" from the shops. He emphasized that owing to the second model of self-financing (*khozraschet*), introduced at the first of the year, the plant had already been able to solve several of the demands raised by the miners, such as new piece rates and norms and additional pay for evening and night work, and was undertaking a program of "social reconstruction" which included the building of housing by the plant independently (*khozsposobim*), giving workers' families trips to the factory's vacation centers as well as to children's (pioneer) camps at no cost, and placing the workers' supply department (for food and consumer goods) under the plant's control.[25]

In all, sixty-four points were discussed at the three-hour meeting and were included in the demands sent to the Supreme Soviet, the Council of Ministers, the Ministry of Ferrous Metallurgy, and the Donetsk Communist Party obkom. Several of the demands were taken word for word from the protocol signed by the miners and the government commission, including the demand for "full enterprise independence"; other demands called on the ministry to supply the plant with electric furnaces and to increase the number of automobiles distributed to the plant's workers.[26]

At another meeting less than a month after the miners' strike began, however, plant director V. Slednev felt the situation to be sufficiently under control to lecture his workers. While acknowledging the validity of many demands, he asked rhetorically, "But what of the other side, where is the responsibility of the labor collective for the fulfillment of the obligations that have been placed upon it? We've learned so very well to make demands." He went on to say that unlike the last meeting, "this meeting will not be turned into a hearing for all these demands, into a night of questions and answers." He repeated management's familiar refrain—if workers worked hard and production problems were solved, workers' social needs would be taken care of.[27]

But others did not agree with placing production problems ahead of social needs. Before the strike, plant newspapers contained many, usually sunny, articles on topics seemingly unrelated to steel production, such as children's summer camps and workers' market gardens. In an article that appeared after the strike about the plant's day-care centers, the plant correspondent reversed the director's argument for solving production problems first:

> The miners' strike graphically demonstrated where bureaucratic, "paper" concern for the working person and his needs might lead. Social problems have everywhere come out into the forefront. . . . If a worker knows that all is well at the home front, if he is not losing his head over where to leave his child, over where to obtain foodstuffs, and over a mass of other such things, which are poisoning our life, then production will grow.[28]

Three months after the open-hearth shop elected a new boss, elected by 78 percent of the shop's workers amid talk of calling a strike, the boss resigned. He claimed the situation was out of his control. He mentioned "the neglect of discipline in the shop, people coming late to work and leaving early." He blamed this on the system of electing managers, which he called a "stupidity," as well as worker turnover, strikes, and "the sharp political situation in the country." As for talk of no strikes among steelworkers, he said the shop's crane operators "sat in one place for two hours" and refused to work.[29] The contradictions between the tough, confident director and the lack of control on the shop floor would continue to grow.

Contrary to some notions of labor conflict, at West Siberian, a more profitable plant with newer, less labor-intensive technology, conflict was greater and more open than at Donetskii. In fact, the complex experienced strikes several months before the July miners' strike, leading some to suggest that the publicity given the strikes may have encouraged the Kuzbass miners in their mass walkouts.[30] The strike was led by an independent "contract brigade," which would have been paid handsomely for fulfilling its norm, but was unable to do so because of the lack of materials. Yet the demands quickly went beyond norms and supplies to questioning why certain categories of workers had rights to additional holiday pay while other workers did not. Criticism also included the formal democratic structures within the enterprise. One woman stated, "I've tried more than once to speak up at meetings, at plant conferences. But as a rule, in the shop, they don't let many of us speak."[31]

Some 238 workers in the shop signed the demands leading to the strike. "Those who had courage signed the letter," said the STK chair of brigade number four. "On the twenty-eighth [of February] I stood up and declared a strike, not because we didn't want to work, but because our pay doesn't correspond to our productivity."[32] When the administration argued about the economic damage the strike caused, one worker retorted, "Three hours is not so long. We stop at other times for longer because we don't have supplies."[33] This strike was followed a month later by another in a different shop with almost identical demands. One local journalist explained these strikes by suggesting that perestroika encouraged workers to take part in plant decision making. "We've summoned the people to activism, and their activism has increased. . . . workers today are fully interested in the economics of production, they want full information about it."[34] This was echoed in one worker's thoughts about the strike:

> This commotion is because we are economically illiterate people. Before perestroika we had no economic information. They tightened the screws and no one thought anything about it. Even now the information is not sufficient. Why did they demand that only thirty percent of the plant's profits [be withheld from the ministry], why not fifty or seventy percent? And maybe, we shouldn't give the ministry anything at all, if this is really *khozraschet.*"[35]

The administration's position, as characterized by the local journalist, was a traditional one: If you want to increase the money the plant has at its disposal, you have to increase productivity. To this workers were said to retort, "How can we do that when the equipment long ago became old, its potential exhausted? There remains only one option—to intensify human labor."[36]

Such were the sentiments of at least part of the workforce at West Siberian four months before the coal miners walked out. Still one month before the miners' strike, workers in the rail transport shop presented demands to the administration, including additional pay for evening and night shifts, an increase in the regional wage coefficient, reductions in the number of managerial personnel—all very similar to the demands the miners were to present. And "to accelerate the resolution of the demands and to not allow them to be shelved," workers in the shop formed an "initiative group."[37]

When the coal strike broke out in full in the Kuzbass, an extraordinary session of the "party-economic *aktiv*" (essentially a party-management committee) took place at the West Siberian plant; it passed a resolution (in language almost identical to that to be used at the Donetsk plant and elsewhere) stating that "we support the demands, but reject the strike as a method." The general director (as at Donetskii) was the first to address the meeting and told of miners who had come to the plant to inspect the plant's coal reserves, but instead, according to the director, held a discussion with him about the plant's successful program of social-cultural and living services (*sotskul'tbyt*).[38]

Soon thereafter, on July 18, the plant's administration, STK, and Party, trade union, and Komsomol committees published an open letter in the plant's newspaper "to the working people of the combine": "Today, from information in our possession, it is known that certain workers of the plant are speaking out, and what is more, taking measures for the organization of strikes in the subdivisions," including "the formation of shop 'strike committees.'" The letter warned that just as the collective was earning, with "conscientious labor," the means "for solving, in the first place, programs for housing, foodstuffs, raising the material stimulation of labor, all our plans might be ruined in the case of a stoppage of the plant or some of its subdivisions. . . . [A]re those who are leading the discussions with the goal of a 'general strike' at West Siberian acting responsibly?" The letter went on to announce that the party-economic *aktiv* had elected a committee, "called not a strike committee, but a workers' committee," to more responsibly gather the demands of workers at the plant.[39]

Thus, as happened at quite a few other steel enterprises, a "workers' committee" was set up by managers, rather clearly with the goal of extracting concessions from the Ministry of Ferrous Metallurgy. This committee met with similar groups from the three other metallurgical plants in the city (the thirty-two thousand-worker Kuznetskii Metallurgical Complex, an aluminum plant, and a ferrous metallurgical plant) to present demands to the government commission and their ministry.[40]

The authority of the workers' committee was challenged, however. Workers in several shops formed an alternative committee, since they believed that the steelworkers "had not supported the miners, had not shown solidarity."[41] This committee was called unlawful by the official workers' committee, but an election was held at a factory conference to decide the issue. Platforms of both committees were published in the plant newspaper, though the plant's deputy Party chair, sharply critical of the alternative committee, provided the only commentary. The official committee called itself "extraordinary and temporary," created as an alternative to the trade union and STK, since these "legal organs . . . do not enjoy the necessary level of support from the workers." The workers' committee proposed to disband when these organs had undergone reelection.

The alternative committee, on the other hand, saw itself as a permanent organ, based upon workers' committees in the shops, which would be given access to information, such as norming documents; would have its own specialists; would participate in elections for shop bosses and local soviets; would organize meetings, demonstrations, and strikes (including "solidarity strikes"); would demand access to local press and radio; and would work with the city and regional strike committees and other organs to, among other things, "observe the principle of equality and justice in the distribution of material goods."[42]

The alternative committee fought to have the election take place in the shops, where each working person in the plant would vote, rather than by delegates at a conference, because "only the administration's yes-men (*ugodniki*) will end up at such a conference, and the work of the committee will be ruined." But the election did take place at such a conference, and there the official committee, a month and a half after presenting demands in the name of the labor collective, received its mandate.[43]

While neither West Siberian nor Donetskii nor any other major industrial plant struck along with the miners in July 1989, these plants hardly were without conflict of their own. Clearly, in contrast to the coal mines, the administration retained the upper hand in steel and other plants, but how they managed to do so remains at question. The explanation given most often by the participants themselves—whether members of the plants' administration, trade union or STK officials, or worker-activists who were in favor of a strike—has to do with the role these enterprises play not only in producing steel, but also in reproducing the labor force. It is the role of these enterprises in solving the "social problems" of its workforce to which we will now turn.

Enterprise Dependence

The Soviet industrial enterprise, in the face of shortages of consumer goods and services, as well as shortages of labor, developed a range of services that it provided to its workforce, from housing to food. At the Donetsk plant, as with many others, the factory provided vacations at its centers on the Azov Sea and elsewhere and had a close relationship with a state farm to which it provided "seasonal workers" and material inputs in exchange for foodstuffs. The plant also had a shop for subsidiary agriculture, which, among other things, asked steelworkers to take in pigs for eight months for fattening. The enterprise also distributed such scarce durable goods as automobiles. By providing nurseries and day care for workers' children and payments for workers' funerals, the plant's services quite literally extended from cradle to grave.[44]

The plant provides much of the services to the borough, including housing and transportation to and from work, so much so that the plant's general director, it was argued, should be elected to the Ukrainian Congress of People's Deputies from the borough. In nominating Director Slednev, his deputy argued that it was time to recognize the significance of the factory, since "without the factory the borough's dwellers would not be able to live normally. See for yourself: every second day-care center in the borough belongs to the factory, half of the dwellers depend on the plant's stores."[45] Slednev, easily making the transition from industrial manager to political candidate, promised that if candidates from the "steelworkers' bloc" were elected to the *raion* soviet, the plant would build a children's amusement park around the "Steelworker" stadium.[46]

About five months after the first coal miners' strike, the director at Donetskii reflected on why steelworkers had remained at work. The economic and financial position of the plant allowed for the solution of a series of problems, including a 100-ruble payment to single mothers, free food to certain categories of workers, aid to labor veterans on pension, a free vacation or monetary aid to large families once every three years, additional bonuses both to workers in the plant cafeterias (for quality food preparation) and to the plant's subsidiary agriculture shop, which over-fulfilled the plan for pork by 120 tons. The sphere of social services was continuing to grow, as there were plans for a shop for smoking meats, another shop for meat products, construction of greenhouses for vegetables, and contracts with Hungarian and other foreign firms for the provision (through barter) of shoes, clothes, stereos, cars. "In a short interview I can't talk about everything. . . ." said the director.[47]

Yet there were clear signs that the situation was not quite so harmonious. "It is no accident," one worker stated, "that the demands of steelworkers directed to the higher levels of power, gave great attention to questions . . . in the social sphere, whose development until recently was carried out on the principle of whatever is left over." The social sphere concerned "not only pay. It includes also the housing problem, transportation, the satisfaction of the needs of working people in day-care, and much more."[48]

At West Siberian, the dependence of the workforce on the enterprise's goods and services was even greater. The plant's location, far from Moscow and in harsh Siberia, made the alternatives that much starker. At the same time, these conditions increased the problem of attracting and retaining workers. Moreover, the plant, with thirty-two thousand employees, was twice the size of Donetskii, and its newness and relative profitability left greater resources at its disposal. If the Donetsk plant, the biggest in the city, had dominated the borough in which it was situated, with half the residents connected in some way to the plant, the West Siberian plant had an entire borough to itself—unimaginatively named "Factory Borough."

The plant sent 110 workers a day, at full pay, to patrol the borough streets with the militia. The plant controlled several vacation centers and eight pioneer camps, as far away as Alma-Ata and Crimea. The plant had its own state farm, to which various shops sent workers to help with harvests and to which the plant sent gas, oil, and other materials.[49] This farm was apparently insufficient to feed the workforce, so the plant set up a rabbit farm and an aquaculture program. The entire operation was supervised by the steel plant's "deputy director for agriculture." To continue the process of food production, the plant contracted with the Moscow engineering cooperative Progress to build a shop for producing sausage and other meat products at the plant. In addition to the plant cafeterias, which provided workers with their main meal of the day at subsidized prices, the plant had twelve stores for selling foodstuffs inside the production shops and two more selling consumer goods. (They were expanded to nineteen in 1991, with six more at the plant's stadium "West Siberian.")[50] The factory's "workers' control" organization inspected and conducted "raids" on the cafeterias and distribution points to prevent pilfering.

Oddly enough, in preparing for the coming market economy, the plant—one of the newest and strongest in the industry—began to devote more and more attention to activities outside of steel production. In 1990, it contracted with a Turkish firm to construct a surgical wing for Hospital No. 29. With the help of a German company and a Yugoslavian construction team, the plant began building a furniture factory inside the steel complex. With three shops, including a sawmill, the volume of production was projected to be equal to that of the largest factory associations and to produce two and one-half times more than all the furniture factories in the Kemerovo region. "We will fight so that first our workers will receive furniture, then people of the borough, then the city, the region, then all of Siberia," said the shop boss.[51] In July 1990 a plant journalist wrote that "the production of consumer goods is occupying an ever larger place in our plant's activities." The plant opened a shop for the repair of computers and the preparation and assembly of electronic devices, including VCRs. "This year the shop will produce 10,000 VCRs, and the next year 20,000."[52]

The plant's general director, B. Kustov, in presenting his program for the steel complex "in the conditions of transferring to market relations," informed his workforce (also sounding like a politician), "A person cannot live with only steel, rolled metal and iron. That is why this program begins with the solution of social problems." Among other plans, he discussed West Siberian's investment in a series of joint ventures that would provide linoleum, car tires, and trucks for personal use, as well as radios, tape players, and videocassettes. "And West Siberian workers will be able to buy these goods."[53] Besides furniture and VCRs, the plant intended to produce televisions (with Japanese tubes and Soviet housings); in addition to linoleum, the plant would produce cinder blocks and even set up a paint canning operation.

As time went on (and under pressure from the workforce, as we shall see) the plant newspaper began to print more and more information about the distribution of consumer goods and vacation trips. A single trade department was formed to handle the distribution of the many consumer goods "more responsibly." In one such instance, under the heading "The Trade Department Informs," it was announced that, in the first half of October, the department received 400 pairs of winter boots, 979 pairs of fall boots, 628 VCRs, 256 videocassettes, 100 boxes of tobacco products, 315 kilograms of macaroni, 7,990 kilograms of cheese, 19,800 cans of meat, 8,974 kilograms of chicken, 20 tons of meat products, 467 tons of beef, 28,000 cans of meat stew, 1,400 bottles of alcohol products, and 1 ton of coal.[54]

In all this, talk of investment to increase steel production—the plant's reason for being, after all—was largely absent, though it would seem all the more compelling under market conditions. But Director Kustov told his employees not to fear, for the plant's paternalistic policies would continue under the market. "Many are afraid of the market, understanding that unprofitable production means they could lose their jobs. But within our wide social program there is something to offer both workers and engineers (ITRs) in the case of [staff] reductions. We have furniture production, a linoleum plant and more. So unemployment won't threaten us."[55]

Divisions

In listing all the characteristics of the social infrastructure at these enterprises, one creates the impression that every worker under the wings of the enterprise has been quite well provided for. But given the enormous size of the workforces involved—seventeen thousand in the case of Donetskii, thirty-two thousand at West Siberian—the benefits seem rather less imposing on a per capita basis. More important, these benefits were not distributed equally, and therein lies a major source of conflict within the enterprise, one that workers challenged when they found greater political opportunity to do so.

Enterprise paternalism in the Soviet Union has been closely related to the labor shortage—privileges are distributed very unevenly, above all to keep skilled workers at the plant.

Questions from the workforce about the politics of distribution arose quite early on, even before the first small strikes at West Siberian. The plant newspaper, on the eve of the first strike, sought to justify this uneven distribution in the following terms:

It seems that it is a secret to no one that at the complex workers of certain professions enjoy privileges—including machine toolers, wire-drawers, pipe fitters, mechanics, . . . Among the privileges is the distribution of apartments. Of course apartments can be received [in this way] only by *peredoviki* [exemplary workers]. At first glance it might seem that machine tool operators, pipe fitters, and others don't deserve such status. But that's only at first glance. Five to ten years is needed to prepare a skilled machine tool operator. Given the deficit of machine tool operators it's impossible to carry out . . . capital repairs of equipment. Or take pipe fitters, whose labor conditions do not bear any criticism. So the STK adopted a just decision: to give apartments to representatives of deficit professions.[56]

Such justifications were not accepted uncritically by the rest of the workforce. When the strike in the contract brigade broke out a month later over a lack of supplies, the demands immediately spilled over to the unequal distribution of vacation time.[57] And despite entreaties that pay and privileges should correspond to the demand for one's skills on a labor market, many workers argued that pay should correspond to labor conditions and intensity rather than skill. One worker involved in the strike complained of differences between two shops. Of one shop she said, "work there is much simpler—the intensity [of work between the shops] is different but the pay is the same." Another woman protested, "There's a discrepancy with vacations. For example, a packing machine operator and a stamper work in absolutely the same conditions, but the length of vacations is different."[58]

At the same time, differences in pay between workers and ITRs in the shop (322 rubles per month in 1989 for the former, 497 for the latter) did not go unnoticed. "Workers are bothered by this difference," wrote one local journalist. "Reworking of rates has the goal of giving skilled labor more earnings." Responded one metal cutter, "That's fine, but they have to earn it."[59]

The divisions were not simply between skilled and unskilled workers, but were part of a hierarchy that existed throughout the plants. If skilled workers were privileged because of the need to retain them, service workers, peripheral to production, were practically ignored. This treatment concerned, above all, women. According to the director of food services at West Siberian, the cafeterias were suffering due to an acute shortage of workers. "We are now short 100 people out of 280. . . . They've just taken sixty away to work in the pioneer camps. The position is especially critical with cooks, who are leaving because of low pay and especially difficult work, both physically and morally." Skilled cooks were leaving the kitchens to work in steel production, where the shop bosses, themselves short of workers, were reluctant to let them return to their former jobs.[60] When cafeteria workers asked to be given additional vacation time as a means of making the work more attractive, they were told that according to a Council of Ministers resolution, additional holiday time was given only to production workers, "to prevent turnover" (*zakrepit' kadrov*).[61]

The uneven distribution went far beyond pay and pensions to include, among other things, such durable goods as automobiles. While two thousand people were "on line" for cars at Donetskii in August 1990, the forty-eight cars received that month were distributed to "exemplary workers, war veterans, veterans of labor."[62]

The second model of *khozraschet*, a further step toward the market, not only decentralized some decision-making power from the ministry to the enterprise, but also made each subunit "economically accountable." As a result, pay and conditions began to vary widely between shops, with some of the more disadvantaged shops seemingly left on their own. In short, divisions were created not only between workers of different occupations, but between shops as well.

For example, while pay for food workers was generally half of the average for production workers (which was 322 rubles in 1989 at Donetskii), the level varied greatly. With economic reform, different production shops were free to pay their own cafeteria workers more for better food preparation in order to in turn help retain their own skilled production workers. (The average pay for cafeteria workers varied from 126 rubles a month in cafeteria number 29 to 200 rubles in cafeterias 9 and 16.)

By far the shop in the worst position at Donetskii was the open-hearth shop, a technology now rarely used in the West. As already mentioned, the July 1989 miners' strike brought the open-hearth shop very close to a strike itself. "The problems of the open-hearth shop are no secret to the people in our plant," the factory paper reported. The situation in the shop became so critical that workers in other shops were asked by the administration to "render aid" to the open-hearth workers, to increase their pay, as if they were a third world country.[63]

Once the euphoria of the first miners' strike died down, the plant's managers sought to regain their authority over the shop. Workers were blamed for the shortcomings, their efforts described as lazy, and they were deprived of their "thirteenth month" bonus and their payment for years of service (*vyslugi let*).[64] Interestingly, the director blamed the shop trade union for not "bringing anyone to account" for "violations of order, technology and discipline," while others spoke of the open-hearth shop "electing those who won't punish them."[65]

Not surprisingly, the workers of the shop had a different perspective on the matter. One steel founder argued that not one brigade in the shop was able to fulfill the plan due to "the poor organization of work, when, as it happens, you show up for work, and sit with nothing to do—there's no raw materials, no refractory materials, no molds. The equipment is bad, the personnel problem has not been solved. Steel founders are leaving to work in cooperatives! And they're sending us unprepared replacements—from this comes our misfortune."[66]

Indeed, while the management stressed the "human factor" as the cause of the shop's problems, workers spoke of shortages, both of materials and of workers. "There aren't enough machinists, young workers just aren't staying here."[67]

Turnover

Almost a year after the proposal to "render aid" to the open-hearth shop, the plant's STK met to discuss "measures for the reduction of turnover in the shop." The discussion that followed revealed the interrelation of production, turnover, and "social problems." Rather than turnover, "the discussion in the hall began with a no less important problem today, and one, unfortunately, very interconnected, as open-hearth workers more than once underlined, with the worsening of production in the shop. This is the housing problem." According to the steelworkers, "people are leaving production [work] because of the absence of housing, [since] the line at the factory stands for fifteen to seventeen years." The acting head of the shop (a permanent replacement still had not been found one year after the old boss resigned) announced that "of 228 people who came to work at the shop in the last year, only 159 remain." The problem "is in all specialties. The managerial staff is almost nonexistent. There are no foremen, we have no experienced workers in the shop. . . . Now there are some materials, but no one to work them. By the way, open-hearth is the basis of metallurgical production."[68] When the acting head introduced a proposal to give steel founders and assistant steel founders housing before others, so they would receive it in five years, the meeting grew heated. The STK decided, after sharp discussion, to help the shop, since, while "housing, undoubtedly, isn't the only cause [of the shop's problem], it's one of the main problems."[69]

Others confirmed the connection of "social problems" with retaining workers at the plant. The deputy secretary of the Komsomol, in charge of youth questions, asked, "How can we attract young people to the factory, if in the co-ops pay is higher, and the work conditions better? A powerful social policy—there's our trump card. But what do young people see? How are social problems being solved? The wait for an apartment is twelve years at least."[70]

In the Kuzbass, as with Siberia generally, the situation with regard to the "cadre question" was more difficult. The problem of attracting labor to Siberia and the Far North was of long standing, one that was solved for many years by exiling convicts. (Such practices still continued, as was evidenced by one of the demands sent to central authorities in the name of Novokuznetsk steelworkers at the time of the July 1989 miners' strike. Demand number 32 read in part: "Stop the transformation of the Kuzbass into a place of exile for those released from prison . . . and stop solving the problem of the Kuzbass's labor resources at the expense of the convicted."[71])

Yet at first glance it appeared that at West Siberian, with all its resources, the labor shortage was somewhat less severe than at Donetskii. A month prior to the first miners' strike, workers at West Siberian were complaining about "reductions" of certain workers. The rail transport workers, who had formed an initiative group to push their demands, complained that train compilers, assistant machinists, switchmen, and train engineers had all been cut back. Ironically, they complained that they could not take their section on lease-holding, as reformers were asking workers to do, because there were not enough train engineers.[72]

Indeed, it is likely that the "reduced" workers simply were transferred to another part of the plant. In 1989, the plant was said to be short 1,640 workers, primarily fitters, electricians, welders, machinists, and train compilers, the last group among those that had been "reduced" in the rail transport shop.[73] One year later, the city as a whole was said to have eighteen thousand vacant work positions. The plant newspaper reported that 360 Vietnamese "guest workers" had been at the plant for the last three years, with many more Vietnamese in mines and other enterprises throughout the region.[74]

While both steel plants suffered from the shortage of workers, the two plants responded in ways that reflected their different strengths and weaknesses, as well as those of the regions in which they were located. During the second miners' strike of March–April 1991, the Donetsk plant joined others in the steel industry in signing an appeal to Prime Minister Pavlov warning of the "explosive situation" occurring in the "coal-coke-steel" industries. Due to

> unregulated growth in prices, inflation, the sharp deficit of food and consumer goods, living standards are sharply dropping for workers of those branches that make up the basis of our country's economy. . . . This leads to turnover and consequently a shortage of workers of basic professions. If you don't raise pay immediately, there will be demonstrations and strikes.[75]

While Donetskii and other unprofitable plants appealed to the prime minister for more funds, West Siberian, along with the Kuzbass miners, pleaded for greater independence. When President Gorbachev issued a decree limiting the use of hard currency received by enterprises as of 1991, the chair of West Siberian's STK sent a telegram to the president arguing that the government was trying to place the burden of economic reform on the "shoulders of the labor collectives," since hard currency resources were used by steelworkers to close gaps in production "and also for the carrying out of the enterprise's social policy for the minimal reduction of turnover by means of acquiring imported goods." "We will defend our freedom to cut barter deals," said the deputy director for economics. "There's no other way. We are forced to trade metal for foodstuffs: meat, fruit, canned goods."[76]

Housing

One of the scarcest goods in the former Soviet Union was housing, a source of great conflict throughout society. Since the industrial enterprise has been the largest source of housing in many cities, it is not surprising that the distribution of housing caused much conflict within the enterprise. Moreover, the distribution of housing provides the greatest single example of the interrelationship of enterprise dependence, management's battle with turnover, and the divisions among workers such distribution created.

On the wave of the first miners' strike, for example, families living in the plant dormitories protested the provision of plant housing to *peredoviki* (exemplary workers), rather than to them (the most needy group).[77] The enterprise and the city government also conflicted over housing distribution. Members of the Donetsk plant's STK blamed the city council for favoring the miners since their strike in the distribution of housing, though, they argued, "the labor of steelworkers, although not underground, deserves the same privileged conditions in this problem. The miners have their decree No. 608. Should it really be fulfilled at the expense of steelworkers?"[78] The plant's STK chair, joined by other representatives of the Donetsk oblast, sent an appeal to deputy prime minister Ryabaev, in charge of fulfilling the miners' decree No. 608, with the demand to solve steelworkers' problems. The representatives warned the minister: "The mood to solve the problems of steelworkers in the same way as the miners—by strikes—is ripening," since the government was solving "the social problems of the miners at the expense of other categories of working people, including steelworkers. We are talking about housing, pensions, and other social goods."[79]

West Siberian, with its stronger economic position, was less dependent on local government for its housing stock but had ample problems of its own. The plant's housing-communal administration was said to hold 345 apartment buildings, with more than 960,000 square meters.[80]

Such a seemingly large amount of housing did not prevent sharp conflicts over its distribution. Some three months after the miners' strike first exploded in the Kuzbass, the plant's trade union held a conference of record length—14 hours—focused especially on the housing problem. Thousands remained on a line that was growing every year. One approach taken by the plant was the construction of individual houses by plant workers, to take some of the edge off the problem. But in order to insure the sufficient provision of materials, it was suggested that the plant build a shop for brick production and that necessary steps be taken to see that such houses would be provided with plumbing and electricity. The trade union conference also struggled with the question of a single line for the distribution of housing. But the debate dragged on so long that a formal decision could not be reached.[81]

Nevertheless, "delegates turned down the proposal of the administration for the provision of apartments on a privileged basis to certain categories of workers, with the goal of keeping them at the plant. The conference proposed seeking other means for this."[82]

As the trade union chair explained the situation, the Russian Housing Code allowed for a privileged list for provision of housing to "exemplary production workers," but in violation of the legislation, the plant began in 1981 to solve the labor shortage by means of additional privileges in the allotment of housing.[83] "This brought forth completely well-grounded questions from the plants' workers. Why does belonging to a certain profession (machine tool operator, wire drawer, metal worker) become the basis for receiving an apartment outside the line? Why are rollers, steel founders, and members of other professions worse?"[84] Yet many workers objected to the idea of rewarding management-defined "exemplary workers" and fought for a single line for housing. For if the distribution of housing was connected in the eyes of management with turnover, it was connected in the eyes of the workforce with social justice. And for most, social justice meant distribution according to a single line, rather than according to one's position in the labor market or one's status as a *peredoviki*. One article in the plant newspaper began, "Housing—a worn, painful theme. Fewer and fewer apartments are being given out every year, and the line becomes longer and longer." Some ten thousand workers were in line to improve their living conditions, the article reported. Two people had first requested an apartment in 1968, 10 in 1970–72, 11 in 1973, and 21 in 1974, all waiting because they had not been on a priority list for apartments. "Only a year or two ago, when people first began to speak of a single line, the idea seemed absurd. . . . But now the work's done (it took over three months to compile the list) and it's already clear that the principle of such a line is quite simple."[85]

Some were opposed to the single list, the plant journalist argued, especially those in new shops where one could receive an apartment much faster. "But is this just? Every person has a right to normal housing. We're all equal under the law. Is it really just that some get apartments, having waited in line for five to seven years, while others have waited ten to fifteen years and still don't see light at the end of the tunnel?"[86]

A trade union chair from another shop wrote an article in the plant paper entitled "A General Line Is Social Justice." While every third worker at the plant was said to need improved living conditions, workers were responding variously to the single-line proposal.

> Workers in the new shops are against the general line more than anyone. As is our custom, when starting up a shop, "well here, please, take an apartment." . . . I personally doubt that all the people that are receiving apartments during the start-up of a shop remain as workers at the plant. . . . Let's find a new means of incentive, reward, stimulation, etc. [of labor], and leave housing for those who really dedicate themselves to West Siberian.[87]

Once again, if workers in certain skilled professions and those working in new shops received privileges in housing, as with other goods, workers in the plant's large service sphere, being peripheral to production, were largely ignored. A worker from the housing-communal administration (ZhKU), composed almost exclusively of women in charge of cleaning and maintaining the plant's housing stock, wrote to the plant paper that while 697 workers in the ZhKU were waiting in line, in the last three years the ZhKU had been given only three apartments.

> The workers of the ZhKU don't deserve to be forgotten. They, though not working in production, do necessary and difficult work. They maintain West Siberian's housing fund, do sanitary work in the basements of dilapidated buildings. It's the hands of women in yellow jackets that keep the streets clean. . . . It's hard, unmechanized labor, the manual lifting of garbage and leaves, working on the streets in heat and cold for miserly pay.[88]

"People work for the sake of housing, even if only temporary, service [*sluzhebniye*] housing," said the ZhKU's trade union chair. "If there's no housing soon, no one will work here." According to the worker, "the single line is just, so that normal housing is given to both janitors and metallurgists. The single line gives workers of the ZhKU the possibility to receive housing equally with workers of all shops of the combine. People are waiting for social justice."[89]

Ironically, as with enterprises' social services generally, the steps being taken toward market reform did not alleviate the housing problem, but rather aggravated it; the greater independence of industrial factories and local governments from Moscow's tutelage did not lessen the factories' position as suppliers of housing, but rather strengthened it.

Because the state construction industry was short of bricks, other materials, and "catastrophically short of construction workers," the West Siberian plant formed its own construction unit (SMU) to fulfill the plant's housing plan with only the plant's funds (*khozsposobim*). According to the chief engineer, three hundred workers were now in the SMU, and "the only thing that will keep them (*zakrepit'*) is housing." He proposed that 10 percent of all housing built by the group be given to its workers. Then "the inflow of labor will allow a yearly increase in the tempo of construction."[90]

Yet by the end of 1990, a year later, West Siberian's general director Kustov, in presenting his program for "how we will live tomorrow . . . in conditions of the approaching market," first focused his attention "on the most sore point—housing." The plant's attempt to avoid the city government's housing system by building housing through self-financing had failed. "We build more and more housing through self-financing, and the construction workers keep more and more for themselves. They've built all of one building. Therefore, we've decided to create our own construction firm on plant territory, so we won't be dependent on anyone." According to the plant's economic director, "The city construction agencies have weakened and fallen apart, so we, having invested 2.5 million rubles, organized the construction firm 'Siberia.' We will build housing with the help of foreigners."[91]

Unquestionably, managers of these steel plants controlled vast resources on which their work forces relied. These resources were sought by management in large part to prevent workers from taking advantage of their one strength—leaving for a better job in a labor-short economy. Yet such individual level strategies were clearly limited in their ability to improve one's position: it simply exchanged one dependent position for a slightly better one. Undoubtedly, steelworkers would benefit from the ability to act collectively; but workers were hampered in that they lacked organizations that might enable them to do so. Why were existing workers' organizations, such the enterprise trade unions, so ineffective in counterbalancing, at least in part, the power of management? And how can the dependence on the enterprise discussed here explain why strikes and other collective actions did not happen in one industry, but did in another? It is these questions we turn to in the following chapter.

CHAPTER 4

Steelworkers, Workers' Organizations, and Collective Action

Why were existing worker organizations in the steel plants a hindrance rather than a help to workers' collective action? And how might these worker organizations, together with other elements of what we have called mutual dependence, account for strikes in coal, but not in steel? This chapter will address these questions in turn.

In theory, workers had an array of organizations that were charged with defending workers' rights. Besides the Communist Party, they were represented by the trade union and the Council of the Labor Collective (STK). After the strikes, workers were also represented by so-called workers' committees. Yet most often, these groups were seen by workers as part of the problem rather than its solution.

The striking feature of the enterprise Communist Party organizations during this period is how little they seemed to matter to the life of the collective as they withered and disappeared. Though Party activists continued to participate in plant meetings, the Party organization itself began to withdraw quietly into the background at Donetskii, while it was placed on the defensive at West Siberian, as the Kuzbass miners, among others, began calling for removal of the Communist Party from all enterprises.

At West Siberian, the question, "What does the Party do at the plant?" was increasingly raised. In answer, one former member sarcastically cited hay making, harvesting vegetables, and repairing houses. The Party found itself in an increasingly defensive position and printed articles in the paper with such titles as, "With Whom Is the Party Interfering?" and "Communism—It's Not a Pejorative."[1]

Toward the end of 1990, as miners began kicking Communist Party organizations out of mines, the question of the Party's existence was debated at the labor collective conference that "had no end." The subject had created stormy debates before, and "in a series of shops at worker meetings the demand was raised to remove the party from the complex." The debate at the conference was said to be hot, with all the speeches, both pro and con, extremely emotional. "The line to the microphone standing in the hall did not shorten." Communists were called parasites and spongers—epithets used by the Bolsheviks for the previous ruling class—and it was said that "they enjoy all kinds of goods, they grab, they steal everything for themselves." The representative of the foundry shop announced that "the founderers at a meeting voted by absolute majority for the party to be removed from the plant." Others called for "the full depoliticization of production" and "forbid[ing] the carrying out of political acts at the complex." The Party secretary for the plant defensively answered the question of what the party had done at West Siberian: the provision of foodstuffs, work on the plant's vacation centers, the construction of housing and of new shops producing consumer goods. In the end, the Party secretary succeeded in putting off the question until the adoption of the constitution of the Russian Federation, which was to decide the question.[2]

The Labor Collective Councils (STKs)

The Communist Party was not the only organization forced to justify itself in the face of the miners' strikes and wider political change. The STKs, intended to increase workers' self-management, were also called into question. They were exposed in both mines and steel plants as organizations unprepared to defend workers' interests and as not enjoying the trust of those who had elected them.

As to the nature of past elections, the STK chair at Donetskii argued, "Given the recent strikes, the STK should become a real organization. It should be 80 percent workers, no less, representing all the shops and services. Elections will be conducted not by already compiled lists [of candidates], but with alternatives." Elsewhere it was promised that electing would take place "on an alternative basis, without the *vydvizhentsi*"—workers promoted by management to administrative posts.[3]

But for some workers, elections "on an alternative basis" were not sufficient. Objections were raised that the process of indirect elections allowed much manipulation by the administration. Representatives from the blooming mill shop wrote an open letter to the collective, arguing that:

1) Elections for the STK—the factory's parliament—should be direct, and not multi-stage, when first electors are chosen, then members of the STK, and then the STK chair; 2) only those people, who are well known by those voting, have a right to be elected . . . Since there is not enough information on each concrete candidate, it ends up like lotto.[4]

In the end the STK was elected in the old way, though it was promised that the STK would be "principally new in character," and the director vowed that it would not be "a collegial organ of the plant's administration" as in the past.[5]

At Western Siberia the STK was also struggling for legitimacy. According to one member of the council, "Our problem is that we are adopting decisions which are not supported in our collectives. People don't support us." Even before the miners' strike, STK members were self-critical, with one member stating, "With many problems people go to the general director, avoiding us." It was said that among workers of the plant the "reasonable question is arising of 'what does the STK do?'"[6]

Indeed, at both plants the STK was having difficulty, not only for being undemocratic and ineffectual, but in defining a mission for itself. In particular, the question was asked why the STK was needed when there was already a trade union. As for the STK itself, its task as defined by law and as interpreted by council members was to work with management to increase production and therefore increase the plant's income, which it would then help distribute. At Donetskii, working with management on production questions included punishing workers. At one meeting, the STK chair criticized the "irresponsibility" of the STKs in the shops, which

> didn't punish workers for costly mistakes. During last year alone there were eleven accidents in the plant, with losses of 346 thousand rubles. Of 729 cases of violations of production and technological discipline, there were all of four disciplinary penalties, 127 cases of deprivation of bonuses, and not a single case of indemnity for material losses.[7]

But if the STK was unsuccessful in applying the stick, it spent most of its time holding out the carrot or, in the parlance of the Soviet enterprise, on social problems. The Donetskii chair claimed that because of the ineffectual work of the trade union, "the STK was forced to occupy itself with problems that were not its own. In particular, there were many appeals for the allotting of cars, apartments, etc." At West Siberian, the STK had worked on such questions from its inception. Before the first miners' strike, the STK's most contentious meeting occurred when it was called on to ratify the lists of those on line for housing. Several months later, in his speech accounting for the STK's activities for the past three years, the STK chair at West Siberian first spoke of "one of the most acute and important problems—that of the social development of the complex, including the construction of housing, social-cultural and consumer (*sotskult'byt*) institutions, work on vacation centers, widening the sale of consumer goods at the plant." The chair spent eight paragraphs of his speech on the housing program, then went on to food ("the next very important program"), and then other distribution problems. He added, finally, "we don't have time to list all the problems handled by the STK, but we've counted fifty-seven."[8]

Indeed, at a typical meeting of the STK in one shop at West Siberian, the items on the agenda were the distribution of housing, the distribution of cars, and the plant's service for repairing workers' cars. However, at the same meeting there were many criticisms leveled at the STK, including that it had "no glasnost" and that its members "don't account for themselves before the collective." At the meeting, a member of the workers' committee was elected to chair the shop STK.[9]

By January 1990, six months after the coal miners first walked out, increases in the prices of transportation, heat, and energy placed the Donetskii and many older steel plants in a crisis situation.[10] (That West Siberian as a newer plant seemed unaffected and unconcerned by these changes is yet another indication of how different these two plants are.) A meeting of the STK discussed the difficulties of the plant. As explained by the STK chair of one department, given the new prices for inputs,

> the level of our pay is remaining the same, but the fund for social development is decreasing. That means that the line for housing will get still longer by several years, the number of vacation trips will become less, there will be less means to allot for day care and school institutions. Maybe there is reason for a warning strike.[11]

Others at the STK meeting also supported a strike. However, the discussion was not simply between elected representatives of the workforce. Two members of the Communist Party committee, present at the meeting, spoke out against the strike, as did the general director, saying a strike would be a "crime against future generations." "Thus while some saw the solution to the crisis in a strike," the majority voted against the strike as "an extremely dangerous measure." Instead it was decided to hold a demonstration and to dispatch representatives to Moscow.[12]

Conflicts continued to arise within the STK. For instance, at a meeting of the labor collective in one shop, many questions were raised about the shop's STK: "It's existed for two years now, but what has it really given the labor collective?"[13] A proposal was raised to strengthen the contacts of steelworkers with the miners by joining the Union of Working People of the Donbass. V. Volkov, a worker in the shop, introduced the proposal, saying that a workers' movement has been born in this country, one that has existed for more than a year. In the Donbass the miners are actively participating. They are the initiators of many political acts, including demonstrations and strikes. I propose that we put up for a vote the question of steelworkers joining the Union of Working People of the Donbass.

According to the plant correspondent, shouts of "Support the miners!" rang out in the hall. However, once again a representative of management, the deputy shop head, asked, "Support the miners in what? In strikes and demonstrations? The miners have made many mistakes, this is no secret." The manager proposed sending "our official representatives" to the group to learn more about it first, and the proposal was adopted.[14]

Nevertheless, and notwithstanding the administration's efforts to keep the situation under control, less than a year after the miners first struck, the STK had moved from discussing the "small questions" of distribution to broader political questions involving the life of the plant. The agenda of the meeting of May 12, 1990, for example, included a report from the plant's delegate to the first Congress of Independent Workers' Associations, steps to aid the victims of Chernobyl (including plant workers who had helped in the cleanup), the holding of a demonstration tied to the opening session of the local soviet, and the question of independence for the plant newspaper.[15]

Conflict within the STK continued at West Siberian as well. When the Kuzbass miners, on the first anniversary of their strike, announced a one-day political strike demanding the resignation of Prime Minister Ryzhkov and his government, a joint meeting of the plant's STK, trade union committee, workers' committee, and administration decided to continue to work, but to withhold the day's proceeds, which would be directed toward "the solution of social problems" at the plant.[16]

Yet, on July 11, 1990, the workers of one section of the steel-wire shop and those in mechanical shop number 2 decided to support the strike fully and refused to work, the latter group for three hours and the former for a full twenty-four hours. A joint meeting of the STK and the trade union committee denounced the groups that struck, since they did not "support the decision of the majority, which is the basic principle of democracy." It was resolved that no punishment would be levied, "although they all punished themselves materially, and the entire collective as well," by not working.[17]

But like the STK at Donetskii, the council at West Siberia continued to struggle with its relationship with the miners' movement and broader political change. The plant sent a representative to a meeting of STK representatives of various enterprises, which took place in the automobile factory town of Tol'iatti. At the meeting, a major disagreement broke out over whether to call for the resignation of the government and a recall of the people's deputies who voted for "the anti-peoples'" law on state enterprises (which essentially removed the STK's authority). The position was backed at the meeting by Nikolai Travkin of the "Democratic Russia" party and the coal miners. But the West Siberian representative joined others in opposing the position, and together they left the hall when the question came up for a vote, depriving the meeting of a quorum. "There is a paradox: on the one hand we are requesting help from the government, and on the other hand we are saying 'give up your portfolio.'"[18]

The Trade Union

If the enterprise STKs, institutions that had hardly existed before 1987, were having difficulty transforming themselves, the trade union committees, with a much longer heritage and part of a large central bureaucracy, had a most difficult time. As mentioned earlier, at Donetskii the trade union committee, less than three weeks after the region's coal miners had filled city squares and seized control of mines, met to discuss fulfilling the plan, violations of labor discipline, and results of the latest round of socialist competition.[19]

Yet four days later new elections to the trade union committee were proclaimed, of which it was said, "[q]uestions of carrying out the trade union's defensive functions should hold the central place in the election campaign including defending the legal rights and interests of workers, securing social guarantees for workers and employees, who were laid off as a result of economic reform." However, how these defensive functions were defined in practice would prove extremely important. As for specifics, it was said that laws should be observed in distributing pay; the provision of food to the population should be improved; the number of garden plots should be increased; the market should be saturated with consumer goods; "workers' control" should be strengthened over enterprise trade; good hot meals should be organized at the workplace, schools and hospitals; and glasnost should be observed in the distribution of trips to vacation centers and health spas.[20]

Yet the miners' strike continued to shake Donetskii's trade union. Within two months of the strike, and with the approaching elections to the plant's trade union committee, one committee member argued, "In our city, our attention has been riveted to trade unions, and their re-election in the coal enterprises of Donetsk. The process occurring there is characteristic for the trade union movement as a whole. Now it is very important that we don't fall in an anarchistic mood, but instead show a sober and considered approach to difficult problems." He added that seven new chairs had already been elected to shop trade union committees.[21]

A factory correspondent wrote, "After the July miners' strikes, and after careful study of their lessons, many asked the question, why were the miners' trade unions given a vote of no-confidence?" To answer this question, the correspondent turned to the blooming mill shop. The shop trade union chair stated that "above all, the task of a trade union is the defense of workers' rights." When asked to give examples of how a successful shop trade union was defending workers' rights, she enumerated several: special milk rations were being given out to metal cutters, welders, and certain other categories of workers, "all who work in the shop receive soap," shop workers' children all received trips to pioneer camps and workers trips to the vacation center, and a small store was set up to sell meat right in the workplace. "Now the matter is only to organize the uninterrupted supply of meat."[22]

The conflict within the trade union between the desire to defend workers' rights and the need to distribute the plant's largesse was evident in the campaign for trade union chair, which at Donetskii was between the current chair and his deputy. In his platform, the incumbent argued that the trade union should unite with the administration to raise workers' living standards and that while it should "get rid of the distribution functions that don't belong to it," there was a long list of such functions in his platform that apparently did belong to the trade union.[23]

His deputy, nine years younger, presented a dissenting view. "We need to solve many problems . . . so that the trade union will not be remembered only when you need a vacation trip." He divided his platform into three points: (1) "The main thing is to defend the legal rights of workers in the sphere of pay and norm-setting . . . through the collective contract"; (2) "social problems" and the distribution of goods and services, which included the need for social justice and glasnost in housing distribution— those first in line should be invited to trade union meetings that allot apartments; and (3) the further development of inner trade union democracy.

The incumbent chair was eventually reelected by delegates to a plant conference. One conference delegate from the blooming mill shop discussed serious problems in the shop: due to the lack of steel, for the second month it had not fulfilled the plan, leading to drastic cuts in workers' wages. However, this situation apparently was not a problem that concerned the trade union. "As for the trade union committee," he added,

it has solved the problem of the family vacation center on the Azov Sea. I consider this a social victory for the trade union committee.

And our children vacation at the pioneer camp "Metallurgist" [on the Black Sea]. . . . Now many are saying that the trade union should not be occupied with the problems of providing workers with potatoes, meat, soap. But who will take care of these problems? I consider this the trade union committee's job.[24]

Others were not so sure. Some connected distribution questions with issues of trade union democracy. One complained about both the shortage of vacation trips and their unjust distribution, for which he sharply criticized the trade union committee and its chair. "As for the collective leadership of the trade union committee, for the last two years the committee has not even met! And even questions of the distribution of vacations, which according to regulations the trade union chair does not have the right to distribute alone, are being distributed by him alone."[25]

Yet another delegate put the question more sharply:

Frankly speaking, it pains me that you have organized this conference as if it were ten to fifteen years ago. We don't talk about the sore points here. We won't revolt, if we find out that apartments are being given to Afghan war invalids ahead of the line, or that a vacation trip in short supply [defitsitnaya] is being given to a steel founder, a furnace worker or a rolling mill operator. But we demand the just distribution of social goods. We need glasnost here, so that all will know, who obtained what. . . . I think we've ruined this conference.[26]

Thousands of kilometers away, the trade union at West Siberian struggled with the same problems and contradictions. When the two shops struck in the spring of 1989, prior to the coal miners' strike, workers received no help from their trade union. After the first shop struck and while the second was threatening to do so, the secretary of the central steelworkers' union and the union's chief legal inspector flew in from Moscow. The national trade union secretary told the workers of the need to give "a decisive no!" to the strike: "The state is socialist, here everything is ours—strike against whom?"[27]

But the shop level strikes pushed the trade union committee at the plant to reassess itself. Two months after the strike, but still a month before the miners walked out, the trade union published an article entitled, "We Are Learning Democracy."

Never before has the trade union committee had to face the question of its place in a strike. The word was only used when speaking of the class struggle somewhere abroad. Therefore, the events in the blooming and the merchant mill shops caught trade union leaders unaware. . . .

It's no secret that some trade union representatives see their basic function as distributive, letting the chief problems in our work go out of control, which immediately leads to conflicts between working people and the administration. . . . In the course of many years, people began to relate to the trade union in a purely consumer sense. The distribution of this or that good . . . became the chief indicator of the work of the trade union committee, and the ability of a trade union chair to obtain something from above was seen as an excellent capability. The most important questions, such as workers' safety, pay and rate setting, cultural and living problems fell to the second level.

The article promised "real elections" to the trade union committee, "on an alternative basis, . . . elections in the direct sense of the word."[28]

The meeting to elect a new trade union committee took place within three months of the miners' strike, just as at Donetskii. It was the first such election in more than three years. As with all such meetings, the trade union was to account for its actions since the previous meeting, and the trade union chair devoted roughly three-fourths of his long speech to social problems and the distribution of goods and services.[29]

Besides the problems of distribution, the discussion also touched on the miners' strike three months earlier. "The trade union was an observer [during the strike], that's why the workers' committee appeared," said one. Others spoke of the need for independence for the trade union. "We don't need an organ such as the regional steelworkers' union," said one shop chair. Addressing the question of keeping trade union dues at the plant, he added, "Without deciding the question of financial independence, there's nothing to say about the independence of the trade union."[30]

The point about financial independence was important, for without it the trade union committee at the plant level was tied to an entire bureaucracy that was seen as soaking up the dues paid by the rank and file. According to the trade union chair of the merchant mill shop, "For many, including for me, the whole structure of the old trade union is part of the repressive-distributive apparatus."[31]

Others chose even sharper words. Around the anniversary of the first miners' strike the dissenting voice of N. Novikov, a fitter in the rolling lathe shop and a former member of the workers' committee, appeared on the pages of the plant newspaper. In an article entitled "The Result of Our Passivity," he wrote that the meeting to ratify the collective contract, in which the trade union formally takes a leading role, was in the spirit of the "good" Brezhnev times. The collective contract was composed and discussed before in the offices, where they laid out the course of the conference, prepared the lists of commissions, the protocol, the resolutions, etc. Half of the hall was composed of the staff participants of all such meetings, and part of the delegates came just to get the food and goods laid out [otovarit'sya]. After two recesses less than half remained. Our living conditions, our pay and our health depend on the decisions of such forums. It's time to wake up and look around. Besides ourselves no one will improve our lives.[32]

Shortly thereafter, Novikov wrote an article entitled, "We Need an Independent Union." With the congress of the steelworkers' union coming up, there would soon be a plant conference to elect delegates to the congress.

We must now prepare delegates to the [plant] conference from democratically and radically oriented workers, nominate candidates to the congress on an alternative basis. We must not allow appeasers, apparatchiks, and lovers of these sorts of meetings to end up at the congress. We need to create the kind of trade union that will be independent and free, like the miners are doing.
    With the help of an independent trade union workers can really take the economy of our enterprise under control, and really influence the political processes in the country. . . . [T]he trade union is obligated to take control of all the means of production. We must decide ourselves, how to distribute the profit, and determine, who and what we need.[33]

Yet, one delegate to the steelworkers' union congress complained upon returning that the meeting "went the old way," just as Novikov had warned it would. The delegate continued: "The organizing committee had everything prepared and thought out before hand—what will happen at the congress and in what sequence." Another delegate, a young shop trade union chair elected after the miners' strike, reported back:

It became clear, very clear, what trade unions do. Now, we must look truth in the eye, we devote ourselves to whatever we like [chem ugodno]—weighing out tobacco and candy, distributing consumer goods in short supply and so forth—anything but defending the interests of workers. Occupied with these trifles, we less and less sense people's problems. People are beginning to look for the defense of their rights on the side . . . wherever they can. . . . We need to defend our workers from the capriciousness [*proizvol*] of management, because very many arguments break out.[34]

Another delegate to the conference said, "many speeches were along the classic lines of the stagnation period: they complained to each other, talked about how everything is bad, raised production themes. In short, everything except why you came." The minister of ferrous metallurgy and his deputy addressed the trade union conference. "The basic thought, heard in their speeches, was 'Comrades, you have to work. Thanks for not striking last year.'" He added his general disappointment with the trade union. "With such 'defenders', life will be very difficult under the market."[35]

In March and April of 1991, the miners were out on the streets again, this time with demands that the government, including Gorbachev, resign, that the Supreme Soviet disband, and that the Communist Party be removed from power. And if the miners, being extremely cautious during their first major strike in more than sixty years, had asked other workers to remain on the job before, they were now actively agitating for a general strike. Yet, almost without exception, steelworkers throughout the Soviet Union remained at the mills.[36]

There were some exceptions. If West Siberian had experienced its first strikes five months before the miners walked out, Donetskii had its first strike, in a single shop, in April 1991.

Six months after advancing demands to the plant's administration, workers of the locomotive brigades called for a two-hour warning strike. The demands included raising pay twofold, increasing vacation time to twelve days a year, and lowering the pension age to fifty. The complaints included a constant shortage of materials, which along with new tariff rates reduced pay considerably. Further, 350,000 rubles that the department earned were being withheld. The director, in a written response, answered that because of the sorry financial state of the plant, he could not presently raise wages or return the 350,000 rubles, and (despite all the talk of enterprise independence) the questions of vacations and pensions were not within the plant administration's competence to decide.

April 15, the day the 350,000 rubles were supposed to be returned to the department, coincided with "an expected city-wide strike" called by the miners. According to the head of the department, miners' representatives came to the plant "agitating and making demands of a political character. We did everything to convince workers not to strike—the party secretary came to the shop, as did other leaders. The workers were told, 'if

you strike for a day everyone will lose pay. All the shops will have to pay
a fine because of you.'" In monetary terms, one hour of a strike, workers
were told, would cost 20,000 rubles. Yet, "three days later, the general
mood was in favor of a strike."[37]

And while the strike was originally over specific economic grievances,
as it was initially with the coal miners, that quickly changed. According to
Yurii Morozov, a senior machinist and the strike's informal leader, "Many
have talked about economics, but here the stress will be placed not on economic, but on political demands." By eight o'clock a column of 150 people, including some workers from the night shift, marched to the square to
join the miners. Said Morozov, "We were the first in our plant to come forward with demands which are on everybody's tongue, which others only
discuss in the bath-house."[38]

Analysis

As we have seen, the Donetskii director explained the absence of a strike at
his plant by being able to solve many "social problems." Similarly, at West
Siberian, director Kustov met in July 1989 with striking miners, who had
come to the plant to check on its coal reserves. According to Kustov, "the
miners had many grievances on social and living problems: few day care
centers, hospitals, vacation centers, high rates of children's illnesses. . . .
The miners listened with great interest to [the steel factory's] plans for the
social development of the borough, about what was built here by the plant
and what was being planned." He spoke of a planned children's hospital,
how additional pay for night shifts—one of the miners' demands—had
been introduced at the plant on July 1, and suggested to the miners that
they could invest together in the construction of day-care centers, housing,
and sociocultural institutions. They could even form an association, he
suggested, such as the one West Siberian had already formed with a
Kemerovo chemical factory, "which allows us to receive a large assort-
ment of consumer goods." The miners were much taken with all of this,
according to the director.[39]

But if the directors could be expected, in self-serving fashion, to
explain the lack of strikes from "what we have done for the workers," the
same could not be said for steelworkers who were actively opposed to the
enterprise system of distribution. One steelworker from the Kuznetskii
plant, who had joined the Novokuznetsk city strike committee, put it this
way:

We have barter at the plant, so we receive goods. At the plant they put
together Japanese VCRs, we get Chinese consumer goods, well, they

give out shirts, other duds. Though all this, I understand, all these things are crumbs, but a worker, who doesn't have anything, and might be able to get a little something, he of course tries to withdraw from [any labor conflict], to stay on the side, to show the administration his good side. People are held back by these crumbs. It's very hard for steelworkers to shake themselves loose.[40]

The representative from West Siberian on the Novokuznetsk city strike committee, though less critical of the administration, as would be expected from a member of the enterprise's official workers' committee, had this to say on the differences between miners and steelworkers:

It's not simply a matter of better conditions. Take housing, for example. Our steelworkers build their own housing. If you go to a mine, the administration's buildings are nice, OK, but the miners' housing is bad, while for steelworkers it's the other way around—the workers' housing is nice, but the administration's housing is not so great. That's one nuance.

Our plant, West Siberian, worries more about its workforce. We spend money on Japanese Toyotas, on other things—well here, these duds I'm wearing. We have our own agricultural production at the plant: milk, meat, and potatoes, we'll have all the food we need.

Many shops supported the demands of the miners, but didn't stop production, because if they stop, they'll also stop the agriculture, the financial picture will be ruined. We'll break our own plant. Yes, there are people who want to stop.

I'm a member of the workers' committee, but it, how should I say it, it works more for the social good of the plant.[41]

In his detailed study of Magnitogorsk, Stephen Kotkin, while not focusing on this question, reaches a similar conclusion after speaking with steelworkers there. As one worker told him, "We're completely dependent on them. Food, clothes, apartments, furniture, day care, summer camps, vacations—everything is allocated by them according to their lists, with which they rule over our lives. Everyone has something to lose."[42]

Conscious of the divisions that such distribution caused, Kotkin says of workers:

All remarked that the authorities' careful attention to 'favorites' strongly inhibited the development of worker solidarity. . . . Workers were only too well aware of how the trade unions, the Komsomol, and the party retained control over the distribution of goods and services, favors and rewards, at places of employment. Indeed, with all workers dependent on the authorities for everything from their housing to their daily bread, there was less a sharp line differentiating 'favored' workers from the rest than a continuum of the slightly greater or lesser rewarded.[43]

Explaining why the miners were the first to break out of this dilemma is not so hard. In many respects, the coal miners' strikes are overdetermined. There is indeed something unique about the labor process in coal mining, working underground in dangerous conditions, and this very likely helps engender professional pride and solidarity. But more important are the specifics of the Soviet coal industry.

We have seen how the "brake" applied to the coal industry in the 1950s created a whole series of problems. Not least of these was the extremely hazardous conditions under which Soviet miners were forced to work; while mining everywhere is a dangerous occupation, the problem became particularly acute in Soviet coal mines, where accident rates were extremely high—much higher than the next highest industry, steelmaking.[44]

Yet declining investment not only created difficulties with working conditions, but also with "social problems," like housing, day care, and the rest. Miners' living conditions were often appalling: in Vorkuta and the Far East, for instance, miners could work underground for twenty to thirty years and still live with their families in a single room in barracks.[45]

Moreover, the problems in the Soviet coal industry worsened with economic reform. The introduction of full *khozraschet,* or self-financing, in the coal industry, the only "planned-loss" industry, had a perverse effect. With bonuses and social expenditures now intended to come out of plant profits, the already austere living conditions of the Soviet coal miners were strained even further.

Here we seem to have a case for relative deprivation.[46] Yet there are problems with such an argument in this context. First, a decrease in investment was experienced by the miners themselves only very slowly, over a long period of time. Second, in the case studies of the steel plants and in interviews with steelworkers met randomly, the sense of anger, frustration, and deprivation is quite clear.[47] The very same issues raised by coal miners are raised forcefully by steelworkers again and again.[48]

More importantly, coal miners have been the highest-paid category of workers, with many miners making almost twice as much as the average industrial worker and considerably more than steelworkers.[49] Yet coal mines, due to decreased investment in social infrastructure, had less goods and services to distribute to their workforce. While industrial-level data on social infrastructure do not exist, regional-level data show this to be the case. One graphic statistic is the following: the Kemerovo region of Siberia (Kuzbass), Russia's largest coal basin, ranked thirteenth in 1989 in industrial production in rubles, even at artificially low prices for coal, but was forty-third in the provision of housing, fifty-eighth in children's establishments, and eighty-ninth for social clubs.[50] In the Donbass, new housing construction was 20 percent lower in 1989 than in 1964, so that housing queues had lengthened by 50 percent just since 1980.[51] In an examination of housing units built in 1979 in twenty-eight large Soviet cities, Donetsk, the coal capital of Ukraine, was twenty-third; it was not only greatly outpaced by the Ukrainian cities of Kiev and Kharkov, but by the nearby metallurgical center of Dnepropetrovsk, which came in first out of all twenty-eight cities.[52]

Thus, steelworkers were compensated with lower wages and higher in-kind benefits, making them more dependent, while coal miners were compensated with a low level of goods and services but high wages, giving them greater autonomy. The strategy some workers pursued was to begin their career as a highly skilled steelworker, get an apartment quickly on a privileged basis, and then to leave for the coal mines, getting both the apartment and the high wage.[53]

How did compensation with high levels of in-kind benefits create greater dependence than high wages in rubles? First, when workers are tied to a job through a paycheck alone, the "cash nexus" becomes a fragile connection because it is single-stranded: a disruption in wage levels can quickly transform quiescent workers into militant ones.[54] Second, unlike many of the benefits distributed through the enterprise, wages can be saved to be spent later, such as when certain scarce goods became available or during a strike. Third, wages have been easier to replace, even in the event of losing one's job, than in-kind benefits. Due to the labor shortage, workers fired for disciplinary reasons were able to find new employment soon thereafter, in many cases with wages higher than in their previous jobs.[55] Yet for a worker who had invested years waiting for an automobile or an apartment and was nearing the top of the list, losing one's position in line would be a terrible blow.[56]

Alternative arguments remain, in particular those pertaining to the technology of production and the resulting organization of work. One such argument has to do with the wide variety of skills required in a modern, integrated steel mill. These differences in skills extend in two directions, vertically and horizontally: job ladders create a greater hierarchy within the basic professions of steel manufacturing as opposed to coal extraction, while the different tasks in which each shop engages means that workers are often facing quite different production problems.[57] With the workforce more stratified along job ladders and across shops, the potential for solidarity is lessened.

While this argument appears forceful, and may provide some of the explanation for why steelworkers found organizing difficult, there are reasons to question several of its assumptions. First, the steel industry is highly strike-prone in some countries but not in others, suggesting that such factors as unions, the state, and cultural and other institutions are more important than technology.[58]

Moreover, as Katherine Stone has argued with reference to the origins of job structures in the American steel industry, there was actually a "lack of important skill differentials between the jobs in steel-making," and the job ladders and classification schemes that arose were largely the artificial constructs of management rather than the result of technological imperatives.[59] And while it is certainly true that workers in different shops at Donetskii and West Siberian were engaged in different tasks, those differences were exacerbated by the peculiar institutions of economic reform, specifically *khozraschet,* whereby shops were cut off from one another and pay and conditions varied widely, even among cafeteria workers servicing different shops.

More importantly, the divisions of workers along skill lines were most significant for the workers themselves when they involved the privileged distribution of goods and services. This privileged distribution allowed managers to respond to a taut labor market, for skilled labor especially, despite the often rigid central determination of wage structures.

Thus, the divisions that result between workers over skill stem less from technical necessity than from management's perceived need to reward groups of workers differently, while at the same time trying to hide that fact from a workforce whose sense of justice includes the notion of pay according to labor.

Furthermore, these divisions, and the attempts of other workers to reduce them, are a direct result of the mutual dependence of the worker and the enterprise—tied to both the labor shortage and the enterprise as central distributor of vital goods and services. One implication of this system of distribution is that it creates further divisions between workers. For example, housing, a source of great conflict inside the steel plants, surely becomes less of an issue for those who have already received an adequate apartment, whether through one's position on privileged lists or through years of waiting.

One further significant difference, also rooted in technology, between the coal mines and the steel mills examined here is size. With a mine's workforce ranging in size from one to several thousand, the barriers to successful collective action are considerably lower than at giant steel plants, such as Donetskii, with seventeen thousand employees, or West Siberian, with thirty-two thousand.

Some, dating back to Marx, have hypothesized that in small plants workers would associate and identify more with their employers, while "the larger the factory, the more workers interact with one another, and the less they interact with their superiors."[60] Others, referring to the collective action problem as an explanation for the failure of Marx's prediction of working-class mobilization, have argued that large plants deter collective action. Like Marx's classic description of the French peasantry as a sack of potatoes, the "manifold relations" between workers may be reduced as plant size increases and workers become isolated and divorced from informal communication networks. "Contrary to what Marx predicted, the spirit of solidarity is reduced in [large] plants, and with it the capacity for effective collective action."[61]

In both arguments, technology is the explanatory variable: for the first group, increasing plant size will lead, eventually, to working-class mobilization, while for the second it will decrease the possibilities for mobilization. In the case of Soviet enterprises, however, technology was not the only variable: the decision was made, for various reasons, to concentrate production in a few very large plants, a process often referred to as "gigantomania."[62]

Whether as a result of technology or not, the plants remain gigantic, and their lack of full-scale strike activity would seem to be a confirmation of the thesis of large plant size as an obstacle to workers' collective action. Indeed, in terms of its workforce, a mine is more comparable to a single shop than an entire steel complex. As the worker-activist from the Kuznetskii Works put it: "We have thirty-two shops, it's like, practically, thirty-two mines in quantity. We have some shops with even more workers than in a single mine."[63]

However, when stated in this fashion, the explanation is insufficient. While the difficulties in communicating and organizing between the shops of these large plants would certainly be significant, this was no less an obstacle than that faced originally by miners in separate mines. In fact, the obstacles were even greater in the case of the miners, since mines were spread out over vast regions and even over the entire country. And yet miners in these disparate mines combined: while at first several individual mines struck in the spring of 1989, by July the Mezhdurechensk miners had set off a "ripple effect" throughout the Soviet Union.[64] Individual shops struck in the two steel plants studied, both before and after the miners, yet they failed to spark similar action in other shops, despite seemingly fewer obstacles in the way.

What is missing in discussions of plant size and collective action is the corresponding size of management at these large plants. In the words of the Kuznetskii steelworker:

> We're all in one group, in one place, with one boss [*kulak*] . . . if some kind of revolt begins in one [shop], then the administration tries to somehow pacify it, and somehow frighten workers with its actions, so there is no solidarity. Here I'll give one example from my own shop: when the shop announced that there would be a strike, then the administration literally immediately got together and there was a leaflet sent around, that participants in the strike will suffer this, and this, and this punishment: lose their wages, lose subsidies for their children, then all the privileges that workers get.[65]

As we have seen in the cases of the two steel enterprises, management, not only on the level of the shop but on the level of the enterprise as well, intervened often to maintain control over the plant and its workforce. Plant conferences, where worker-representatives were elected to plantwide posts and where the collective contracts were ratified, have been a recurrent theme in the case studies presented here. These conferences were one way in which the plant administration could use the size of the workforce to its advantage. Thus the problem for workers of electing representatives to the trade union, the STK, and other organs was not simply a function of plant size, but getting around the rules and other obstacles put in place by the enterprise administration.

And yet, as the last part of the previous quotation indicates, the issue was not simply the problem of management domination, but also of the levers that it controls: the privileges extended to workers to prevent them from acting individually (to take advantage of the taut labor market to "exit") can also be used to prevent them from acting collectively. Once again, we return to the importance of mutual dependence.

At present we are left with partial explanations. Even the "most similar cases" of coal mining and steelmaking still leave many differences in the work experiences of the two groups, which may account for differences in strike activity. How to untangle these alternative explanations? Fortunately, for present purposes, as the comparative case method would call for, counterexamples can be found—coal mines that did not strike.

As we shall see, participation during the 1991 strike was spotty, with some mines joining in the middle of the strike, others dropping out, and still others producing coal for local use with the blessing of the strike committee. Yet there were also examples of mines that did not strike at all. Though the mines that did not strike were often quite different from one another, they shared a common characteristic: they were all linked to a trading partner in such a way that a strike would cut off the provision of vital goods or services to the workforce.

One group of mines less prone to strike, as described earlier, were those mines making up the very "isolated communities" that were expected to be most strike-prone. These mines, removed from urban areas in settlements of their own, were certainly hindered by their inability to communicate with other mines. But such mines were also able to establish strong links to nearby state or collective farms. Had the mines struck, they would have violated their contracts with these farms and in turn would have lost their source of food supplies, which were especially hard to obtain in industrialized coal basins with arid land or otherwise harsh climates.[66]

A second group of mines that did not strike were those more often located in urban areas, which, either through rich geological endowments or through managerial skill, had created links not only with state farms but with producers of consumer goods, domestic or foreign. These arrangements typically involved barter.

One such mine, Zasiad'ko, is something of a local legend in the city of Donetsk.[67] In July 1989, while other mine directors made themselves scarce, Efim Zviagil'skii, the Zasiad'ko director, retained the loyalty of his miners by expressing his support for their demands and their decision to strike.[68] When in the spring of 1991 Donetsk was again engulfed by a strike, Zasiad'ko workers remained on the job. "The director thinks, above all, about the people," explained a face worker in an article entitled "Why the Zasiad'ko Mine Is Not Striking." The article went on to describe how the mine had developed "an entire trade and industrial complex," which included a department for housing construction, two vacation centers, greenhouses, a livestock station replete with a slaughterhouse and a smokehouse, and its own farm whose produce was exchanged for consumer goods. Contracts with trade organizations brought in clothes, shoes, furniture, and automobiles, while barter deals provided the miners with cassette players, VCRs, and televisions at subsidized prices. The mine was purchasing an Italian bakery that would use the farm's wheat, had built a new cafeteria "with a vitamin bar," and had acquired several stores for the "Miner" trading complex. To transport all these goods, the mine had obtained its own truck depot, and to improve export prospects, it had purchased jointly with other enterprises a freight ship.[69] As for striking, the face worker explained:

We . . . well understand that, having shut down the mine, we will worsen our material position, since no one will pay our wages . . . . There will be no means to maintain the sanitoria, meat and vegetables will disappear, housing construction will stop, the day care centers will close.

What's more, our trading partners will demand our forfeiture. We will suffer enormous losses.[70]

There is a third category of mine that did not participate in the 1991 strike, though the number of examples are few. As will be shown in the following chapters, the Kuzbass miners, with their relatively new and rich coal fields, often sought to maintain control of their mines independently of the state. One miner-activist who was able to achieve this for his mine rather effectively was Yurii Gerol'd.

Having come from a long family of coal miners, Gerol'd was elected chair of his mine's STK after the July 1989 strike, despite having just started work there as a foreman. Young and forceful, he was elected deputy chair of the Kuzbass regional strike committee and helped prepare the protocol, signed by the miners and the government commission, which ended the strike. He was later elected co-chair of the Confederation of Labor, as well as a people's deputy of the Russian Federation, the latter on a program of "enterprise independence" and end to "the alienation of the working person . . . from the product of his labor."[71]

By March 1991, when the Kuzbass miners were striking to bring down the Soviet government, Gerol'd, while remaining a people's deputy, resigned from the city and regional strike committees and the Confederation of Labor. His mine, Polosukhinskaya, continued to work. Remaining true to his principles of creating independence and ending labor's "alienation," at least in one mine, Gerol'd had sought and helped find a British partner for a joint-stock company, which could promise a relatively high standard of living for all of Polosukhinskaya's employees. Participation in the strike would have meant an end to the joint-stock arrangement.[72] Thus, Gerol'd and his colleagues were faced with a choice between maintaining solidarity and remaining part of the workers' movement, or keeping their relative independence and prosperity—the final goal, in the miners' eyes, of their political strike against the Soviet government.[73]

What each of the three categories of mines shared in common was a contract arrangement with horizontally linked trading partners, which provided the mines' employees with goods and services at levels significantly higher than the average mine. Of course, miners who did strike sacrificed a good deal, as we shall see. But while striking miners were provided with a strike fund, however meager, these contract arrangements provided miners with goods and services that a strike fund could not buy.[74]

Thus, across differences in plant size and production processes, and even across industries, dependence on the enterprise as the distributor of vital goods and services has remained a strong inhibitor of strike activity and workers' collective action. If the presence of enterprise dependence can account for the lack of strikes in steel enterprises and certain coal enterprises, can the lack of a high level of enterprise dependence account for the presence of strikes in industries other than coal mining? While a definitive answer lies outside the scope of the present study, the industries and sectors where strike activity has occurred suggest that such may indeed be the case. As we have noted, the provision of goods and services at an enterprise's disposal varies greatly between enterprises as well as between industries. Between September 1990 and August 1991, strike activity, outside of coal mining, occurred mainly among transportation workers (railroad and public transport), dock workers, merchant marines, other miners (gold and iron ore), and white-collar employees (doctors, teachers, and air traffic controllers),[75] and these general patterns have continued to hold in the years since. While there may be alternative explanations for strikes among these particular workers, all lie outside the traditional heavy industrial sector, where worker collective action could be expected to occur and where enterprise goods and services have been concentrated.[76]

In the longer term, the future of enterprise dependence is limited, even if it is difficult to determine when the longer term might arrive.[77] An end to subsidies, leading to bankruptcies and widespread unemployment, would remove the main reason that enterprises supplied workers with goods and services in the first place—to attract and retain skilled workers in a taut labor market. At the same time, unemployment and the uncertainties of a market economy would likely create new obstacles to, and opportunities for, workers' mobilization. We will return to this question in part 4 of this book, to find that the relationship between the market forces and enterprise paternalism has not been straightforward.

If the concept of mutual dependence is historically limited, it is theoretically limited as well. As was argued in the first chapter, rational choice and structural perspectives, from which this concept has drawn, assume that the interests and ideas that motivate and inform collective action are static (and relatively unimportant). But as we shall see in the case of the coal miners, ideas—and ideology and culture—were a central influence on the direction taken once the miners mobilized. The concept of mutual dependence, or rational choice and structural explanations more generally, cannot account for how miners moved from self-described "economic" to "political" demands or from supporting the goals and the language of perestroika to demanding the dismantling of the state. Nor can it account for the miners' shift from appealing to the state for more goods and services to pushing for the market as a solution for, of all things, the country's least profitable industry. We turn in the following section to understanding the relationship between the cultural frameworks crafted by miners and their leaders and the transformation of their demands.

Part 3.
Hot Coal: The Radicalization of the Miners' Movement

CHAPTER 5

Building a Workers' Movement

At the end of their first strike, coal miners in different regions sought to institutionalize their newfound power, in order to defend their gains. The obstacles to creating a viable workers' movement would prove formidable, as we shall see. These obstacles were both internal to the miners' movement and external, including above all dramatically changing political and economic conditions. As for the latter, the miners' gains were being defended in deteriorating economic conditions, so that concessions achieved on paper quickly dissipated. They also faced a weakening Soviet state, less and less able to deliver the goods it promised. Further, during their struggle with the state the miners were being exposed to various and increasing denunciations of the very institutions of the Soviet political economy. In this atmosphere, the miners were to grapple with several contradictions—most fundamentally, between the sense that the state owed them a decent standard of living and a desire to end their dependence on the state; and between their belief in the ideals, though not the reality, of the Soviet system, and the understanding that this system was being irrevocably altered while something else, quite different and almost unimaginable, lay in store.

In this chapter we will examine the miners' attempt to build a workers' movement, including the difficulty of uniting coal basins with very different structural conditions and the attempt to create viable institutions, including newspapers, trade unions, and workers' committees. The argument to be made is that the miners' evolving demands and strategies were driven not simply by structural conditions, or the rapidly changing political economy, or the organizing skills of miner-activists, but rather by the tension between each of these and the miners' sense of justice. This sense of justice stemmed largely from Soviet institutions but was interpreted and reinterpreted by miners and their leaders in quite new and imaginative ways. To begin to document this sense of justice, we will return briefly to the anger and euphoria that immediately followed the first strike.

The Kuibyshev Trade Union Conference

Days after the 1989 strike, as was the case in mines throughout the country, the Kuibyshev mine of Donetsk held a trade union conference.[1] The discussion of Kuibyshev demonstrates a mixture of traditional concerns and militant rage.

The meeting began in typical fashion, with trade union chair Viktor Efimov reading his report on union activities since the last conference. He proposed increasing the social benefits distributed by the trade union, such as "when someone dies, let's make arrangements to have a coffin, music and flowers." Again in typical fashion, he enumerated the recent violations of labor discipline: 77 people missed 371 days of work in the first half of the year, 49 people were taken to the sobering-up station, and 58 people were involved in "violations of public order." But when he began citing a Gorbachev speech calling for "discipline and order," he was cut short by cries from the audience.

When the commotion died down, Efimov replied, "We [the trade union] didn't support the strike. Right? That's why you've withdrawn your support from me. And I think you were right. Then there is no need to make a report." With this the floor was opened for questions.

At least initially, most of the questions revolved around the trade union's role in distributing the goods and services of *sotskul'tbyt:* who received material assistance, cars, and apartments; how Efimov obtained an imported refrigerator from the mine when others didn't even know they were available; and why miners and their families so rarely received vacation trips, when Efimov took a trip every year and strangers were often seen vacationing at the mine's own summer resort.[2]

As disgust with Efimov mounted, there were calls from the audience to strip the trade union chair of his awards: three Miner's Glory medals and one Honorary Miner of Ukraine. The conference voted to remove the latter title. But the complaints only grew. One pensioner cried, "When people like myself work in industry for 43 years, we feel we're making the country grow. We feel it becomes powerful and prosperous. Then people like you come and shit all over her." Still another argued:

> I don't think comrade Efimov was completely correct when he reproached himself for not taking part in the strike. This is wrong: with his years of work as trade union chair, comrade Efimov was preparing this strike. He was preparing it with his wrong actions, with his injustices, and with everything we're discussing here. . . . "They" didn't even think of the future. They thought it would last forever. . . . We see comrade Efimov not as an advocate for workers' rights, but on the contrary—especially since our dues pay his salary—as an oppressor of workers' rights.[3]

With this the complaints moved beyond Efimov himself; several are worth quoting at length.

In addition to [the strike] committee, we must nominate our comrades to local soviets. It's time to take power into our own hands, and place trust in comrades who can defend the working class and full restructuring [perestroika] of Soviet power. This vicious circle has gotten so bad that the working man can't get an apartment, has no rights, and so many people are pushed to suicide. . . . The working class must rise and defend its rights; we will support our government, which has woken up and begun caring for the people because now the end is coming and a crisis is upon the country. Because our leaders have begun robbing our people instead of helping the working class in building our communism for which Lenin raised us, for which our old folks fought for Soviet power, so people could live like human beings.

And another:

When I was on the square—that square will probably be called Solidarity square in honor of our success—from that big 11 story building [the regional Party headquarters] they looked from behind the curtains on all floors and smiled, those people. What kind of people are they if they couldn't come out to the miners, and talk, and engage in dialogue? . . . We must turn back to Lenin more often. The ideas that Lenin had for workers were not reaching them. I took a class on scientific communism. We talked about how workers live, but where? In France, Italy, but never in the Soviet Union.

Still another:

Our leaders gorge themselves on the sweat and blood of the working class. Why? Because every month and every year all the mines of the Soviet Union create new cripples and new dead bodies, because mines can't exist without injuries and without people dying. And I will tell you who enjoys the benefits. . . . You know comrades, how you work, the slave labor at the mine, in the dust, dirt, the worker leans on the jackhammer, and it shakes all over. [But the managers get paid] 500, 700, 1,000 Rubles. [cries from audience.] This is who gorges themselves on the blood and sweat of the working class comrades . . . Everything Efimov said was lies.

The conference ended with elections for a new trade union chair, amid accusations that past elections were not fair.[4]

Thus a single trade union conference, in the wake of the strike, moved from official rebukes for violations of labor discipline and complaints about the distribution of vacation trips, to stripping the trade union chair of his post and honorary title, and finally to questioning the very foundations of Soviet power. But the conference also illustrated a curious mix of demands and concerns: bread-and-butter issues with charges of exploitation; disgust at the corruption of a single trade union official with calls for workers' self-management; talk of "comrades" and the invocation of Lenin, with the allegation that the Soviet revolution had been hijacked; specific demands for handing out apartments, cars, and vacation vouchers, with the indictment of Soviet leaders for gorging themselves on workers' blood. Above all, the tone was one of anger expressed explicitly in class terms.

But if the Kuibyshev miners succeeded in removing, and indeed humiliating, their trade union boss and other managers, in order to meet many of the concerns they had begun to raise, they would have to push beyond their mine. Together with miners from around the country, they were to try to transform their spontaneous strike into a workers' movement, to insure that their strike agreement was fulfilled, and to jointly influence the direction of "the full restructuring of Soviet power." Yet there were many unanswered questions. For instance, what did a workers' movement entail: reforming the old trade union structure or creating a new one? Building a political movement or even a party? And if so, who would be included as potential allies— miners, all members of the working class, like-minded members of the intelligentsia?

Before answering these questions, the miners had to overcome other obstacles in the way of a united workers' movement. Not least of these were the significant differences between the mining regions: The basins were an extremely long distance from one another, in different republics with different histories of development. Most significant were the very different structural conditions, which would seem to suggest different strategies for the workers of each region.[5]

The Kuzbass

On seeing the Kuzbass, one gets the sense of being on a frontier: vast stretches of land, jagged hills, wooden houses often made from rough-hewn logs, and an unforgiving climate, with extremes in both summer and winter. This was a land of political prisoners: Dostoevsky was exiled to Novokuznetsk, and the area became a base for the Stalinist gulags of the 1930s. (Many miners speak with pride of their "heritage" as descendants of former political prisoners of one stripe or another.) Indeed, it was during the 1930s that coal mining in the area was first expanded.

The housing in the Kuzbass still reflects its days as a former prisoners' colony. Many miners and their families, as many as one-quarter in all, live in barracks intended years ago to be only temporary housing. These wooden barracks, it is said, become almost unbearable in the intense Siberian winters. When attention was finally paid to this region because of the strike, the residents painted these barracks with such slogans as "Welcome to the Stone Age" and "Thanks to our government for a happy childhood."[6] The housing conditions reflect the level of investment in social infrastructure generally, including medical care, schools, and consumer services. The region is further handicapped because it is an industrial center far from the agricultural heartland: only 6 percent of the population works on the land, making the region dependent on others for its food supply. This dependence became very clear when reform measures decentralized the supply system, since in the absence of a market or administrative pressure it was difficult for regional officials to insure that supply contracts with distant regions were met, with the result that less food and consumer goods arrived in the Kuzbass.[7]

Such problems were compounded by the unrestrained fashion in which the region's environment had been exploited. The city of Novokuznetsk has two steel mills employing more than thirty thousand people each, in addition to another ferrous metallurgical plant, an aluminum factory, several mines, and other industrial enterprises. The city has some of the worst pollution in the Soviet Union, if not in the world: one-half of children born there are in need of resuscitation at birth, eye disease is 72 percent higher than in the nation as a whole, and asthma and cancer rates are also considerably higher.[8] Elsewhere in the region, coking and chemical plants further reduce the amount of food that can be grown. The Tom' river, flowing through the Kuzbass, became a "dead" river from the effluents of the steel and coal industries. The open-face mines, which cut off the riverlets and tributaries to the river, were a further source of discontent, since they were often located right within the miners' communities and were called "pigsties" by the inhabitants, while the area in general was referred to as a "lunar landscape." Far from being an abstract, postmaterial concern, ecological demands were of vital importance to miners of the region.[9]

Yet in contrast to such abysmal living conditions, the Kuzbass is blessed with coal, its reason for existence. The coal is of high quality and is located near the surface, thus allowing for open-face mining and lower costs in underground extraction. That, and the coal ministry's heavy investment in modernizing the coal machinery, meant relatively high productivity, which, along with a regional bonus intended to attract and keep a workforce, meant relatively high wages for the Kuzbass miners.[10]

The combination of difficult living conditions and significant natural resources (as well as Kuzbass's long distance from the centers of political power) created a variation on the theme of exploitation described earlier. The miners of the Kuzbass express a sense of colonialism, in which they were largely dependent on the extraction of a single raw material, for which they were paid an extremely low price by the "center," which in turn provided them with a subsistence level of food and consumer goods. This sense of colonialism was strengthened after the strike, when certain suspicions were confirmed as residents learned the value of goods taken away from the region versus the value of goods returned.[11]

A people's deputy from the region denounced the dependent relationship with central authorities in an address to the USSR Congress of People's Deputies during the strike: "They always said [to the Kuzbass]: 'Give us coal and steel, and we will feed you.' But in exchange for coal and steel it only got smoke, dust, mud, gas, poisoned water, lunar landscapes, sickness and much more. Now they say to the Kuzbass: 'Fellows, we have perestroika now, feed yourselves.' And we don't even have land, since it's all been excavated."[12]

But the Kuzbass miners were to seize upon the irony that while they themselves were poor and extremely dependent on the state, their land was mineral rich, and on it the state was dependent. Hence came the demands, by the deputy quoted in the previous paragraph and many others, for the state to allow 15 to 20 percent of the coal and steel produced in the region to remain there, so that it could be sold to increase the neglected standard of living of those in the Kuzbass or, in the words of the deputy, "so we can build schools, and hospitals, and sports halls."[13]

The Donbass

In many ways, the Donbass contrasts quite sharply with the Kuzbass. Located in industrialized eastern Ukraine, rather than in isolated Siberia, the Donbass enjoys a relatively benign climate. In cities like Donetsk and Makeevka, care is taken to maintain parks and flower gardens, and the proximity to farming regions and centers engaged in the production of consumer goods insure that the region is well supplied, at least in a relative sense. The problems with air and water, while quite serious, are not on the same level as in the Kuzbass.[14]

The long history of mining in the region is reflected in the enormous slag heaps found throughout the Donbass, and in the condition of the social infrastructure. One miner who was visited in his home, for example, within the city of Donetsk, lived much like a rural peasant of the nineteenth century. The little wooden cottage, where he lived with his wife and married son (whose wife and daughter were forced to live with her parents due to the lack of room), had no running water, an outhouse, a wood-burning stove, a pigpen, a chicken coop, and a strip of land for growing potatoes and other vegetables.[15] Besides the region's long history, the housing and social situation generally reflect the cutbacks in investment in the region. Yet relative to the Kuzbass, such conditions were favorable, at least enough for Kuzbass miners, when they finally came to the Donbass almost a year after the first strike, to reportedly joke, "Why did you go on strike here?" But they had not yet visited the mines.

In the Donbass the sense of impending mine and factory closures is palpable. Indeed, a Soviet Academy of Sciences report in the 1970s argued that in the long term the Donbass coalfields were impractical. This analysis led to planned underinvestment and further losses. With few renovations and outmoded technology, production in the Donbass declined from a peak of 225 million tons in 1976 to 197 million tons in 1985. The problem is not simply one of technology, but that the easily exploitable coal has already been mined. As one U.S. study concluded, "In terms of mine depth, seam thickness, and methane concentrations, most of the Donetsk mines would no longer be considered proven reserves by Western standards." The high concentrations of methane mean that mining in the Donbass is particularly dangerous.[16]

The Academy of Sciences report, which suggested accelerating the development of the Kuzbass at the expense of the Donbass, led to a sharp reaction among the miners and others in the coal industry there. When self-financing was introduced in January 1989, a form of triage was developed, and a number of mines in the region were closed that April: twenty-one mines in all were judged unable to meet the self-financing criteria and were to be shut; and another group of mines was scheduled to "continue operating at falling levels until they were worked out." Just days before the strike began, when the Kuzbass miners were to propose economic independence, the region's problems were discussed in *Pravda,* and a headline in the region's paper *Socialist Donbass* asked, "Is This the End of the Donbass?"

Nevertheless, the Donbass, as the Soviet Union's largest coal basin, remained an important source of coal. Moreover, it was the country's principal producer of high-grade steam and coking coal. In response to the academy report, a study by the Donetsk Economic Institute (perhaps not an impartial observer) claimed that while losses from the planned closures in the Donbass totaled 141.9 million rubles a year, the transport costs of coal from the Kuzbass needed to offset the output of the closed mines would total 155.1 million rubles annually.[17] Indeed, the Kuzbass miners complained about the artificially low wholesale price of coal, assuming that the state would continue to subsidize transportation costs to consumers in the European Soviet Union and the Far East.

The objective conditions and future prospects of each coal basin are less important for present purposes than the perceptions that arise from them. While during the strike the Kuzbass miners saw reason for optimism about the future, the Donbass miners truly feared for their jobs. If the Kuzbass miners were drawn by their perceived strength toward demanding greater independence, the position of the Donbass miners would seem to lead them into a defensive, even more dependent, position. The reality, it will be shown, was rather more complex (though in the aftermath of the first strike, the Donbass miners were reportedly less political than their counterparts elsewhere, rejecting efforts to create an alternative trade union, let alone a "Solidarity"-type movement).[18]

Given the very different structural conditions and the different strategies that they suggested—increased autonomy and reliance on the market on the one hand versus continued subsidies and protection from the market on the other—it is difficult to see how miners from the different basins could accommodate themselves to a single movement. At the least it should not be surprising that the miners' movement first developed on a regional level.

Fulfilling the Agreement

If the miners were being pulled apart by differences between the regions, they were united by Council of Ministers' Resolution Number 608, which consolidated the regional strike agreements into one document. It was to this document that the miners on all levels turned their attention, to insure that the government kept its side of the bargain. But problems arose almost immediately.

"Resolution 608, as with such things usually, was adopted hurriedly," said a miner elected to the commission to oversee fulfillment the agreement. "Several of the demands decreed in it are objectively unfulfillable, not only today or tomorrow but in the foreseeable future." Another member of the commission stated that when he and another miner met with Prime Minister Ryzhkov in November 1989, "we ourselves proposed that the resolution be reexamined, in order to make it more realistic."[19]

The biggest demands could not be fulfilled because they implied major structural reform to the economy, something the government had been unable to carry out. While mines were given independence, the change was purely formal in most cases since they were still subject to state orders, often covering 100 percent of their product, with the penalty for failing to meet those orders the state's withdrawal of capital funds. A further problem was caused by the lack of price reform. In the Donbass, miners soon learned that only one mine was profitable at existing prices for coal, rendering the goal of enterprise independence (at least in the absence of price reform) moot. "No wonder the ministry was so keen to agree to our demand for financial independence," said one miner-activist. "Now it is we who have to make up the shortfall in the price!"[20]

The only card the miners held in their struggle to achieve fulfillment of their demands, including an increase in the price of coal, was the strike threat, and it was not long before the miners played their card again. As one miner explained, "in the resolution there is a definite date for the fulfillment of each demand. And the workers think that since the resolution was signed by the government, and a demand has not fulfilled by the established date, then this means outright disorder."[21]

The first time the miners were to sense disorder, and to act upon it, came only two weeks after the regional strike agreement was signed in the Kuzbass. There, with water quality a major source of illness, miners in nearly all cities had demanded a halt to the construction of a hydrotechnical plant on the river Tom'. When construction of the plant appeared to be continuing nonetheless, the regional strike committee called for a two-hour warning strike on August 3. While the call was heeded by only seventeen mines, construction was halted for good.[22] This incident was followed by other strikes tied to the specific dates for the fulfillment of demands, such as a small strike in October in Mezhdurechensk, where the July strike began, and a rather more significant strike in Vorkuta.

Vorkuta is a relatively small mining region in the far north of Russia, first begun in the 1930s as a prison colony, where winter lasts about nine months a year. Though only some twenty thousand miners in all work there, Vorkuta was the site of the miners' first overtly political strike.

The miners from Vorkuta claimed to have advanced political demands during the July strike (which they subsequently described using the Bolshevik slogan, "All power to the Soviets, land to the peasants, factories to the workers") though there is no evidence that this was the case. Several months later, however, with the experience of the first strike under their belt, their political demands were clear.

The strike began in late October and lasted for thirty-eight days. The demands included the removal of article 6 from the constitution, which gave the Communist Party its monopoly on power. "We didn't demand any meat, sausage or money from anyone," claimed one miner afterwards.[23] Yet the political nature of the demands were more complicated than it would first seem. According to one account, "It was only 3,000 miners at [the] Vorgashorskaya [mine] who were espousing the most radical ideas. They gained only patchy support from the 20,000 other miners in Vorkuta, and still less from miners elsewhere in the country."[24] According to a survey of 323 strikers conducted in November 1989 in Vorkuta, only

8 percent considered the strike "mainly political," while 35 percent considered it "mainly economic" and 50 percent "a mixture of the two." Significantly, the strike ended when Coal Minister Shchadov promised full economic independence to the Vorgashorskaya mine.[25]

Despite the unclear direction of the strike and the scattered support it received, it did mark the beginning of a radicalization of the miners' movement. Once the points of the agreement, signed by the government, failed to be carried out by the dates promised, the legitimacy of the government was called into question, and the possibility of political confrontation so carefully avoided in July was now raised.

Building a Movement in the Kuzbass

In the Kuzbass, the miners began by building on the perception that they had been receiving much less than they had been giving to Moscow over the years, and that their mines would be profitable if they cut the links of dependency to Moscow and instead relied on the market. This sense of power helped them to create organizations to strengthen their position and carry their struggle directly into the political arena. Within little more than a year after the first strike, they had formed—in addition to the workers' committees—the Union of Working People of the Kuzbass (intended to be a more broadly based organization than the workers' committees); created their own platform for elections to the local and Russian soviets, established the Confederation of Labor to link workers' groups and like-minded radicals throughout the country, conducted demonstrations and strikes to advance political demands, and fought to create an independent trade union, in a country that had not seen one in more than sixty years.

Yet despite all this organization building, within a year and a half these efforts were to appear fruitless, and what on the surface had been a powerful movement now seemed to have expired, overcome by its contradictions: dependence on the old system while seeking to become independent from it and indeed to transform it; uncertainty about where that transformation should lead, particularly in the economic sphere, with calls both for the self-management of the economy by working people and for a Western-style market economy; and the difficulty of a self-proclaimed workers' movement to find and maintain support from workers other than miners, let alone others outside the working class.

Still, the movement began auspiciously. At the Fourth Conference of the Kuzbass Workers' Committees, held four months after the first strike in November 1989, the Union of Working People of the Kuzbass (UWPK) was formed. The more-inclusive name "working people" (*trudyashchiesya*) was chosen deliberately to contrast with "workers" (*rabochie*), since the latter refers exclusively to the traditional, industrial, typically male workers. The union's founding program described it as a sociopolitical organization uniting workers, peasants, engineering-technical personnel (ITRs), or "all working people." "The revolution from above, started by the Party, may suffer defeat if not supported from below—this is the function that the Union takes upon itself." It called for the acceleration of perestroika, for democracy, for glasnost, and for social justice, and stated that its main goals were enfranchisement of workers through direct elections to the soviets and the independence and management of enterprises by their labor collectives. Its significance surely lay in its attempt to widen the base of the movement begun with the spontaneous miners' strike to enhance "all working people" and to include within that movement overtly political ends, if only by legally sanctioned means.[26]

Yet members of the Union of Working People were still unclear as to what the organization would become: "a popular front, a Solidarity-type trade union movement, a new party," in the words of one, or something else entirely. In fact, underneath the general goals proclaimed in the union's platform lay sharp conflict and "heated arguments" at the founding conference between the workers' committees that dominated the organization and others in attendance. The arguments were over the movement's tactics and strategies as well as, in one delegate's words, whether the new organization was to be "a political organization or a 'Fisherman's Society.'" The question of whether Communist Party membership was compatible with membership in the new organization was sharply debated, since significant numbers of members of the union were Party members. A number of delegates threatened to walk out if the group became a "social-political organization," apparently finding that position too radical. Another person present stated that since speakers expressed "contrary points of view on fundamental questions," it was not accidental that the founding program had difficulty defining what the group was all about, let alone what was meant by such concepts as "social justice."[27]

Perhaps the most important result of this conference was the creation of an independent newspaper, *Nasha Gazeta* (Our Paper), as the organ of the UWPK.[28] The paper was created, as described in its first editorial, "to fight against disinformation" and "attempts to discredit the workers' movement," against those "trying to drive a wedge between workers" and "between the intelligentsia and workers," the latter concern reflecting that the paper's staff was drawn from the intelligentsia. As expressed, an overriding goal of the UWPK was "to consolidate with professional managers, lawyers and others, . . . with those in party organs and other people within the official structures of power, who are interested, not in words but in deeds, in consolidating with the workers' movement, which has stepped forward for perestroika."[29]

The paper was forced first to publish by "partisan methods," which in practice meant finding a different enterprise newspaper (*mnogotirazhnik*) each week to publish *Nasha Gazeta* in place of the enterprise paper's regular edition. Yet within two months it had succeeded in being officially registered, becoming one of the first papers in the Soviet Union to be published officially and independently "of the party, trade union or any other apparatus." This independence surely reflected the strength of the miners' movement in the Kuzbass; yet the paper was also to reflect the movement's continuing dependence on the traditional structures of power. The only printing press in the area large enough to handle such a publication was that of *Kuzbass,* the official publication of the regional Party committee (which still carried on its masthead the slogan "Workers of the World Unite"). Thus, what was to become an increasingly anticommunist newspaper was, through the force of its popularity within the Kuzbass and beyond, published by the very power against which it struggled, but not without the constant threat of being shut down.[30]

Nevertheless, with the founding of *Nasha Gazeta* six months after the first strike, the message within the miners' movement was of support for perestroika rather than a battle against communism. The first edition of the new paper proclaimed "our union—a support for perestroika!" Mikhail Kislyuk, a mining industry economist who was to lead the liberal, market-oriented wing of the miners' movement, named Gorbachev as his favorite political figure, while Vyacheslav Golikov, head of the Council of Kuzbass Workers' Committees, cited Lenin as the political figure with whom he had the most sympathy.[31]

And the Kuzbass miners sought to carry on their struggle within boundaries defined by the state. While one miner-leader spoke of using the *diktat* of the workers' movement against the *diktat* of the bureaucracy (and another favorably compared the strike threat with Margaret Thatcher's policy of nuclear deterrence), the preference was clearly for using the threat of a strike rather than the desire for a strike itself. The UWPK's position was that the Kuzbass miners had shown "maximum responsibility" during the Vorkuta political strike—supporting the demands, but calling for the government to engage in the dialogue.[32] By March the workers' committees were arguing that the government, by its repeated unwillingness to fulfill the agreement, was "urging us to strike. But we will go a different path." Since a strike might actually harm efforts to achieve economic reform, it was argued that the struggle should be carried out through elections to the local Soviets. In June Golikov said that such threats were proving successful. The government's "concessions are not from the love of the Kuzbass; they know we are mobilizing."[33]

It was hoped that after the elections the "revolution from below" would be led by the new Soviets. One hundred candidates were nominated for the regional soviet on the platform of "the workers' movement," and an extensive campaign was carried out in the pages of *Nasha Gazeta.*

Yet the election results did not meet expectations, and the Kuzbass miner-activists were soon disillusioned with their attempt at "Soviet" power. Only 35 "workers' movement" candidates were elected to a parliament with 187 seats.[34] On the first day of the regional soviet, the "workers' movement" deputies and others allied with their platform, having failed to win a majority, walked out of the hall, arguing, "You can't run over minority opinion like a tank." Within a week Kislyuk said that by voting down the platform of the workers' movement, the soviet had placed fulfillment of the protocol in doubt, and he obliquely hinted at the threat of a strike if the movement's position were not adopted.[35]

Within weeks of the convening session of the local soviet, the workers' movement convened a meeting of its own, billed as the first congress of independent workers' organizations in the country, which took place in Novokuznetsk from 30 April to 2 May 1990. Some three hundred delegates arrived from around the country, and the meeting had a strong political and even anticommunist mood, highlighted by a passionate speech by Nikolai Travkin of the new Democratic Russia movement. The congress was deliberately held over the May Day holiday in the hope that "from the semi-official holiday of the hypocritical bureaucracy May Day again [will become] the Day of brotherhood of people of labor." The outcome of the meeting was the founding of the Confederation of Labor, which would unite independent workers' organizations throughout the country into a single political force, a conscious reflection of Poland's Solidarity.[36]

Once again expectations fell short. After the first day, a representative from Solidarity's international bureau reported that the congress was weak, that it lacked a clear goal, and that there was much talk but little being accomplished. The impression of another individual attending the congress was that as many as half of the delegates were not representatives of workers, but were instead "the sort of people who show up at such political meetings wherever they are held," and many others represented only a handful of people at best. Indeed, stringers for one news agency could not even confirm the existence of some of the groups represented at the congress. As evidence that miners generally and Kuzbass miners in particular dominated the new confederation, two of the three cochairs of the confederation, Yurii Gerol'd and Golikov, were Kuzbass miners. Yet even among the miners the organization was not strong: A poll taken six weeks later at the first congress of miners found that 62 percent of the elected delegates, certainly the most knowledgeable among the miners' ranks, had not even heard of the Confederation of Labor.[37]

Building an Independent Trade Union

Having built political organizations, the miners also sought to construct an organization that would focus more narrowly on defending their economic interests. The disillusionment with the official trade union that was expressed during the first strike had grown. Bokarev, then leader of the Donbass miners, said that since a plenum of the official coal miners' trade union had refused the independent miners' request that the coal union leave the central trade union structure, "we will discuss these questions at a miners' congress," which was said to be among the original demands of the July strike. At a congress of the official coal trade union in March 1990, delegates shouted, whistled, and stomped their feet, and the independent miners walked out of the hall. Their major complaint was that only 20 percent of the delegates were underground workers. As a miner from Vorkuta reported: "We saw the correlation of forces at the congress, and we didn't hide our protest against it. The day before we adopted a decision to leave the congress, and didn't ask for the right to vote in it, so we wouldn't be accused of participating in its work." Instead they called for the convening of a miners' congress that would discuss the creation of an independent trade union of miners.[38]

But when that congress convened in June 1990, there was some confusion as to what was meant by an independent trade union. A poll of delegates on the first day of the congress found a plurality—49 percent—agreeing that a radical purge (*ochishchenie*) and renewal of the existing trade union was needed, while 42 percent believed that no type of renewal of the official trade union was possible and that new trade unions needed to be created. There had been some changes in the official trade union to warrant optimism. On the whole, 50 percent of enterprise-level trade union chairs in the coal industry had been changed because of the strike, and reelections had taken place on the regional level as well. The secretary of the regional trade union committee in Vorkuta had recently been a face worker, the most basic mining profession. "Yesterday he worked with a shovel, while today he occupies such a serious position," one of his colleagues remarked. At the miners' congress Lunev, the chair of the official coal union, argued that the union could be transformed, since shops had been given total independence (making it, he argued, the most progressive miners' union in the world), and that anyone could be made to face new elections, including members of the union's central committee.[39]

Yet such changes, in many miners' eyes, were insufficient. The Kuzbass leader Golikov had managed to be elected to the central committee of the official trade union. "We thought we could change things through elections," he said after the official trade union congress in March. "I intend to ask those who elected me to remove me from the central committee." While there was still some support for the enterprise-level trade union organizations, many argued that beyond that level the union could not be controlled from below: "There's too many regulations and too much red tape."[40]

But the problem with the old trade union was not simply one of bureaucracy. The problem was what the trade union did: rather than defend the interests of its members, it distributed goods. As one letter to *Nasha Gazeta* put it:

> What keeps people in the trade union? Mainly this: the possibility to receive aid when temporarily unable to work, to get apartments, to acquire "deficit" goods (from cars to socks) and food, privileged vacation tours, trips to sanitoria, rest centers, etc. But after all these are the prerogatives of the enterprise. The trade union should defend the concrete individual.[41]

A delegate to the miners' congress who had recently been elected as his mine's trade union chair complained about his new position: "Up until the strike I had wide authority in the collective, but now [since the election] I am losing that authority. I am busy with the distribution of goods, but there are not enough for everyone. If the chair of the trade union committee doesn't give out goods, it means he's good for nothing. All these social problems which are shifted onto the trade union should be handled by the city Soviet." Another delegate told the congress, "We might be able to reform the trade unions if they had a single function, but a whole circle of problems weighs on their shoulders from the birth of a child to the death of a pensioner." The Vorgashorskaya mine, which led the Vorkuta political strike, had created its own trade union, and a member advised the miner-delegates to follow their example and "demand the means for state social insurance which has been going 'above'—this is no small amount—and from this pay for health clinics, pensions, trips to sanitoria and vacation centers, social aid, and so on."[42] But the assembled miners apparently preferred that an independent miners' union not be occupied with matters of distribution: while the poll of delegates showed there was no consensus on what a trade union should do, besides "preserve the health of working people" (67 percent), the results indicated that they preferred that the union defend their economic interests rather than be a distributor of privileges.[43]

The problems with the official trade union did not end with what it did and did not do; there was the further problem of its very structure. Soviet trade unions were organized along ministerial lines; just as they distributed goods and services within the enterprise, their membership reflected the great importance of industrial ministries in distributing goods and services as well as producing them. Thus many service workers were needed to accommodate the needs of the basic workforce and the industrial products required by the enterprises. At the congress a delegate argued, "We need a trade union of miners, that is people who have something to do with extracting coal, but not teachers, construction workers, people doing repairs or working in mechanical factories as it is now." He added that in his regional trade union committee there were at least ninety enterprise-level organizations, but of those only seventeen primarily involved miners. Another delegate gave more general numbers about his union local:

> We have a difficult situation. We have a trade union of 9,500 members, and of those 5,000 are underground personnel, with purely underground workers numbering only 2,500. Five thousand coal workers, with the remaining doing subsidiary economic activity, such as state farm workers, hotel workers, even 900 construction workers. I respect the labor of construction workers and peasants, but we have different problems."[44]

But the official union comprised not only subsidiary workers but all people employed in the ministry, up to the top bosses. One delegate stated that miners, including foremen, accounted for only 21 percent of the membership in the union's central committee, but that coal minister Shchadov and his deputy minister were also members. As another said, "All trade unions today are links in the state system, and the state is the single exploiter, so the trade union is also our exploiter."[45]

Indeed, many spoke harshly of the official union, as its chair and the minister of the coal industry looked on. One delegate, for example, groused, "We've wasted a lot of time over the last four days, and only one thing is for certain: let's give the trade union one in the snout, since from July strike it's acted like a schoolmarm."[46]

In discussing the creation of a new trade union, the question of who should be allowed to join became sharp. The debate is of interest since it shows, one year after the spontaneous strike, where the miners saw the boundaries between those inside and those outside their evolving movement. One question centered on whether underground workers should form their own trade union, since they, it was maintained, had special problems. Such a trade union "will not create a split in the workers' movement," one representative stated defensively. Yet the open-face miners understandably saw things differently. One argued strongly for the unity of all miners and workers, while saying that a union of underground workers was particularly dangerous, since open-face mines were creating an "ecological catastrophe" and thus many should be closed in favor of underground mines.[47] Others also argued that dividing workers was dangerous, with one contending that since there was still one ministry, there should be one trade union.[48]

Still others who had been included in the official trade union did not want to be left out of a new one. A representative of the mine rescue workers (*gornospasiteli*) asked that they not be forgotten in forming the new trade union. A worker at a coal enrichment plant argued that "of course, enrichment workers did not participate in the strike as actively as they should," but several associations did actively support the miners, he added, and others joined strike committees and workers' groups. "Many women work at the enrichment plants, because they can't find other work in coal regions while their husbands work in the mines," as did men who were unable to work underground. Therefore, he argued, there should be one united trade union of mine industry workers.[49] Others proposed a trade union along the lines of the final product—coal. Yet some saw a branch-based trade union as too narrow. "Are we not making one more mistake?" a delegate asked. "The whole world is moving from multi-party systems to non-party systems, from nationalism to cosmopolitanism, and we are building a branch fence" around the workers' movement.[50]

Indeed, the language of class and the question of class boundaries permeated much of the discussion. "In our unrestrained striving for the creation of independent trade unions we will proceed from the conception of antagonisms between the working and the dominating class—Let's clearly define who is who!" declared one. Another delegate proposed a union "united along professional-class interests," with its goal to insure that its members "expend less physical force and earn more," while adding, "This is a real chance for a solidary working class in distinction from the idealization of the party." Yet another argued, "We need to reconsider the meaning of the word 'worker.' The Party, ruling in the name of the working class widened the boundary of this concept so far that [Minister] Shchadov might be considered a worker." But success could not be achieved unless

> we get the fantasy out of our heads that the worker is the master at the enterprise. . . . The state is the owner, the minister and the director are the managers of this property, the *apparatchiki* of the ministry or the

enterprise are also managers and they should guard the interests of the employer—the state. He who sells his physical and mental labor is a worker. It's a difficult task to sort out this vinaigrette, but we must do it.[51]

But sorting out the vinaigrette proved difficult. It was clear where Shchadov and the mine directors stood, but on which side of these class divisions did the "engineering-technical workers" (ITRs) belong? They certainly sold their physical and mental labor, yet some performed managerial or supervisory functions. One delegate proposed that while Shchadov should certainly be excluded, the ITRs should be included, "unless they prove to be anti-worker." Another argued from personal experience: "For seventeen years in the coal mines I have gone from face worker to manager. . . . Many ITRs are former highly skilled face workers and tunnelers. How can we be deprived of the right to be members of our own miners' union?" He reported that the question had been discussed in his collective, and "as for workers and ITRs—the working people of our mine are against a split because our strength is in unity."[52]

By the end of the congress, the consensus was to create an independent trade union of workers in the coal industry (including ITRs in some form); a vote found 330 for, 22 against, with 75 abstaining, in sharp contrast to the poll taken on the first day which had shown only 61 percent favoring an independent trade union. Still, the precise definitions and the deciding vote remained with the individual labor collectives. However, continued concern with the question of who should belong in the industrial union, as well as the fear of interference from the "apparat," was reflected in the decision as to who would be allowed as delegates to the second miners' congress, which would be the founding congress of the new union; the decision was that no one higher than foreman was to be admitted.

While the argument over a new union dominated discussion, and was ultimately resolved, the question of the future of the economy was also a source of debate, and the answer was far less clear. Put differently, the miners were to unite in a new independent trade union, but they had not yet decided what to unite for. There was a consensus that the government agreement was not being fulfilled to the miners' satisfaction; 96 percent of the delegates polled felt the agreement was being fulfilled poorly or not at all, and when prompted for reasons, 38 percent responded that "many of the points were unfulfillable." As one angry miner told the congress, "Let's forget about [the agreement] 608, Ryzhkov and Shchadov have been leading us by the nose for nine months, let's bury it and give birth to 609, but this time with thought."[53]

Several Kuzbass delegates pushed for greater enterprise independence through the use of the market.

> What do we do now? Fine, let's go to the square [where strikers gathered], but then what, ask for more sausage and soap? . . . Better that I take care of myself, that no one worries about me. Give me freedom. Let me work freely and receive what I am able to earn so that I may feed and clothe my family. . . . For twenty years I've worked for the Motherland, fed Moscow, the brother republics and developing countries, the defense industry. . . . Enough experiments, let's bring on the market.[54]

Another had a more concrete proposal: 50 percent of all profits should be kept by the enterprise for investment and social needs, 30 percent should go to the local government, and 20 percent to the republican government (and none, therefore, to the union government). He argued that a political strike might be the only way to set up an independent trade union, with a singular demand to the Supreme Soviet and union government: "Grant the natural right of distribution of the basic and surplus product to the very producers of that product."[55]

But what of the miners of the Donbass, where the very existence of a surplus product was in question, and where the market threatened the future of many mines? Since the congress was being held in the Donbass, and the majority of delegates hailed from there, it is no wonder that such a question arose. Fears were also encouraged by the government officials, who argued for continued dependence on the state and the old trade union. Lunev, secretary of the official coal union, asserted that his union would be needed more than ever in market conditions. "The market is going to bring big problems. I'm for it, sure, but we need guarantees . . . in the face of mine closures." The deputy coal minister Garkavenko painted a much starker picture to the congress. "The coal industry is the sole 'planned-loss' branch in the economy," he declared, with 4.3 billion rubles in subsidies in 1990 alone. With market reform, he argued, the need for subsidies will grow and mine closures and unemployment will be inevitable. Deputy Prime Minister Ryabev spoke sympathetically of the miners' desire for independence through leaseholding and other measures that fit within the government's reform program, but warned miners that "the situation in the Donbass will remain difficult."[56]

The Donbass miners clearly heard these statements. One miner responded that while coal mining might be unprofitable at market prices, coal was still needed by many industries. He warned the Kuzbass miners and workers from other industries, "We must hold on to one another. If we die today, you will die tomorrow! . . . Without the help of the state, miners won't survive the market, but without miners the state can't exist—this is a law of life!" Others contended that "miners should be responsible for providing coal in the amount needed by the country, and the government should take responsibility for providing a high standard of living for miners." The survey of delegates also found rather mixed views on what the economy should look like. While 50 percent thought that as far as the introduction of private property was concerned, "the more the better," only 30 percent supported a "free market," while 59 percent supported "a regulated market economy with the strong social defense of working people." Even more telling was that only 15 percent thought that all goods should be distributed by free prices, while 38 percent believed that primary consumer goods (*tovari pervoi neobkhodimosti*) should be rationed, and 26 percent felt that all goods should be distributed by rationing. A further example of ambivalence between the independence promised by the market and the security promised by the state was displayed in the delegates' treatment of coal minister Shchadov. On the one hand he was repeatedly told to resign, and even given a vote of no confidence by the assembled miners, while on the other hand he was asked to continue to solve their concrete problems.[57]

As the delegates to the first congress returned to their mines to discuss setting up an independent trade union, *Nasha Gazeta* sought to convince the Kuzbass rank and file that they needed an independent trade union. As one worker wrote in the paper, "A trade union movement is a more mature form of the workers' movement." Employing the concepts he had been taught in school, he said, "Our economy has lagged because of backward relations of production. And our production relations have not developed because a workers' movement was forbidden. . . . The history of the workers' movement in the world is the history of the struggle for trade unions." The Kuzbass miners also sought to convince those concerned by unemployment and high prices that under a market system, "the need for militant trade unions becomes especially sharp . . . In our country, saving the drowning is the work of the drowning themselves."[58]

While such calls for self-sufficiency made for good rhetoric, the reality was that the miners were still dependent on the old system. A case in point was the second miners' congress, where the new trade union was to be established; to organize the second meeting, the miners needed money they did not have. For this money the organizational committee felt compelled to turn to Minister Shchadov, to whom the first congress had given a vote of no confidence.[59]

When the organizational committee approached Shchadov for financial help in running the second congress, he informed them that he had already set up an organizational committee of his own.[60] Needing the money, the miners agreed to form a single committee. Shchadov proposed himself as chair, though a compromise was reached in which he was a cochair, while the ministry was given "purely technical functions" in the running of the congress. Nevertheless, he succeeded in getting his speech— "The Coal Industry in Market Conditions"—on the agenda and was able to invite dozens of ministry officials and bosses as delegates, despite the ban by the first congress on delegates above the rank of foreman. When the congress began, three miner-activists from the Kuzbass, including Golikov, arrived to find they were not considered delegates, while many managers were; arguments over these questions occupied the congress until the middle of the second day. Shchadov's speech was placed at the top of the agenda, while discussion of creating an independent trade union, the original reason for convening the congress, was pushed to the bottom. While the Kuzbass delegates succeeded in changing that, discussion about the impact of the market began to dominate the congress. And unlike the first congress, many spoke in favor of reorganization of the old, official trade union. When Shchadov finally spoke, his recitation of facts and figures so overwhelmed many delegates that it became unclear "just what they would do under the market." Toward the end of the second-to-last day, the head of the Kuzbass delegation, Anatolii Malykhin, called supporters of a new trade union to meet that night outside of the congress; 130 (approximately the size of the Kuzbass delegation) of 900 delegates met at the Hotel Miner to work out a statute for the new trade union. When results were presented to the full congress the next day, they were not accepted until the Kuzbass delegates walked out of the hall. After a twenty-five-minute recess, the congress reached agreement, made some additions and changes, voted to adopt the statute, and elected an executive committee of the Independent Miners' Union (NPG).

Yet the session reflected and further widened the rift between the miners of the Donbass and the Kuzbass. According to a representative of the AFL-CIO present at the congress, all the talk of the market clearly shook the Donbass miners, so much so that "it was impossible to get the Kuzbass and the Donbass miners just to sit down together." After the congress the Kuzbass leader Aleksandr Aslanidi admitted, "such attempts [by the coal ministry and the official trade union] at disuniting and setting miners from different regions against each other succeeded to some degree. . . . The coal ministry tried to convince the Donbass that only within the ministry and the help of subsidies would it survive. And that the most important question should be the coal industry in market conditions." Golikov asserted, "Shchadov simply deceived people, promising that if you work within the ministry there won't be unemployment and the closing of mines. That's a lie, mines are closing today. Yes the Donbass and the Kuzbass have different conditions. There the mines are worked out, and the state should have begun to take care of those problems twenty-five years ago." He argued that the Soviet state, "or if it doesn't exist, then an inter-state agreement, should include these expenses in its program." Then in a statement revealing how much the rift had widened (a year and a half before the union was dissolved), he added, "If help is needed, we, I think, will not leave the Ukrainian miners without it, just as we helped the English miners in their time," referring to assistance given by the official trade union during the recent British coal strike.[61]

Yet the Independent Miners' Union was created: it was to cover production workers in coal extraction enterprises, with the possibility that other types of miners might eventually join. ITR workers were admitted, though into a separate association within the larger union, and foremen were also allowed "with the acceptance of the labor collective." The NPG consciously modeled itself on Western trade unions, focusing on defending economic interests. Its main goal was to conclude collective agreements with the employer—the state—and to achieve "a fair price for labor as determined by the market." And there was a contradiction between a disdain for hierarchy and the need to create a strong organization in difficult conditions: In strong contrast to the old trade union (and to not a few Western unions), by its stature the NPG was very decentralized, with the center having at most coordinating, or "recommendatory" functions, while the primary enterprise-level organizations would have the last word on virtually every question.

The Workers' Committees

The founding of an independent trade union did not mean that the miners were walking away from their explicitly political concerns. In fact, for many the trade union was able to have purely economic goals because it was only one stream within the broader workers' movement. The workers' committees, for instance—the former strike committees that had risen spontaneously during the course of the first strike—were still in existence and continued to provide the closest link between rank-and-file miners and their elected leaders.

Nevertheless, the workers' committees were not without difficulties of their own, which again underscored the continued dependence of the miners on the old system they were attempting to transform. Traditionally, members of the enterprise party committee, trade union committee, and later the Labor Collective Council (STK) (and others, stretching to enterprise musical and dance troupes) were "freed from production": while retaining the pay and privileges of their former positions, these people were allowed to work full time on their "social functions." The administration largely decided who should be granted such status, and workers, as they were to express it after the strike, detested feeding these unproductive mouths. But if strike committee members were going to organize, they would need to be paid, and with no independent means they too had to be "freed from production." This presented the workers' committees with two problems. First, they had to insure that each mine's collective met periodically to grant this status to its representatives and that the miners within each enterprise were strong enough to overcome any attempts by the administration to prevent such actions. Second, it placed the workers' committee members in the same category as members of the Communist Party committee and others the miners had long detested.[62]

The problems of overcoming the power of the administration were real. Some mines were not represented at the miners' congresses because directors had simply dragged their feet and prevented their collectives from electing delegates. When new elections to worker committees were called, in preparation for a possible strike on the anniversary of the first strike, Golikov warned: "We must preserve our independence," so that "the elections be like they were last year during the strike." Yet in the Kuzbass town of Berezovskii all but one of the members of the city's strike committee had been recalled; the only remaining member was a pensioner, who did not have to be "freed" from anything. Members of the worker committees of Mezhdurechensk and Prokop'evsk had to go around to six enterprises to make sure that genuine elections for new members took place. The chair of the strike committee of the Kapitalnaya mine was told that for the last twelve days, his time spent on workers' committee activities would come out of his vacation time; when the collective voted to pay him, the director, angry at the worker-activist for leading a campaign to remove the enterprise Party committee, charged him with being absent from work instead. In September 1990, the Kemerovo city workers' committee issued a public "appeal to the working people of the city of Kemerovo," stating that there was only one "freed" member left on the city committee and that there were many unsolved problems, including "sabotage, lack of authority, and a difficult situation in society." "We appeal to the labor collectives of the city of Kemerovo—delegate your representatives to the city workers' committee!"[63]

While hostile managers and Communist Party officials posed some of the problem, another part was recalls by the miners themselves. The labor collectives had the right to recall representatives for any reason, at any time, and the workers' committee representatives were responsible for a regular accounting of their activities before their constituents. If the miners had questioned the activity of the strike leaders before, they were even more likely to do so as they became increasingly frustrated with the government's failure to fulfill their demands in worsening economic conditions.[64]

One miner-activist spoke of the problem of recalls not from the workers' committees but from the commission charged with monitoring the government's fulfillment of Resolution 608 (though the problems appear to be the same).

> People are nominating representatives who can shout louder than all the rest. Not only that, but it's also happening that thoughtful, literate specialists . . . are being recalled from the commission, and if not recalled, then not supported. For some reason people think that representatives who can 'grab people by the throat' and 'wave the sword' will be able to achieve more. Around 70 percent of the Donbass representatives have been changed.

The recalls had become, as this representative put it, "our sickness. The plague of the workers' movement." In the Vorkuta city strike committee, it was said that 90 percent of the membership had changed four months after the first strike and within a year was on the fourth round of workers' committee leaders.[65]

The failure of the government to fulfill its promises, the deteriorating economy, and the increasing calls for alternatives to existing political institutions all helped drive the radicalization of the miners' movement.[66] Yet miner leaders were also pushed from below, prodded by the fear of being removed (and returned to the mines) if they failed to bring about results. In May 1990, the Kuzbass Council of Workers' Committees appealed to the region's labor collectives to renew the activity of the worker (strike) committees at enterprises and in cities and to create new ones where they had not existed before. "We haven't achieved our economic demands," the appeal declared, making a political strike possible. At the miners' congress in June, it was said that during the first strike "they outsmarted us, . . . led us away from politics." Miners from Vorkuta sent an appeal to the congress "to support on July 1, 1990 a general strike in all coal regions of the country." The congress agreed, and it passed a resolution stating that since the present government lacked the decisiveness or the ability to end the state's monopoly in the economic sphere and the Communist Party's monopoly on power, it demanded the government resign, calling on President Gorbachev to form a new "government of popular trust" that could carry through economic and political reform. (The delegates did not appear concerned that this resolution contradicted an earlier one, passed 323 to 138, that endorsed completing an agreement with the very same government.)[67]

In the Kuzbass, a daylong strike was called for July 11 in support of the decision of the miners' congress, with the demands that the union government resign, the democratic decisions of the Russian congress be supported, new and direct elections be held to the Soviet parliament, a new constitution be drafted, and the property of the Communist Party be nationalized. A big strike was promised in the Kuzbass, with the possibility of strikes and demonstrations throughout the country.[68]

The strike was smaller than expected. Whereas *Nasha Gazeta* claimed that two-thirds of the mines of the Kuzbass participated, though many for only two hours, *Pravda* stated that only one-third struck. In the Donbass, the regional workers' committee split over the strike vote, leaving the decision to the individual labor collectives, with the result that the strike was said to be anticlimactic.[69]

The rank and file appeared to be split as well over the wisdom of a purely political strike. While in one mining town a *Nasha Gazeta* reporter quoted workers as saying, "Already in the last strike we should have advanced political demands, but we were scared," and "We need to strike longer, two hours is not enough, no one will pay attention to us," in a neighboring town another correspondent asked rhetorically, "Isn't the reason [the strike] didn't find support from many working people of Kiselevsk because the strike advanced only political demands, and completely rejected economic ones?" Yet in another Kuzbass town, miners, while discussing their views on Gorbachev, showed how in subtle but important ways their thinking had changed from their initial support of "perestroika from below": "Gorbachev woke us up, and if a person wakes up, then he acquires a natural ability to think." Another declared,

> I would name Gorbachev himself as the force which leads the miners in the struggle for their rights. He placed us on the rails of perestroika and commanded us to apply pressure from below. But now he alleges there's some dark force [among the miners]. It seems like he underestimated the intellectual ability of miners, considers us undereducated laborers. That's a shame.[70]

A further difficulty with demanding the resignation of the government, beyond getting people to strike for such a demand, was that it required cutting off negotiations as well as requests to improve living conditions and the food supply. And that meant waiting even longer for the satisfaction of some very basic demands. In one telling scandal, Kokorin, the leader of the Mezhdurechensk mine that started the first strike, was kicked off the city strike committee for taking two television sets given to the strike committee for distribution. He succeeded in getting reinstated to the strike committee, at which point he went to Moscow to request increased food and other supplies from the Ryzhkov government, despite a decision by the regional workers' committees to break off all relations with the government. He was called a strikebreaker and thrown off the city committee once again, but the reactions of other members of the city strike committee to the scandal are revealing. When asked if they supported Kokorin, one former colleague answered, "Well yes and no. We can't live like this anymore. Something has to be done to lower the tension." Another responded, "Now people are so apathetic that to them politics isn't what's needed. People are busy trying to find something in the stores. Right now people don't want independence. . . . Some miners say, 'If the powers that be need us, let them support us, give us something. And if not, let them get rid of us.'"[71]

Indeed, the suggestion was that the leaders of the miners' movement had lost touch with their constituents and were becoming increasingly ineffectual. An article entitled "Better Mineral Water than Coal Dust" in the paper *Komsomolskaya Pravda,* which had been quite sympathetic to miners' movement, claimed that because of bureaucracy, political infighting, and being detached from the rank and file, the miner-leaders and their organizations had lost their strength. The suggestion was made here and elsewhere that while they had given a powerful spur to both the state and society with their strike, they should now return to the coal face and let others more qualified handle the complex questions of politics and economics. The only thing that was holding up this process, the article maintained, was that the miner-activists had gotten used to swallowing "mineral water rather than coal dust."[72]

Soviet Miners and Social Movement Theory

A year and a half after the spontaneous mass strike, the attempt to build a strong workers' movement had achieved mixed results at best. The miners had succeeded in building a number of organizations—including the city and regional workers' committees, a Union of Working People of the Kuzbass, the Confederation of Labor, and the Independent Miners' Union. In addition, the miners increased their control of many trade union committees, STKs, and workers' committees in the mines. Yet the Union of Working People of the Kuzbass had ceased to exist as an influential organization ten months after its founding, it was not clear who the Confederation of Labor represented, and the NPG had yet to build a single mine-level trade union organization. Most troublesome of all was the weak link between the regional workers' committees, the real leaders of the miners' movement, and the miners themselves. This problem was clear from the aftermath of the July political strike, from the empty shells that many workers' committees had become, and from the recalls by miners of their own elected leaders.

According to resource mobilization theory—long the dominant approach in the United States for the study of social movements—the Soviet miners' movement would seem to have failed. With its focus on formal organizations as the agents of social change, resource mobilization theory could not have accounted for the first spontaneous mass strike of July 1989, nor would it have been able to predict the second mass strike, of March and April 1991. In both cases, strong institutions that might mobilize, unite, and coordinate miners did not previously exist, and those that did were often pushed to the side. The organizations that did matter were "emergent" institutions, such as the strike committees that arose spontaneously during the first strike, and other organizations, such as the interregional coordinating committee, that arose to meet the needs of the next mass strike.

But while the organizations themselves may not have been strong, one cannot say that the workers' movement was without strengths. In the Kuzbass, for example, the miners had succeeded in creating an independent newspaper, which had grown in circulation from 10,000 subscribers to 130,000 within three months. While its importance as an independent source of information and political views should not be underestimated, the paper was perhaps even more important as a symbol of defiance in a society where for so many years the state maintained a monopoly of the printed word. And while the NPG would have a difficult time establishing itself as a powerful force, the miners' congresses, albeit tumultuous, had established continued contacts between the miners from widespread regions. Moreover, the mere creation of an independent trade union was also a strong act of defiance in a society where the state had long monopolized this right as well—the right to speak on behalf of the workers themselves.

There were other signs of strength, also hard to measure. While the miners in July 1989 had consciously kept their language and actions (outside of the act of striking itself) within acceptable limits and away from high politics, the miners clearly no longer felt confined by such boundaries. And while it was clear that support for "purely political" strikes was mixed, the miners on the ground began to focus anger on the Communist Party. If before individual Party leaders were attacked as insensitive or corrupt, the Party was now attacked as an institution and its monopoly power rejected as mine after mine voted to remove the Party from its premises. Previously, the miners' vexations had fixed upon local-level officials and changes within the enterprise, the community, or the region, and had called on top state officials, including Prime Minister Ryzhkov, to guarantee that their demands be met. But by signing the agreement, the government itself had come into the miners' field of vision, and when it failed to fulfill the agreement to their satisfaction, its legitimacy, from the miners' perspective, became questionable.

The unfulfilled agreement helps in part to answer the following question: In the absence of strong organizations to mobilize the rank and file, how can we explain a two-month-long "political strike" that shook the coal fields once again, challenged the very essence of Soviet power, and threatened to grow into a general strike? The change from economic to increasingly political concerns, however, can only partially be explained by the failure of the state to fulfill the strike agreement. More deeply, the failed promises of Soviet socialism continued to motivate the miners. The anger exhibited at the Kuibyshev trade union meeting only grew, as did miners' criticisms of Soviet institutions. And yet the ideals that were a legacy of those institutions continued to influence miners as they defined such concepts as social justice and even democracy and the market. Indeed, while they explicitly stopped invoking Lenin and addressing each other as "comrade," the miners viewed the world and plotted their strategies through an ideological framework derived largely from the very system they were trying to transform. As we shall see, even as they were calling for the removal of the Communist Party from power and pushing for the market for their heavily subsidized industry, the ideals of socialism, if unacknowledged, remained at the core of their project.

CHAPTER 6

From Economics to Politics

We now turn to the question of how the miners moved from narrow economic demands to such self-consciously political demands, in less than two years. Why, despite so many expectations to the contrary, did these members of the Soviet working class, rather than defend the Soviet system, demand liberal political reforms? More surprisingly still, why did the coal miners, in the single most heavily subsidized industry in the Soviet Union, push not for increased state subsidies, but for the accelerated introduction of the market?

Some have argued that the miners' demand for liberal economic reforms was a result of rational calculations—they sought to take advantage of the relatively high world market price for coal. Others claim the miners were gulled by liberal intellectuals; still others assert that the miners' actions were the result of "contradictory class consciousness" and naiveté. The problem with each of these explanations is that they do not examine how the miners themselves expressed their concerns. Rather than rational expectations or myopia, coal miners grafted their working class concerns onto the rhetoric of liberal reformers, ultimately creating a vision of democracy and the market quite at odds with traditional liberalism.

This chapter begins with a narrative treatment of the second all-union miners' strike, then proceeds with an analysis of in-depth interviews with miners from various regions. These interviews are examined with a view to understanding the source of the miners' resurgence as well as the dynamic nature of their demands and the cultural framework through which they were made.

The 1991 Strike

On the eve of their major political strike, the miners' movement looked particularly weak.[1] In January 1991, the rank-and-file members voted down an attempt by leaders of the Kuzbass miners to lead a political strike over the repression by Soviet troops in Lithuania. A meeting just weeks before the start of the strike found miners sharply divided over what demands were important (only economic demands were discussed), and

123

even whether to strike at all. Moreover, their position was being challenged by the increasingly populist-leaning official trade unions, who were calling for strikes of their own.[2] Even managers were getting into the act: In Donetsk, directors of the Donetskugol association threatened to withhold the loading of their coal until the Ukrainian government made concessions; that they appeared to succeed without any help from the independent miners' organizations was seen as a threat to the independents' standing in the eyes of the rank and file.[3]

Not to be outdone by their own management, the regional council of strike committees of the Donbass threatened to strike on March 1 if there was no agreement with the U.S.S.R. and Ukrainian governments on pay (the demand was for a 100 to 150 percent pay increase, together with additional pension benefits). Yet when they failed to get an agreement by the appointed deadline, the miner-representatives could not agree among themselves on the strike question: some proposed a one-day warning strike; others were flatly against the strike, saying it was premature. When no strike proposal gained a majority of votes, representatives from the city of Donetsk said that they reserved the right to strike regardless, with the final word being given, as always, to the labor collectives.[4]

In this fashion began what was to be the closest the Soviet Union ever came to experiencing a general strike. On March 1, the sixteen mines of Donetskugol worked but halted the delivery of coal; only five mines in Krasnoarmeisk and Makeevka, of a total of 214 in the Donbass, stopped work completely. But the Ukrainian miners were joined by twenty of the twenty-six mines of the Karaganda fields in Kazakhstan. There the demands were for an increase in pay and "normal food supplies," in addition to the call that the "Union treaty be signed immediately on mutually beneficial conditions."[5]

The Donbass strike call also reverberated in the Kuzbass, where the focus became explicitly political: The regional council voted for a political strike on March 3, this time demanding that President Gorbachev resign, that leadership of the Soviet Union be transferred to the Federation Council, and that the KGB, the Army, and the Interior Ministry be "de-politicized" of the Communist Party.[6] However, on the next day only three mines partially downed tools. That same day, the Karaganda strike was suspended, the Karaganda miners having concluded a republican agreement with Kazakhstan President Nazarbayev that included moving the mines to the republic's jurisdiction. Thus the strike began inauspiciously— only thirty of 594 mines struck on March 1. Meanwhile, the demands varied dramatically between republics: they were clearly economic in the Donbass, while in Kazakhstan economic demands were combined with calls for republican autonomy. Even within a single republic, demands were incompatible—while the Kuzbass miners called for the president and union government to resign, the only demand of the miners of Vorkuta was for direct negotiations with the prime minister over economic concerns.[7]

Nevertheless, the strike gathered momentum, taking on increasing importance for the constituent republics. Though only a few mines were out in the Kuzbass, Yeltsin met with Kuzbass representatives to discuss the transfer of the mining and steel industries to the Russian republic. Meanwhile, all twelve mines of Chervonograd in (the more nationalist) western Ukraine joined the strike, arguing that the miners' demands from 1989 would not be fulfilled without a change in the political structure. The demands included abolishing the post of president of the U.S.S.R. and dismissing the Soviet congress; granting the Ukrainian declaration of state sovereignty the status of a constitutional act; rejecting the union treaty; and releasing Stepan Khmara (a Ukrainian nationalist) and other political prisoners.[8] Despite the fact that the strike was initially limited in the Kuzbass, support came across class lines for their political demands, as food and financial assistance was received from Lithuania, and the Democratic Russia movement began a solidarity picket in downtown Moscow. In order to increase the visibility of their demands, four miners and one Russian people's deputy from the Kuzbass began a hunger strike in Moscow.[9]

By March 14, political demands were added in the Donbass, where the strike had originally started over wage and pension issues. Miners there now called for the USSR Supreme Soviet to be abolished, for Ukraine to be given political and economic sovereignty, and an for end to "deductions for the center."[10]

The number of mines on strike continued to grow as well. By April 4, between 100 and 150 mines were out. Because there were varying degrees of striking, it was hard to get a firm count: while some mines stopped completely, others extracted coal without delivering it, and still others shipped coal to local consumers at the request of regional strike committees. Some mines struck one day and worked the next, and others were divided between sections of the same mine.[11]

Faced with such a formidable, if not united, challenge, the "center" attempted to apply both the carrot and the stick. Coal minister Shchadov sought to have strikers fired, while on the local level, miners in Karaganda, Pavlograd, and Tula were taken to court under the law on labor conflict established after the first miners' strike.[12] Miners from several mines claimed that their phone lines were cut, while some mines were threatened with having their electricity shut off for nonpayment (which, miners argued, was a transparent bluff, since such an action would have prevented necessary maintenance and would have destroyed the mine). Others claimed that food shipments to their regions had been reduced, while in several cases social services provided by the mines (such as day-care centers) were suspended or closed off to striking miners.[13] At the same time, the Soviet Council of Ministers proposed to the Supreme Soviet that striking miners be fired and that organizers be sentenced to two years of "corrective labor." The proposal was voted down, but the vote could not have helped dampen the miners' demand that the government be removed from office.

Indeed, when the Soviet government finally managed to extend the carrot, it was rejected. On March 26, the Supreme Soviet voted to propose that the miners suspend the strike for two months, while suggesting that the government grant all their economic demands.[14] Gorbachev and Prime Minister Pavlov, who had agreed earlier to meet with only nonstriking miners, later dropped this condition. In early April, Gorbachev addressed a collection of representatives of the mining industry, where he agreed to double miners' wages (though in stages, an important point given the now open inflation), to increase the number of professions on the list for privileged pensions, to compensate miners for recent price increases, and to allow a certain percentage of coal produced (5 percent for coking coal, 7 percent for energy-grade coal) to be sold at market prices, including markets abroad.[15]

But while these concessions would have been considerable a month or so earlier, in the present conditions they only inflamed the strike. Ironically, the strike seemed to have been waning prior to Gorbachev's address to the miners.[16] Certainly part of the explanation lies in the ill-timed price increases, which took effect on April 1. But the reaction was not only to rising prices, but also to the government that implemented them and to the political system itself.[17] While the sole demand of miners in Vorkuta had been a meeting with Prime Minister Pavlov, they later rejected his offer of a visit to the region. Despite the Supreme Soviet's ban on protests, the invitation to talk with the government, and Gorbachev's later concessions, more mines went out on strike. In the Donbass it was declared that now the "political demands were the most important," while additional economic demands were added to the ones granted by the government, including signing the miners' General Tariff Agreement and paying for the time on strike.[18]

The strike hit virtually all the mining regions of the country. While the numbers within each region varied, even from day to day, miners struck in the Donbass, the Kuzbass, Vorkuta, Inta, the South Urals, Rostov, Tula, Kizel, indeed, as in 1989, from L'vov in western Ukraine to Sakhalin in the far east.

Despite the broad nature of their political demands and the fact that their strike activity had brought economic gains (however unsatisfactory to the miners), workers in other industries, as was true with steelworkers in the first strike, reacted hardly at all. This behavior is all the more puzzling since all workers were suffering great economic hardships, including the recent unprecedented price increases. Workers in other industries were directly affected by the strike, as the lack of coal hampered production in the rail transport, heating, metallurgical, and machine-building industries; in all such industries, workers' wages were tied to production levels.[19] Already by March 23, the national news program "Vremya" stated with black humor that "our economy is sliding further and further into the pits."[20] By April 11, more than twenty blast furnaces at different steel enterprises had been shut down for lack of coking coal, including four of five at the Chelyabinsk works alone, and there were appeals virtually every day in the press, often in the name of the labor collective, for the miners to provide coal to this or that enterprise.

Rail workers, who were paid by the amount of freight hauled, were hit particularly hard. In the Kuzbass town of Belovo, rail workers voted against joining the strike, while in Krasnoarmeisk, a strong center of strike action in the Donbass, rail workers spoke out against the strike, which they said was costing them wages, and in Vorkuta, rail workers gave miners an ultimatum. Even in L'vov, where Ukrainian nationalism played a clear role in miners' militancy, rail workers were said to be against the strike.[21]

All the while the miners, who had asked workers in other industries to refrain from striking in 1989, were now agitating for a general strike. "I don't deny that I'm in favor of a general strike. This might achieve a lot," one miner told a foreign journalist, while according to Volynko, a strike leader in Donetsk, "If other sectors don't support us, we'll never get off our knees."[22]

The support that the miners did receive came as much across class lines as within. Liberals saw the miners as the powerful force that they lacked to push through their changes. Pickets by the Democratic Russia movement grew in size in Moscow and elsewhere, while collection boxes were placed throughout the city for contributions to the miners' strike fund.[23] In Leningrad the city council and the local Democratic Russia organization called for a one-hour political strike, though unsuccessfully. Food, clothing, and money arrived in the mining regions from Georgia, Armenia, and all three of the Baltic republics. In one of the more interesting cases of support across class lines, the Union of Cooperatives (really an organization of entrepreneurs) donated 10 million rubles to the miners' strike fund.[24]

The support coming from other workers was muted. Oil and gas workers threatened to strike, but clearly with the goal of gaining greater control over their valuable resources.[25] The confederation of Labor Collective Councils of the USSR called for a forty-eight-hour warning strike to support political demands, though the strike never materialized and it is unlikely the group would have been able to mobilize any such action. The official steelworkers union called for a "day of demonstrations" to call attention to the industry's economic plight but rejected strikes and called for the miners to return to work.[26]

The strikes that did break out were largely marginal. At the giant Uralmash plant, a bread shortage led to a short strike, where strikers proclaimed support for the miners.[27] Steel plants that struck were exceptions that proved the rule: The Norilsk plant, where steel founding was combined with ore mining, went on strike for twenty-four hours, while in Sverdlovsk a two-hour warning strike led by the local mining and metallurgical trade union apparently had the blessing of the plant's general director. "I want to stress right away that the strike did not have the slightest effect on the productivity rate . . . because it was carried out either between shifts or at dinner time. The main task is to support the miners' political demands," said the regional chair of the trade union.[28]

The major exception to the lack of strike activity was provided by workers in Minsk, until that time considered one of the least politically active regions in the Soviet Union.[29] The strike was sparked by the April 1 price increases, which led to a warning strike at an electrotechnical plant, which in turn led to mass walkouts and demonstrations throughout the city. The initial demands were economic in nature, including compensation for the price increases, especially for the dinners provided in the plant cafeterias, but political demands were soon added.[30]

Despite their unsuccessful calls for a general strike, the miners remained strong until the end. Even after an agreement to end the strike was reached in Ukraine, Donbass miners continued to strike, arguing that their political demands had not been met. In the Kuzbass, the number of mines on strike continued to grow throughout April. In Vorkuta, miners agreed to return to work after receiving a telegram that stated that the Vorkutaugol coal association had been transferred from Soviet to Russian jurisdiction.[31] In the Kuzbass, the strike ended only after Yeltsin, who had recently signed the "Nine-Plus-One" agreement with Gorbachev and the other republican leaders, flew to the region to explain that he had not betrayed the miners, who had been demanding the resignation of the very person with whom Yeltsin had been secretly negotiating.[32] After bargaining with the miners, Yeltsin presented the transfer of mines to Russian jurisdiction as a great victory, which was intended to mean that the mines could keep 50 to 70 percent of their product to distribute as they chose and be granted full economic autonomy, including the right to choose the mine's form of property.[33]

Even though their political demands were not fulfilled, the miners saw this outcome, which they viewed as granting them significant control over their workplaces, as a considerable achievement.[34] Yet even after Yeltsin's reassurances, the decision to end the strike was not taken lightly. As for the agreement that their mines would be placed under Russian jurisdiction, the miners demanded that they have the original document signed by all the responsible parties before calling for an end to the strike.[35] Reflecting both the weakness of the Soviet state and the strike's further aggravation of state power, the strike ended in the three republics involved—Ukraine, Russia, and Kazakhstan—when the miners signed agreements with republican leaders, not the Soviet "center."[36]

Indeed, though the strike's legacy was soon overwhelmed by the failed putsch, its impact should not be underestimated. While Gorbachev's accommodation of the conservatives in January—exemplified by the crackdown in Lithuania—had helped radicalize the miners to call for his resignation, the strike itself and the popular support it received compelled Gorbachev to move back toward the reformers and sign the "Nine-Plus-One" agreement, which was to grant considerable autonomy to the republics. It was the impending implementation of that agreement that provoked the coup plotters to act, with their failure leading to the eventual collapse of the Soviet state.

The strike itself was characterized by the Soviet media as "the biggest social explosion in 70 years of Soviet rule."[37] Even allowing for hyperbole, it is hard to think of another single event that might deserve that claim. In economic terms, the strike placed the coal industry in debt, even with the very low purchase price of coal, for 4 billion rubles worth of coal to other industries.[38]

Political Demands

In discussing the political demands of the 1991 strike, Clarke and Fairbrother have maintained, "The fundamental question is whether the Workers' Committees represented the views of the miners in this regard, or whether they were functioning in the best Bolshevik tradition of harnessing the workers' economic demands to their own political aspirations."[39] They argue strongly for the latter view, contending the leaders were duped by liberal reformers, while "workers themselves showed . . . that they were primarily concerned with their economic conditions."[40] Others have argued that the miners were not duped, but rather were rational actors—

that the coal miners' embrace of political demands was motivated by direct economic interests, especially the desire to market coal for hard currency on world markets.[41] Still others have seen the "extremely radical forms of working class organization in the pursuit of . . . pro-market or even pro-capitalist" demands a result of "contradictory consciousness" and "conceptual confusion."[42]

It will be argued here that the miners were indeed deeply politicized in 1991 and that they were driven above all by economic concerns. Yet they interpreted their economic interests through an ideological framework of their own making. This framework was comprised of elements of the ideology of liberal reformers, but these elements were appropriated by the coal miners and reinterpreted to meet their own needs. Yet miners also interpreted their situation through core elements of the old dominant ideology, even as they were demanding that the old system be dismantled. The result was that Soviet coal miners fought against the Soviet system and for liberal reforms, including the market, but for reasons that were at odds with those of their liberal allies, reasons that at root were quite socialist.[43]

We have seen that the miners were unorganized on the eve of this major strike. A meeting of miners' representatives from around the country found sharp divisions over the strike issue only two weeks before it began.[44] Some called for thorough planning and acting only in unison. Delegates argued that without a coordinating organ for the spontaneous nationwide strike two years earlier, the results had been mixed at best.[45] Another argued that strikes in only one region would be doomed: "Tanks can't crush unity. But local strikes they will crush."

Others were concerned about a lack of consensus among rank-and-file miners. One delegate reported about a trip among the mines of Karaganda and the Kuzbass: "It's no secret what the miners said, 'Let's get something, demand something.' But how? There are those who want to strike, while others say that we have to think everything over seriously, we are now talking with the government, it's cold now, winter, and so on."[46]

On the other hand, the miners were clearly concerned with recent strike calls by the official trade unions, which were seen as a provocation. The representatives of the independent miners' organizations feared that a successful strike by the official trade unions would greatly discredit the independent miners. Argued one delegate, "I'm against ignoring a strike called by [the official trade unions]. We need to participate. If we don't seize the initiative, we won't be worth a damn." Others contended that it was simply time to take action. "There are those who say we shouldn't strike," declared Yerokhin from the Kuzbass. "But we don't have any other weapon and we never will."

Given such prompting from official trade unions and even mine directors, the strike followed a path quite independent of that of its leaders. Such was true even in the Donbass, where the strike began. "When the strike started we were already catching up with a moving train," Mikhail Krylov, cochair of the Donetsk strike committee, later confessed.[47]

Indeed, one interesting aspect of the strike was how much the demands changed, not only from the strike two years earlier, but during the course of the two-month strike itself. At the meeting of representatives just before the strike, political demands played a very small role. The concerns raised at that time were clearly economic, as miners were troubled by inflation that was eating up past gains and rampant rumors of future price rises. One of the main economic concerns was for an additional fourteen days of vacation for those employed in dangerous work, a demand that had been decreed by the state but not implemented locally at mines.[48]

A further question, seemingly quite small, involved the number of professions entitled to a privileged pension. The issue, as with others concerning privileges, divided miners: "Will a tunneler fight for a timberer, when he himself is three years from a pension?" asked one, while another added, "Some tunnelers say, I've got my pension, but remember, you got it thanks to the timberers—everyone struck." Still a third maintained, "We should have one principle: everyone from shaft to face is an underground worker. We all have to eat." Others argued that the issue was meant to divide miners: "They're dividing us amongst ourselves, what will happen next?" Another alleged, "The government is trying to knock our heads together."

Even though the miners themselves would be calling for a general strike within weeks, the more parochial question of solidarity was one that initially concerned only miners, involving issues about different regions, different professions, and so forth. And on the eve of a "political strike," the concerns remained almost exclusively economic: according to Pavel Shushpanov, then chair of the NPG, "The main task is improving wages and social conditions."[49] The trade union's means of obtaining that goal was the General Tariff Agreement (GTA), a labor contract based upon the American model. "The GTA is the basis of all trade union activity," Shushpanov explained. "All the other trade unions are waiting. If it works out for us, then they will also follow this path." Argued Yerokhin, "All these questions: pensions, vacations, . . . the cost of living—all are in the GTA," which he said was the miners' decree no. 608 on a higher level.

As for the rapid shift to political demands, we have seen how the state's inability to fulfill its past promises helped turn the miners against the state. There was continued anger over the fact that their past demands had not been fulfilled, followed by a belief that a government that had signed a document guaranteeing action by specific dates and had yet failed to do so could not be trusted. The miners who had helped bring down Prime Minister Ryzhkov in the search for satisfaction of their demands now moved up the political hierarchy to Gorbachev himself. One told of a message he had passed on to the Soviet president: "Mikhail Sergeevich," the note read, "you guaranteed that these questions would be fulfilled, but they haven't been: pensions, vacations, ..."[50]

But the miners began to focus attention on the state not only as potential guarantor of demands, but also as employer and owner. In regard to the enterprise-level labor contract, one miner argued, "Go ahead, conclude a contract. But remember one thing—where is the money you need? You can remove the director, but you won't find the money. You can force him to take the money from the fund for social development to pay your wages. I see a different answer—The contract should be with the owner, and we have only one owner—the state."[51]

In this way even bread-and-butter trade unionism meant confronting the state. According to Sergeev, then deputy chair of the NPG,

> The main task of our trade union is to oppose the employer, that is the state. For many years we were told that we, the workers and peasants, were the masters of our country, and that property in the USSR belongs to the entire people. However, in 1990 the USSR Supreme Soviet adopted the Law on Property, and it turned out that it no longer belongs to the people: [the majority of it] belongs to the state. . . . Therefore, this law confirmed that a certain opposition exists in our country between the state . . . and hired labor. This opposition is part of an objective reality, and that is why trade unions should reckon with it.[52]

But the push toward political demands came not only from the state's stature as employer. Ever since their first strike, miners had been accused of "taking all the blanket for themselves," since, it was argued, any concessions the state granted to the miners had to be taken from someone else.

Thus, on the eve of their strike, Ukrainian Prime Minister Fokin addressed the Donbass miners on Soviet television about their economic demands: "Tell me please, from which part [of the budget] are we to cut out these billions, or to be more precise, from whom are we to take them?" His rhetorical response to the question included teachers, health care and day-care workers, pensioners, and invalids.[53]

Likewise, Volynko of the Donetsk city strike committee argued with peculiar logic that this strike began because miners were unhappy with press coverage of the workers' movement and their demands. "Miners do not want to look like spongers ready to snatch a piece of bread from some-body else's mouth," as the press would paint them.[54]

One way around the charge that miners were demanding more than their share from the state coffers, seen by all as a zero-sum game, was to orient the strike to political demands, which were directed only at the state. As a result, political demands were seen as less selfish and representing a higher consciousness than economic demands. Kuzbass miners did not hide their pride that they had first raised political demands during the strike; thus Golikov of the Kuzbass would claim that they had stopped asking "for more deliveries of carloads of goods and sausages" from Moscow.[55] Even miners in the Donbass, where the strike had begun over raising miners' wages and pensions, would argue during the strike that they had "no purely miners' demands."[56]

If political demands were better than appealing for more goods from the state, then demanding independence from the state was seen as best of all. As one Donbass miner explained of their demands in 1989, "We worked on a package of demands that would be ridiculous to discuss in a civilized society, demands about providing more soap—this in a country of triumphant socialism. . . . I think that the only point necessary and worth anything in those demands was a paragraph demanding full auton-omy for enterprises."[57]

Exploitation and the Labor Theory of Value

More important still than the concern for how their demands were being perceived by others was the miners' strong sense of exploitation—a sense that they were not justly paid for the product of their labor. Paralleling that was the notion that if there was to be a market, their goal should be to sell their labor power for a just wage on the market for labor. Yet in their considerable rhetoric in support of the market, just payment for their labor was seen as based not on its market value determined by supply and demand, but on a materialist-based labor theory of value.[58] For instance, miners were outraged that workers in trade—who produced nothing—were getting paid more than miners. As one delegate to the miners' con-ference explained:

> You don't have to think, from where to get the money. You only need to sell your labor power. There's money. We've concluded a contract for 10.5 million Rubles with people who do absolutely no labor what-soever. There's a [small] state cooperative, which has a wage fund of 1.1 million Rubles. While [at our mine] we have 3.5 thousand people and our wage fund is 1.2 million Rubles. So, there's money.[59]

Indeed, many miners had calculated that they were earning only a very small percentage of the true value of their product, though on what basis this calculation was made was hard to determine. Thus Yerokhin argued at the conference before the strike that there should be only two demands—the GTA and monthly wage indexation. "Then we will sell our labor power every month. While now we sell ourselves for 10 percent of what we earn and live like slaves."[60] As one miner explained to the author, "For every dollar you earn you get 60–75 cents, while we get only 13 kopecks from every ruble. And from that 13 kopecks they still take out taxes. With the remaining 87 kopecks 'they' buy whatever they want. Even if I work in a mine I can't afford to feed my family." Others made much the same argument: "By our data, in the coal industry from 8–12 percent of the value of our productive labor goes into the wage fund. If we don't solve the political question, then that [additional] pay isn't going any-where."[61]

Moreover, the resentment generated by this sense of exploitation had a strong class character. When miners railed against Communists, they spoke of them as ranging from their section boss up to General Secretary Gorbachev. One Donetsk miner, at a demonstration on the square before the oblast party headquarters, spoke of class antagonisms within the mines this way: "Look around—on the square there isn't a single foreman, not one section head. In 1989 they weren't here either. They say 'go ahead and strike, if you get something, it will come our way. And if you don't get anything, we'll live well just the same.'"[62]

As for why miners were justified in getting paid more than mining engineers, despite the latter's education and relative scarcity, miners argued that their life expectancy was considerably less than an engineer's, and so, as one put it, "a miner wants to live the life he has better than an engineer."[63]

Other miners based their argument not simply on class antagonisms, but on their labor theory of value. Bosses, after all, produced nothing. At Donetsk's October mine one worker argued, "A lot of people live at the expense of others. Take our mine for example. During the last strike we counted the number of people who work directly in the mine producing coal—3,800. Of these 700 were managers. We have some sections in the mine where 4 workers are supervised by 3 people." Another October miner, discussing the mine's accountants and support staff, put it more strongly: "Look at how many mouths we feed! This system must be smashed."[64]

Given this materialist sense of what different people deserved to be paid, wage differentials within a single firm, which would seem overly modest in a capitalist economy, were simply not tolerated where miners had the ability to challenge such an arrangement. Valery Samofalov, a strike leader at the Kuibyshev mine who disagreed with this prevailing view, recalled with exasperation,

> We have to change our consciousness. When we drafted the [labor collective] contract . . . and read it to the workers, no one was listening until we got to a paragraph stating that the director's salary should depend on the performance of the mine. The idea was that if the entire mine . . . fulfilled the plan, and all the workers earned a good wage then the director should get triple. And if the plan was overfulfilled, then the director would get more. Let him have an incentive too. So, we got to this point, and people have this consciousness—it's not their fault, it's our misfortune, it's how we were raised. "Look," they said, "the director sits in his office and makes R10,000 whereas I work with a shovel."[65]

There was more at work in these sentiments than populist envy. Rather, miners expressed a strong sense of injustice, a sense of being robbed. While gathered with his fellow workers at the demonstration in Donetsk, one miner exclaimed, "Right around one of our mines, 'they' are building villas. You should see such villas! Us, with the money that we get, could never build something like this. Give us our money, so we can build things! It turns out, that everything is their property. Those who don't work, can live. While we are impoverished."[66]

This exclamation led his workmate to protest,

> The fellows in the brigade know, where I served [in Afghanistan]. I'm entitled to certain privileges. But look how I live, and how they—the section boss, the director—live. I live in a barrack-house and before that a dorm. It's fifty years old, if not older. They've done no repairs on it. It leaks all the time, no one should live there. But the section boss, the head mechanic somehow get houses outside the line. They have privileges, a special line. Why this line for them, and not for me?[67]

This sense of injustice was tied not only to local bosses but also to bureaucrats in Moscow. In the coal ministry, one miner argued, there were 2,656 people, excluding service workers. "What do we need them for? They buy coal from us for 18 R a ton, then sell it abroad at world prices. And we don't get anything from it. While they drive around in foreign cars. And that's with a salary of 350–400 R. Where does this money come from?" The answer, he implied, was theft. "They're fleecing the country right now. They're carting away everything, and bringing back only 10 percent."[68]

The problem, according to many miners, was that people were not getting paid according to their labor: those who worked hard and produced something of material value were being cheated out of its value, while those who distributed and redistributed this wealth were enriching themselves without real work.[69] "We don't earn, they give out, and they give out not according to labor but by how much they figure you need."[70] When pressed to define the "normal" society that they claimed to be striving for (beyond a desire for what seemed like the West's boundless wealth), one described, "A new, civilized system—where people live as well as they work."

It appeared that the market was better disposed toward paying according to labor than a state where distribution was regulated by the self-appointed Communist Party elite. As one miner-activist explained:

> For what is all this wealth (*blaga*) lumped together from above, and then handed out, to whoever needs it? Like some great uncle sitting on a sack—to you Vanya, I'll give you this, but to you Fedya, nothing. This is no market. A market is this: I earn my own, I buy my own, having sold my labor power. But we don't have this. Here they say to you, Vanya, you'll receive this much. Receive, and not earn. There's a big difference in this—everyone should get according to his labor.[71]

Miners began to argue that the essence of the Soviet system was its ability to distribute and redistribute, and they complained, as in a typical remark, about "our whole idiotic system, our distribution system."[72] The market was seen as the antithesis to this system, and attempts to dilute the influence of the market were seen as self-serving. "What they are trying to introduce now, a regulated market, is simply the same system trying to save itself, survive, remain on top and continue to distribute everything."[73]

With the questioning of the state's essential right to distribute the national wealth, miners, long assumed to be part of a working class that was conservative and patriotic, strongly criticized the state's military expenditures: "We have many generals—each general has his own plane. On one plane, a TU-154, they carry one person around the country. Seventy percent of machine-building in Russia works for the military-industrial complex. How are we going to live well? Cannons, tanks—they can only shoot."[74]

As funding for the military was called into question, so were what were once considered to be the benefits of such a system. According to a textile worker from Donetsk, whose plant had struck and formed an independent trade union with close ties to the miners,

I think that our education and health care under socialism, if we can call it socialism, was never free of charge. [In our trade union] we've analyzed what was happening in our society, and we came to this conclusion: it would have been much less expensive for us if we just got our share of the wealth of society and paid ourselves for health care and education that would have been better than being supported by the system. It's easy to calculate that.[75]

Miners also began to question some of the most basic and universal forms of state support such as social security and pensions, arguing that they should have control of their own money. In doing so they failed to answer the question of how, once they withdrew their money from such funds, those who did not produce any wealth, such as pensioners and invalids, might survive.[76]

In challenging the Soviet state, the miners realized that they were pushing on a door that was already at least partially open. If the miners found good reason to attack the state's self-proclaimed right to distribute surplus, it made even more sense to do so when the state was increasingly less capable of performing this role.

When the Soviet government granted virtually all of the miners' economic demands in early April, the miners were advised by liberal economists (such as Vasily Selyunin) on the worth of these concessions. Selyunin told them that of the 57 percent of their coal they would be allowed to export for hard currency, 40 percent would immediately be removed by presidential decree to a fund for servicing foreign debts, and of the remainder 90 percent would be paid into the "Union-republic currency fund." Enterprises would be left with 6 percent of the earnings, "and this currency must be bought with rubles." Yet beyond taxation, Selyunin also questioned the state's ability to allocate the goods promised in the document, a central function of what had often been described as a centrally allocated economy. He referred to the document that provided

> for allocating to miners a very considerable quantity of materials for the construction of housing and social amenities. But what does allocate mean? To issue funds, that is a voucher conferring the rights to buy goods, and to tie these funds to specific suppliers. Gosplan and Gossnabzhenie will undoubtedly carry out such actions. But then— whatever will be will be. The funds are only paper, nowadays compulsory deliveries are met only as an exception.[77]

He thus confirmed what many miners had already perceived: that the state, while retaining its ability to take away, had lost much of its ability to deliver.

And while the Soviet government was trying to placate the miners through the promise of an additional allocation of goods, the Russian government was trying to woo miners by promising to expropriate less of their product. As Russian Prime Minister Silayev said to miners of the Kuzbass, "I cannot give you anything, because Russia itself is poor. The only thing that I can give you is freedom—more freedom to dispose of the output you produce."[78] As reported by *Pravda,* a publication very critical of both the miners' movement and Yeltsin, "Boris Nikolaevich has played the miners' card very successfully to achieve his power goals" by asking them to switch to Russian jurisdiction. In doing so, *Pravda* said, he promised to raise the amount of coal that could be sold at free prices from 5 to 20 percent.[79]

For all these reasons—the sense that they were being cheated out of the full value of their product, that the state was no longer able to distribute, that the republics were now each offering better deals—it is not surprising that some miners began questioning the continued need for the Soviet state. "What do we need a President of the Union for, when we have republics? The republics should elect their representatives to the Union Federation, the so-called free states. And they, as a coordinating center, will decide."[80] Anatoly Malykhin, a Kuzbass miner who had just negotiated with Yeltsin for an end to the strike in exchange for a transfer to Russian jurisdiction, explained his rationale for why the agreement answered their political demands:

> To take such powerful branches as coal, energy-heating, and metallurgy under your wing, that's big politics. We'll let the president sit in the Garden Ring [in Moscow]. . . . The rest will follow like a chain—machine building will come under Russia. And then the center will have no control over industry, they'll have nothing left to command, all will be in the Republic, and that will be sovereignty.[81]

The Market

But if miners in disparate regions with very different economic conditions agreed on the desire to bring down the state, they had not decided on what to put in its place. Many hoped for an answer in independence for their mines, an outcome, as we have seen, especially desirable to the miners from the relatively profitable fields in the Kuzbass. Coal could be extracted from these newer coal fields fairly efficiently, and world prices were considerably higher than the state purchasing price. After the agreement with Yeltsin on transferring the coal industry to Russian jurisdiction, Malykhin began to draw up elaborate plans for the transformation of mining enterprises. The form of property would be "any form of property that the collective agrees on—joint-stock, national (*narodnaya*), collective (but not private, that's still a big question)." For his own mine, his plan was to create a "national association" (*narodnoye tovarishchestvo*): "we are now writing up the statute, we will get credits, we will buy the whole enterprise," together with others who wanted to buy shares, such as the mine's suppliers and customers. At a meeting of the Novokuznetsk city strike committee, Malykhin addressed the miners about the enormous prospects before them—"the market is a cruel thing," he told his fellow miners, "some mines will get colossal profits, while others will be pushed towards bankruptcy." Thus a system of profit-sharing among the mines in the region would have to be set up. Pensioners and others will also be hurt, so they needed to establish a fund for social security (*obespechenie*) and so on.[82] The clear assumption was that the market and independence meant that the miners themselves were to have control of their mines.

While most miners in the Kuzbass had a clear economic interest in gaining independence for their mines, support for such moves went beyond pure economic rationality. Enterprise independence was seen as more worthy than demanding that something more be ladled out of the common pot. Thus, miners from Rostov, part of the economically distressed Donbass region though administratively located in Russian territory, were pushing alongside other Russian miners for enterprise independence, though as one miner conceded, perhaps optimistically, "In our mine, we know that if we switch to economic independence, it won't be easy for a long time."[83]

Indeed, even as they were calling for the end to the Soviet state, miners in the Donbass understood all too well that they would remain dependent on the state, some state, for survival. The support of the Russian-speaking Donbass miners for Ukrainian sovereignty was based not on nationalism, but on the hope that a Ukrainian government with more independence would provide a better deal than the Soviet government in terms of subsidies and support for the mining industry. Most miners and others interviewed in the Donbass held two contradictory viewpoints without particular concern: that the "center" in Moscow was exploiting them and that they were dependent on state subsidies for their survival.

Given these fundamental differences in economic positions between miners in the Kuzbass and the Donbass, even "Western experience," the lodestone that guided so many in at the end of the Communist era, meant entirely different things in these two regions. For most, including the Kuzbass miners, the experience of Western countries showed the need to rely on the market; for the miners in the Donbass, it showed the need to rely on the state.

Hence while Kuzbass miners were debating the merits of joint-stock companies versus collective property, Donbass miners were coming to different conclusions: "From what I've heard, mines abroad are also subsidized by the government. A mine should be state owned, because it's an unpredictable enterprise. You can't get profit out of it. We don't want our mine to be private, no one would agree to buy it." Said another, "We aren't good enough economists to be able to say what type of economic system there should be. For now we are orienting ourselves by foreign experience. As for mines, that experience shows that mines should remain state property, and live on subsidies."[84]

The same sentiment was found among miner-activists as well as rank-and-file miners. "Frankly speaking I support privatization," argued Mikhail Krylov, cochair of the Donetsk city strike committee. But privatization of specific enterprises depended on the market value of one's product. "It's clear how an automobile plant can be made private. Cars are scarce in the CIS. Any worker in such a plant is interested in privatization." The coal industry, however, was another matter. "Now they are talking about the privatization of mines. I'm against that." There was another issue, perhaps even more important than the unprofitable conditions in the industry: "Where would the workers get the money to privatize their mine?"[85]

There were also dramatic changes over time in attitudes toward the market and its effect on the mining industry and the lives of miners. Valery Samofalov of Donetsk had this to say shortly after the second all-union strike in 1991, when the Soviet Union was crumbling and Ukraine was seeking independence:

> The mines should not be asking the Union or republic governments to raise the price of coal, but set it themselves instead. They should establish horizontal contracts and find those who need their coal. Let them buy it. If there are no takers at R500 we should look for those who would buy it at R400. In my view, this is how we should be shifting to a market economy. Protecting us from it will turn out badly.[86]

Just over a year later, when Ukrainian independence appeared to be leading to greater hardship rather than prosperity, and it became clear what the unbridled market would mean for the Donbass, Samofalov had an entirely different take on the question. "If we had been thrown on the market, we would have been closed down long ago. The state should take care of the people, it should retrain them and give them the chance to get another profession."[87]

Yet even as they demanded that the state take some responsibility for their well-being, the countervailing and contradictory sense of exploitation continued. With a new state in Kiev seen as unresponsive to their needs, and with the perception that subsidies notwithstanding, they were not getting paid a just amount for their product, the Donbass miners continue to call for greater independence from the state.[88] The reasons were not purely economic: they argued that the new Ukrainian state was not democratic, that it favored Ukrainian-speaking regions over the Russian-speaking Donbass, as well as the building of an independent state over greater economic stability and trade with Russia and the former Soviet republics. But surprisingly, in addition to calling for greater political autonomy, miners and others in the Donbass began demanding the status of a "free economic zone," a plan with surely disastrous consequences, at least in the long term, for the economically distressed region.

Explaining Radicalization

Rational choice and collective action approaches were used previously to understand why steelworkers did not strike while miners in the same communities were striking, organizing, and calling for the economic and political transformation of the Soviet state. As an analytical tool, the rational-choice perspective offers a simple yet powerful explanation for certain social and political phenomena. Given a set of preferences, one can, in game theoretical terms, determine how different decisions will lead to different payoffs, and hence determine which choice is the most "rational."

But how are preferences formed? What happens when preferences change dramatically over time? Even if preferences remain the same—arguably coal miners ultimately wanted a decent standard of living and some control over decisions that affected their lives—how do some means toward achieving those ends get placed on the decision-making agenda and others not? How, for instance, did the miners transform their demands from asking that the state give them more to asking for independence from the state? How did the miners come to see that their demands required solutions less economic in nature than political, ones that called for changing the political system itself? How did they come to see the "market," rather than a return to the past or some form of democratic socialism, as a means to a higher living standard?

We have found several reasons for the miners' shift toward political concerns, each of which could be said to follow from the miners' rational self-interest. Raising political demands rather than asking for further economic concessions allowed the miners to avoid the charge that they were once again "taking all the blanket for themselves." More important, to be sure, was that the state was not viewed merely as the enforcer of private contracts, but as the employer: in short, to raise demands with management was to raise demands with representatives of the state. The Soviet state had thus assigned itself responsibility for the plight of the entire economy, from the macro-level conditions to everyday conditions on the shop floor. And once the government had signed an agreement, whose implementation was not visible to the miners by the dates promised, the legitimacy of the government itself was soon called into question. But more important still was not what the government failed to provide, but what it took away in its role as distributor and redistributor, which leads to the question of the market.

The explanation for the miners' strivings toward the market is rather more intricate, since it involves not only economic self-interest but also the cultural frameworks through which self-interest is interpreted and strategies are chosen.[89] Certainly one overriding reason that the miners' movement supported market reform has to do with the by-then ascendant tendency in Soviet (and later post-Soviet) society to look to the West as a model, as miners and many others began understanding that their own standard of living lagged considerably behind that of the "normal" and "civilized" capitalist democracies. The use of the "West" as a lodestone for their own transformation was in part due to new information, but also was the result of the uncritical use of the West as a utopia.[90] Conversely, miners and many others decried efforts to implement further "experiments," referring not only to the seemingly endless attempts at reform during the post-Soviet period, but to the entire Soviet experience as well.

Ironically however, while explicitly rejecting the old system, miners and others continued to use that system's cultural concepts to interpret their situation and to choose strategies of action. As the preceding pages have shown, even the striving for the "market" was as much a product of the old ideology as it was of the new. The miners had no direct experience of the market, which had become for them a new utopia; their conception of the market was shaped by a very vague notion of how people lived in the West and much more by their own ideals for a just society.

In this way, the demands for independence were driven by the miners' acute sense of being exploited, a sense based only thinly on the market value of the coal they produced. While miners pointed to the enormous disparities between the world market price for coal and the state's purchasing price, they also acknowledged the substantial subsidies they received in the form of low prices for material inputs, energy, and transportation. More important was that miners produced a material value (as opposed to workers in service or trade, accountants, or bureaucrats, who produced nothing tangible). This material value was needed by the country, they argued, and yet they were not being paid fairly for their product. This contradiction—between the desire to withhold their product from the

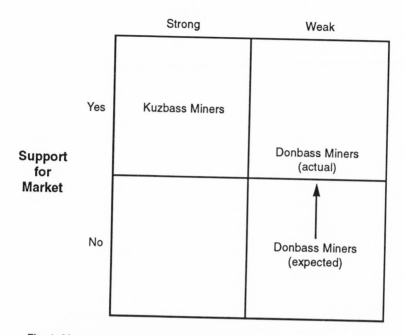

Fig. 1. Market position and support for the market in the Donbass and the Kuzbass

state and sell it on the market and the understanding that, without state subsidies, such a move could be disastrous for many, if not most, mines—has not been easily resolved, as we shall see in coming chapters.

Further, the term *market,* ambiguous as it is, had different meanings for miners in the Kuzbass and Donbass than it did for liberal economists and intellectuals in Moscow. For miners the market meant workers' ownership and control rather than traditional capitalism.[91] They had no intention of replacing the exploitation of the state with that of a private owner; workers' management, or at least comanagement, would insure that the market worked to the advantage of miners, or so it was hoped. Thus while speaking favorably of the market and the desire to live in a normal, civilized society, miners also invoked one of the unfulfilled promises of the Bolshevik revolution—"all factories to the workers."

Nevertheless, one could argue that such a culturally based argument is not necessary to explain the radicalization of miners of the Russian

Kuzbass. In terms of economic interests, the trajectory of the Kuzbass miners has been fairly straightforward. The relative newness of their mines and the perception (mistaken, as we shall see) of potential profitability led them to seek greater independence to dispose of their product, including the right to sell their coal abroad. On the other hand, the richness of the coal they extracted contrasted so sharply with the squalid living standards of the region that miners could argue that they had been colonized by Moscow. This clear interest in independence helped spur political demands, including the dismantling of the Soviet state, as a means of gaining that independence. Somewhat more tangibly, as resource mobilization theory would predict,[92] the economic position of the Kuzbass miners was parlayed into greater organizational strength as they created stronger local organizations, established an independent newspaper, and pushed through the founding of the Independent Miners' Union.

But the situation in the Donbass was rather more complex. Here miners have long been dependent on subsidies, and the battle has been less for enterprise independence than against deindustrialization and unemployment. Even before the first strike, which united miners across the Soviet Union, workers in the Donbass understood themselves to be in a position almost directly opposite that of their counterparts in the Kuzbass.[93] In terms of structural position and resulting economic interest, the Donbass miners would surely need a strong, paternalist state; yet they followed the lead of the Kuzbass and called for the downfall of the most paternalistic state in modern history (see fig. 1). While the Donbass miners were not as successful in building organizations and were less decisive in their demands, they were no less prone to strike than miners in the relatively rich Kuzbass. They too experienced a strong sense of being exploited by the state, even as they understood their dependence on state subsidies.[94]

Indeed, the Donbass miners joined the Kuzbass miners during the 1991 strike in calling for the dismantling of the Soviet state largely because of this sense of exploitation by the "center." However, the hope of the Donbass miners that Ukrainian independence would improve their material situation and the accountability of the state proved short-lived. Less than a year after the failed putsch, miners in the region were complaining that everything was worse, and that the "center" had simply moved from Moscow to Kiev. But even while calling for greater state support, they remained ideologically committed to decentralization, calling not only for a federal system for Ukraine, but even for making the economically dependent Donbass a "free economic zone."

As the foregoing discussion would indicate, the contradictions the miners faced became no less sharp with the fall of the old regime and the rise of independent Russia and Ukraine. They now for the first time had direct experience of the liberalism they helped bring about, an arrangement that challenged their very existence as industrial workers. After a time they were gripped by the realization that their vision was almost completely at odds with that of their liberal allies. It is to this dilemma that we turn in the section that follows: first to the dire economic challenges faced by coal miners in Russia and Ukraine, and then to the miners' political responses to those challenges.

**Part 4.
Liberal Economics and Labor
Politics in Post-Communist
Russia and Ukraine**

CHAPTER 7

Labor and Economic Transformation

By the end of 1991, virtually all of the miners' political demands had been fulfilled: Gorbachev had resigned, the Communist Party was removed from power, and the republics not only gained "sovereignty" within a Soviet federation, but became independent states. Not long afterward, they realized they had gotten more than they had bargained for. While the miners and other workers well understood the Communist system and their opposition to it, they were ill prepared for the bitter struggles that awaited them after the downfall of the Soviet system.

This chapter will examine the economic challenges faced by miners and other workers after the Soviet collapse by focusing first on Ukraine and then on Russia. After investigating the impact of economic liberalization on the coal industry in these now independent nation-states, we will turn to the effects of liberalization and privatization at the mine level, looking in particular at the impact on paternalism, trade unions, and the labor market in the post-Soviet period. The chapter will conclude by exploring the interrelationship of these changes by returning to one of the steel plants examined earlier—the West Siberian Metallurgical Complex. Having done so, we will be in a position in the chapter that follows to examine the political response by coal miners and other workers to these enormous challenges.

Coal and Ukraine

With the end of the Soviet Union, Ukraine's miners found themselves heavily dependent on state subsidies, but ironically also with virtual veto power over the country's economic and political future. Ukraine's miners are concentrated strategically in the eastern Donbass, the most heavily industrialized area of Ukraine, albeit with obsolescent plants and worked-out mines. Outside troubled Crimea, the Donbass is the predominant center of Russian language and culture in Ukraine. Hence the region compromises a central part of the large cleavage in Ukraine between East and West, between Russian and Ukrainian speakers, and between industrial and agricultural interests, with industrial managers interested above all in

149

rebuilding ties to Russia and the CIS and nationalists interested in building a strong independent state. Last, and by no means least, the dominant sector of the region's working class—the coal miners—is organized and ready for battle over the nation's economic future.

As we have seen, the Donbass miners pushed hard for a sovereign Ukraine during the 1991 strike. With the sense that Moscow was cheating them, that they were putting more into the central coffers than they were getting out, the call for a sovereign Ukraine, when it came, struck a deep chord.[1] As one miner from Donetsk's October mine put it during the 1991 strike, "There's chaos now in the USSR, no one is subordinated to anyone else. If Ukraine left, we might be able to bring about order." Underscoring the ambiguity of the notion of independence that was prevalent among those who used it, his friend added that sovereignty was needed "so it will be like you have [in the United States], each state has its own laws, its own governor, and so on. A small country is easier to manage." Said another Donetsk miner, if Ukraine gets sovereignty, "above all, Ukraine will become an independent state. Moscow will not be able to capriciously cross out everything we've obtained here."[2]

As Yurii Makarov of the Donetsk strike committee explained after the 1991 strike:

It's my opinion that in such a big state as ours it is impossible to administer all regions from one place, from Moscow, and to issue laws that would be acceptable to everyone. I think that if Ukraine were independent, it would be better able to fix the economy and everything else on its territory.[3]

But the hope of the Donbass miners that Ukrainian independence would improve their material situation and the accountability of the state proved short-lived. When asked a year later what had changed since the 1991 strike (in which the miners' political demands had been achieved), Makarov replied, "everything has gotten worse." He explained,

Ukrainian independence did not improve the situation—the "center" just moved from Moscow to Kiev. In the past we fought for the existence of Ukraine as an autonomous state. But we didn't want Kiev to become the center instead of Moscow, we wanted power to be given to the localities, to enterprises, to cities, we wanted the living standard of the population to grow. But not so Kiev could grab the reins of government in its fist.[4]

These dramatic changes in sentiment, evident throughout the Donbass, are rather clearly driven by Ukraine's thoroughly dismal economic performance. Though prior to gaining independence, Ukraine was seen by many observers as being the best endowed and most viable of former Soviet republics, the years since have been anything but kind to Ukraine's economy.[5] The more optimistic forecasts on Ukraine's viability overlooked Ukraine's tremendous interdependence with the economy of Russia and other former republics, and disruptions in trade and shocks in oil prices have hit Ukraine hard.

Moreover, while Ukraine is certainly industrialized, it has suffered from years of intensive exploitation from Moscow, geared toward the needs of the now defunct Soviet Union. While Ukraine was an engine in Stalinist industrialization, upon gaining sovereignty and control over its resources, Ukraine has been saddled with obsolescent and environmentally harmful industries.[6]

Independent Ukraine soon faced the twin problems of hyperinflation and enormous deficit spending. By the end of 1993 the karbovanets, which had started at par with the Russian ruble two years earlier, was trading at 27 to 1 ruble, and inflation for 1994 reached 461 percent.[7] Living standards dropped precipitously.[8] Industrial production in 1994 alone declined by almost 28 percent. While industry has survived through subsidies, such payments, fueling the inflation rate, have reached their limits. In 1994 the budget deficit reached 49 percent of GDP, with subsidies to industry alone reaching 28 percent of GDP.[9] Certainly, any reduction in the budget deficit would have to come at the expense of subsidies to industry.

Ukraine's industrial workers remain one of the biggest roadblocks lying in the path of such a policy. Putting a brake on such a high level of inflation and deficit spending implies a correspondingly high level of unemployment. While most workers in Ukraine remain unorganized, the Donbass miners are already prepared for just such a fight.

Though the Russian miners continued to be heavily subsidized by their government after independence, miners in the Donbass, more directly dependent on the state, were soon given a taste of free-market economics. When Russia began lifting price controls in January 1992, forcing Ukraine to take similar action, the government in Kiev lifted price restrictions on coal, while leaving the prices of most other inputs fixed. At least initially, this action allowed for windfall profits in the coal industry, and miners' wages rose dramatically.

According to Yurii Boldyrev, then of the Donetsk city strike committee, "That was not an economic, but a purely political decision. [Prime Minister Fokin's] goal was to avoid a miners' strike. . . . He understood the sequence: prices go up—strikes—the government falls down."[10]

The euphoria from the sudden increase in wages was short-lived.[11] As Bychkov, the deputy chair of the Donetsk city council, put it, the miners "were deceived." In addition to letting coal enterprises sell their coal at market prices, the Ukrainian government granted the industry tax-free status, thus giving the miners total independence from the state. The miners, however, soon understood the danger of this step. While wages soared, "they started to realize that there are less and less buyers of coal, and more and more coal in warehouses. Now miners understand that in a year or so there will be lots of coal, but few buyers, and no need to keep mining. What will happen to the miners then?"[12] As for total independence from the state, "the miners are ready to pay taxes to the state budget," Bychkov explained, "on the condition that the state should be responsible for the mines, like in the Ruhr Basin in Germany, in Britain, and even in America. When a mine is closed, the state decides to develop new work in electronics or some other industry, creating new workplaces. That's state policy."[13]

As Makarov, deputy chair of the Donetsk city strike committee, argued in reference to recent mining deaths in the Donbass,[14] "We object to having miners work in these dangerous conditions. We will agree to close down those enterprises, but the people who work in those mines should have the chance to be retrained and to work at something else." He continued, "They can't simply close the mines and throw us out of work. Retrain us, let us build cars, whatever."[15]

As his colleague Boldyrev argued:

Certainly, Ukraine received the Donbass when it was in terrible condition. The Donbass is like the Ruhr. The Ruhr is being shut down, there are very few mines left. The same process should start in the Donbass. It's necessary to close the mines. But it should be done slowly, gradually, while creating new workplaces, to prevent an outburst by the miners. . . . The authorities in Kiev seem to be hostage to the situation: if there were mass closing of the mines, there would be a great outburst and social unrest, and they know that perfectly well.[16]

As argued by Krylov, "Maybe those who say the Donbass should be closed as a zone of ecological catastrophe are right. It's necessary to close [certain] mines and factories. But if the Donbass mines are closed, 120,000 underground miners will be jobless. There will be a social explosion—a war."[17]

Coal and Independent Russia

When courting the support of miners before and during the 1991 strike, Yeltsin promised them greater control over their resources. Ostensibly, this meant the increased use of market forces, or giving mines the right to independently market their coal; in practice, as Yeltsin became president of a sovereign Russia, it has meant rewarding miners for their political loyalty through greater subsidies to the coal industry. When the Yeltsin government, led by Prime Minister Gaidar, embarked on a policy of "shock therapy," leading to sharply rising prices and falling real wages, the "only serious challenge to the Gaidar measures came in the coal mining regions," despite the fact that their strike threats and actual work stoppages "met little resistance from the government."[18] A strike by the miners ended with the tripling of miners' wages—despite a declared policy of tight money—to 7,000 rubles, while the national average was 900 rubles.[19] Nevertheless, the miners remained restive.

Given a nearly twentyfold rise in general price levels and corresponding further wage increases, the government was hard-pressed to print enough money to keep up with wage payments. By February 1993, some mines in the Kuzbass had not received wage allocations since November and it was estimated that by the end of the year the government would be in arrears to the miners by some 200 billion rubles.[20] The high wages paid to miners together with the still artificially low prices for coal meant that by May 1993, subsidies to the coal industry alone were absorbing 20 percent of the revenues of the Russian state budget.[21]

Yeltsin's significant promises of "independence" for Russia's coal mines went largely unfulfilled. Moreover, and despite Russian miners' avowed support of the market in the past, when the Yeltsin government proposed "freeing" coal prices as a means of cutting subsidies and the budget deficit, the proposal met with strong opposition. Yeltsin's decree on the freeing of coal prices as of July 1, 1993, was ill-timed, in that miners from Rostov were already picketing government buildings in Moscow demanding payment in arrears for wages and subsidies.[22] They demanded that the decree on price liberalization be rescinded, since they feared, with justification, that market prices would not cover their losses and might lead to the closure of half of Russia's mines. The Rostov miners were soon joined by miners from the Kuzbass and other regions, arguing that the government should continue to provide the subsidies promised in the past.[23]

With coal prices before the decree approximately 4 percent of world market prices, coal prices quickly shot up by a factor of nine, forcing the price of steel above world prices.[24] The resulting protests, both by miners and such coal consumers as the steel industry, resulted in a considerable softening of the decree and continued subsidies for the coal industry, thus reversing much of the intended effect on the budget and inflation.[25]

Yet after gaining wage increases and promises of continued subsidies, the mining regions were hit with proposed pit closures. Within weeks of the announced liberalization of coal prices, miners in Vorkuta staged a warning strike over a proposal to close mines, stating that guarantees needed to be in place to provide new jobs for any miners let go.[26] The proposal to close mines was also softened, so that in October 1993 the plan was to shut down forty-two mines by the year 2000; yet further strikes were called over the government's failure to provide any social guarantees for unemployed miners in the event of layoffs.[27]

Nevertheless, a World Bank proposal for the Russian coal industry called for laying off within five years half or more of the eight hundred thousand people directly employed in mining.[28] In what was certainly a bitter blow to Kuzbass miner-activists, once so optimistic about their prospects under market conditions, under the World Bank's plan, *"The most difficult situation will be in the Kuzbass, where total employment could fall from about 300,000 to 70–80,000 workers at the end of the restructuring period,"* ideally three to five years.[29]

Yet for all the talk of market prices for coal and the closure of unprofitable mines, little changed in the mines themselves, in Russia or Ukraine.[30] Many in the industry realized that given the expectations of the miners—such as the provision of new jobs and resettlement from isolated mining towns in the advent of closures—as well as the cost of transferring each mine's extensive social infrastructure to municipal governments, it was simply cheaper to continue subsidizing coal production than to pay for closing mines down and all that entailed. Even at the Russian mines that were among the forty-two first slated for closure, miners expressed little sense of impending doom or the need to look for new employment.[31]

At mines with more average conditions and prospects, workers complained that little had changed.[32] Miners continued to be paid by the amount of coal extracted, which preserved the practice of encouraging miners to violate safety standards and risk their lives for higher pay.[33] And despite the changes meant to push more mines to sell directly on the market, directors continued to complain about the plan (though now officially referred to as state orders). In fact, because of the interenterprise debt, it was more favorable for mines to sell coal to the state than directly to consumers, and even to substitute subsidies for market earnings. Payments for state orders and subsidies were delivered on time, while payments for coal from other enterprises could be delayed for several months, which became greatly discounted given the high rate of inflation. Further, the current scheme directly compensates lost market revenue with subsidies. Well into Russia's program of economic restructuring, "mines that receive no or small subsidies are in the worst financial situation."[34]

The subsidies are also handed out on a discretionary basis, first by

Rusugol[35] and then by the coal associations to the individual mines. Mine managers must spend a considerable amount of time and energy competing with one another for subsidies; subsidies are often handed out first to the most outwardly militant mines, encouraging strikes and strike threats. Mines and miners are thus divided by the extent of their subsidies, which can determine when miners are paid (on time or months later), creating divisions between regions and even neighboring mines.[36]

Paternalism Revisited

Enterprise paternalism has continued to flourish in mining regions, both in Russia and in Ukraine. In the Kuzbass, after demands by miners to be able to market some of their coal independently were met, the region was swept by a series of barter deals of coal for foreign consumer goods. Some mines were overwhelmed by a wave of Toyotas and Korean VCRs, while others, lacking quality coal or the contacts to pull off a deal, were much less well off. One miner conveyed the problem of a sudden influx of Korean refrigerators at his mine: the first was more than welcome at his home, and he even brought home a second, then later supplied refrigerators to friends and family, and even sold a few. But after a time, payment in refrigerators became a rather bulky currency. So the mine, as with many others in the Kuzbass, created their own scrip (or "dollars" as they became known) that could be traded for consumer goods available from the mine's store. Miners from the Dmitrova mine might post signs offering to trade "Dmitrova dollars" for "Badaevskaya dollars" to have access to another mine's store of consumer goods.[37]

Barter deals were the purview of the mine's administration, and the fruits of the deals were distributed according to management's wishes. As with other enterprise goods and services, unless the mine's workforce was particularly well organized, bartered goods were handed out according to lines (such as "privileged" or "ordinary") and managers typically retained 5 to 15 percent of each deal to distribute as they chose through the "director's fund."[38]

As a wider variety of consumer goods became available for rubles, barter deals declined somewhat in importance. Yet consumer prices have remained out of reach even for the relatively well-paid miners, even more so in that their wages have often gone unpaid for months at a time. As with other workers, this increased dependence on goods and services provided at the workplace: without pay, workers got their meals at the plant cafeterias and bought goods at company stores, open even on holidays, on account.[39]

Indeed, contrary to expectations, enterprise paternalism has not lessened with the onslaught of a market economy and in many cases has thrived. It is the least successful enterprises that have, in the absence of market revenues or sufficient credits, begun to simply abandon many of the social services, such as housing and vacation centers, on which workers so long depended, leaving workers to fend for themselves.[40] On the other hand, the enterprises most successful on the market have often increased their expenditures on social infrastructure. Clarke et al. describe several fascinating cases of continued paternalism among the first privatized enterprises in Russia.[41]

Why might managers of state and even privatized enterprises continue to expend scarce resources on providing goods and services that, in a capitalist society, workers would be expected to buy on the market or receive from local governments? One reason is that incentives still favor the continued provision of these goods and services, since these funds often come from the state, and such expenditures for "social infrastructure" are free from payroll taxes, leading managers to shift compensation into these funds.[42] But a more fundamental reason is the precarious position of managers themselves. Once appointed from above through the nomenklatura system, managers appointed in the Soviet era have been cut off from political patrons and are isolated and vulnerable within the firm.[43] While managers were always dependent on the workforce to a degree, particularly on skilled workers in short supply (as suggested by the concept of "mutual dependence"), managers must now placate their workforce in order to retain their positions. This continued mutual dependence has been reinforced by earlier institutional changes within the enterprise. One was the Law on the State Enterprise, which instituted a system of elections for enterprise management, from the foreman to the director. The law was rescinded within a couple of years, but its legacy is still felt within enterprises, where workers can recall the right to elect their bosses. While in most cases this right was more formal than real, the situation was different in the mining regions; there, as we have seen, miners often used the enterprise election law to remove managers after their first strike.

A Tale of Two Mines

The precariousness of mine managers, the continued importance of paternalism, and the varied trajectories of individual mines beyond 1989 can be seen by comparing the cases of two Donbass mines, Kuibyshev and October, both located in the same borough of Donetsk.[44] Both mines erupted during the 1989 strike, and the anger of the Kuibyshev workforce has been amply documented in the trade union meeting just after the strike.[45]

Yet the path of the Kuibyshev miners sharply diverged from those of neighboring October. While the October miners quickly sacked their director, the Kuibyshev miners continued with their old director for another year before removing him for a younger replacement. The new director, Alizaev, was elected on promises of "working for the good of the collective" and proved energetic and able to put the mine on solid footing. Despite the mine's long life and average geological conditions, the mine was soon able to deliver high wages and a variety of consumer goods. In 1991, while other mines were striking throughout the Soviet Union for independence for the republics and the removal of Gorbachev, Alizaev convinced his miners that they had too much to lose from stopping work.

Alizaev succeeded in having the strike committee disbanded, and the mine's STK simply stopped meeting. When asked why such institutions were no longer needed, the director explained that "if there's a dispute, people speak to me." The one workers' body that did remain was the old trade union, which as in the past spent its time handing out goods received from barter deals and vouchers for trips to the mine's vacation centers.

The atmosphere at the October mine, only several kilometers away, could not have been more different. In contrast to Kuibyshev, the October miners struck for a full two months in 1991. Only one Kuibyshev miner had left the official trade union, but at October, five hundred miners had joined the NPG by July 1992. While Kuibyshev's trade union chair entertained questions in his spacious, air-conditioned office, the independent union's committee at October was quartered in a crowded, dimly lit room, the only piece of equipment being a telephone that looked like a relic from a World War II bunker. And whereas the Kuibyshev chair had spoken at length without interruption, his secretary guarding the door, at October the door to the NPG's office was constantly opening and closing, as miners came in between shifts to ask questions, scrawl out requests on pieces of scrap paper, and discuss the same political issues that one or two miners had raised to their colleagues to no avail at Kuibyshev.

As mentioned, the October miners replaced their director in the wake of the 1989 strike. "He ran things with terror," as one of the members of the independent union's committee remembered him, while another recalled, "The director was like a tsar." The replacement turned out to be ineffective, both in improving the mine's economic position and in controlling the workforce. After the 1991 strike, the collective fired the second director and hired a third. While this director was a better economist, according to the miners he was no less accountable to the workforce (the removal of the enterprise election law notwithstanding). As explained by Bobunov, the chair of October's independent union, "We don't have many problems because management respects us. We speak to our director this way: 'Here's the law, here's the [boss] responsible for breaking it, and if you don't act, we have the right to declare a strike. So you can expect an explosion any day now.'"[46]

There appears to be no compelling structural explanation for the difference in these two mines, since both have geological conditions average to the Donbass and both are equally dependent on subsidies. Rather, the different experience each workforce has had with its managers provides the best explanation for the presence or absence of labor militancy.[47] Whereas Alizaev secured the barter deals and state concessions necessary to provide a material base for his mine's return to paternalism, the experience of the October miners with their first director—the "tsar"—spurred their militance and would likely have led them to reject a return to the safety of paternalistic dependence.

More important for present purposes is how this case underscores an important reason why managers prefer to spend scarce resources on workers' social welfare. Western economists and others advising the Russian and Ukrainian governments have asked with vexation: Why not simply transfer state subsidies for social services from enterprises to municipal governments, as is done in the West? At least part of the answer is that managers want to prevent Kuibyshev from becoming October, with the risk not only of a restive labor force but of managers' possible dismissal. (Another reason is that such a move, while getting coal and steel enterprises out of the business of providing housing and vacations, might not save the state much money, since subsidies would simply be transferred. And while in theory unprofitable enterprises stripped of their "social functions" would be easier to shut down, the state would have to substitute subsidies for unprofitable production with unemployment pay, job retraining and job creation, resettlement from single "company towns," and so on. Any savings would be small, especially when the social and political costs are considered.)

Trade Unions

Whether at a single mine like Kuibyshev or on the level of national union federations, it is still hard to disentangle trade unions in the former Soviet Union from their traditional role as distributors of enterprise benefits. Largely as a result, the former state trade unions continue to dominate the representation of labor. In Russia, the Federation of Independent Trade Unions of Russia (FNPR) claims more than 50 million members from a total labor force in Russia of approximately 73 million. The union also wants to establish itself as labor's exclusive bargaining agent with the state.[48] This bargaining was intended to occur as part of a "social partnership," through which representatives of labor, private employers, and the state would meet to hammer out agreements explicitly modeled on Western European-style corporatist pacts.[49] Such pacts were not successful in this case, in part because the Russian state remained the main employer, and not a mediator between capital and labor as in the corporatist ideal. Rather, the FNPR and enterprise managers cooperated in efforts to maintain wages, subsides, and high employment. Moreover, another essential element was missing for the building of a corporatist labor pact—the peak labor unions able to mobilize workers to strike in order to have bargaining leverage, and able to convince or coerce members to refrain from striking once the pact has been accepted. The FNPR has proven unable do either.[50]

The once-official unions not only survived the fall of the Soviet Union but have continued to thrive, because with the collapse of the old regime, they found themselves holders of enormous amounts of property. One percent of members' salaries were automatically deducted as dues, the unions owned large buildings in the center of most cities plus an array of vacation and cultural centers, and they are increasingly involved in commercial activity.[51] The unions also control the distribution of social security funds, as they did in the Soviet era; many workers mistakenly believe that these payments come from union dues rather than the state, or that the union can legally refuse payment to nonmembers, and so they are reluctant to sign a form stating their desire to leave the trade union. While Yeltsin decreed that control of social security funds be taken from the trade unions, in effect this has meant that the unions are just more accountable for the spending of these funds.[52]

At the level of the enterprise, where workers most need a strong ally to help them combat falling living standards and deteriorating working conditions, the trade unions remain mired with the distribution of goods and services. That further increases their dependence on management for funding, subsidies, and goods from barter deals to hand out to the workforce, which can be used in turn to retain membership. In workers' eyes, the unions are still seen as another arm of management. As Clarke and Fairbrother argue, "The official unions are so discredited that most workers do not see any need for a union at all." This perception is not surprising, given workers' experience with unions, for as even "many union officials explicitly recognize, their organizations are not trade unions, but a particular form of welfare administration."[53]

The miners' NPG, however, one of the few independent trade unions in Russia, placed itself in a contradictory position. In terms of economic demands and strike activity, it was the most militant union in Russia, but it remained allied politically with Yeltsin, whose policies were responsible for the generally disastrous economic conditions. The NPG's membership was rather small, even when compared to the once-official coal union, but its influence extended beyond its numbers.[54] While the once-official union still encompassed virtually anyone employed in the coal industry, including cooks at mine vacation centers and teachers in mine day-care centers, the NPG confined itself to "basic professions" of coal mining, which meant privileged male workers.[55] From the outset, the NPG chastised the old miners' union for being mired in distribution issues rather than problems of pay and working conditions. But in order to compete and retain members, especially among workers who had expectations of unions taking care of "social problems," the NPG had to provide tangible benefits to members, from consumer goods to garden plots for growing food.[56]

The NPG also fought the monopoly held by the once-official unions over the distribution of social security funds. Yet with the desire to control the wealth they produced, the NPG attacked the social security system as a whole. According to Krylov, head of the NPG in Donetsk, "We want everyone to be the master of the fruits of his labor. . . . We proved the state is robbing us, and we took our money back from it. . . . We've calculated how much they take and how much they give back. It turned out they don't give back one-sixth of the amount they take away."[57] Indeed, the NPG challenged the very notion of social security: It sought not merely to establish a generalized social insurance fund for its own members, but in essence to place social security withholdings into individual savings accounts without any shared insurance coverage at all.[58] This reaction against the old system at times bordered on the absurd, as when one Donbass miner explained that he, being healthy, should not have to pay for the health care of his sickly coworker, but should be able to keep his money for himself.[59]

Yet the NPG's most significant, and perhaps fatal, problem, was trying to square the militancy of its membership in greatly deteriorating economic conditions with its support for the political status quo embodied in the Yeltsin government. This question deserves considerable attention, which will be provided in the following chapter. But the problem was not merely deteriorating economic conditions, familiar to trade unions everywhere. Another profound change was having significant impact on miners' and other workers' lives—Russia's drive for the privatization of state enterprises.

Privatization

While Ukraine has lagged behind considerably on privatization, Russia has taken considerable steps to privatize state enterprises. As we have seen, the miners themselves pushed not simply for the market but also for control over their mines, and the agreement to end the 1991 strike was understood by miners as bringing that about.

The attitudes of mid-level miner-activists toward privatization from January to March of 1992, roughly a year after the strike, were captured in a study by Leonid Gordon and his collaborators.[60] Many of their respondents were said to favor collective ownership by labor cooperatives, in which members would participate in management and the distribution of income. As one respondent put it, "The main thing is that those who work can dispose of the fruits of their labor."[61] Yet for others, collective property was derided as "*kolkhozez* [collective farms] in industry," with the negative experience of socialism discrediting the notion.[62] In the three months of discussions, Gordon and colleagues reported a shift by the activists toward less support for collective property as opposed to classical private property; one wonders, however, about the impact on this perceived shift of the concurrent threefold wage increase given to miners by the Yeltsin government, as well as Gordon's adoption of Touraine's methodology of "sociological intervention."[63]

Regardless, there appeared to be a consensus that the immediate dissemination of private property, especially the prevailing "nomenklatura transition," was widely unpopular. According to respondent Igor G., "We are all populists inside; everything belongs to the collective, everything is mine, and suddenly an owner comes in. There is a big danger of social upheavals here."[64] And even if these miner-activists were convinced about the apparent benefits of private property for their coal mines, they all conceded that the views of their work collectives were another matter entirely. On the possibility of transferring a mine to private ownership, Pavel R. had this to say: "Let someone ask about it at the mine, call the collective and say: 'the owner will arrive tomorrow; we're giving the mine away.' What will the answer be? He will be torn to pieces!"[65]

Some have argued that "if there is a basis for the development of a progressive and democratic workers' movement in Russia," it lies here, "in the struggles opened up by the process of privatization."[66] At first glance, workers seem to have benefited considerably from privatization in Russia. Any privatization scheme proposed by management had to win the approval of two-thirds of the enterprise labor collective, giving the employees veto rights over how their plant would be privatized.[67] Ironically, having led the drive for enabling work collectives to decide the form of ownership of their enterprise, and having been promised just such an arrangement by Yeltsin at the end of the 1991 strike, the coal industry was excluded from this possibility, with Moscow retaining control of individual mines.[68]

Yet in other industries, a majority of enterprises did in fact choose something resembling "collective property." When 11,000 out of a total of 14,500 eligible enterprises had been formally privatized by the end of 1993, about 80 percent of enterprises had chosen the "second model," under which 51 percent of all shares went to enterprise employees. Some liberal reformers began to decry the creation of "collective ownership," with the claim that under such an arrangement all income would go toward wage payments.[69] The continued provision of social services and consumer goods for employees at the expense of profits seemed to prove this point. Moreover, despite the steep decline in production, workers were rarely laid off. Indeed, interviews with enterprise managers found their greatest concern to be "keeping the labor collective together." In a poll of managers at the end of 1992 by the Russian Union of Industrialists and Entrepreneurs, a plurality of 33 percent chose "keeping the labor collective together" as their first goal over the choices of "increasing production," "increasing sales," and "profit-making."[70]

It may seem that such preferences are a result of collectivist notions such as those expressed by coal miners, or at least the desire to prevent social upheaval, and surely that is part of the equation. Yet other concerns appear to motivate managers during the privatization process. Although workers nominally hold the controlling shares, enterprise directors are able to employ Soviet-era tactics to control shareholder meetings much as they did for meetings of the labor collective, since only delegates are able to attend such meetings.[71] Managers appeal to the labor collective as a strategy to prevent outside interference or ownership, which might question the continued stewardship of the firm by present management.[72] So enterprise directors choose "employee ownership" much like managers might employ a "bitter pill" strategy to prevent a hostile takeover in the American capital market.

Yet this situation is very unstable, especially from the viewpoint of workers; "worker ownership" appears to be tolerated by liberals as a necessary but temporary phase leading eventually to the concentration of capital in the hands of managers and outsiders. It is so because employees' shares are transferable. Managers from many large enterprises have set up separate trading companies to buy enterprise shares on the secondary market, increasing management's portion of the holdings. Shares shift gradually from employees to managers, outsiders, or both.[73] This process is facilitated further since many workers are mystified by the complex steps involved in privatization, investment funds advertise often outrageous returns in exchange for vouchers, and workers, often unpaid for months at a time, are clearly tempted to trade away paper wealth for something tangible.

Since employees nominally remain the controlling owners during the privatization process, managers are in a delicate position and must prevent collective action by workers against management or their uniting behind the privatization proposals of outsiders or rival management groups.[74] For this reason managers seek to maintain employment levels, despite slumping production, in order to placate the "labor collective" during the privatization process. If managers lose in the conflict over privatization, they could easily lose their jobs.[75]

Managers are also interested in maintaining the employment levels of auxiliary workers, who, while largely unskilled and of limited use in production, act as "a political counterweight within the enterprise to the aspirations of [core] production workers" and thus help form "the political base of the administration."[76] With these workers more dependent on management, they are more easily persuaded to act in the interests of management, something crucial during events such as enterprise shareholders' meetings.

Further, skilled workers on their own might prove better able to lead a united and more militant trade union. In fact, the miners' NPG, representing core production workers, has argued that its constituency would actually be better off in the event that unneeded auxiliary workers were let go:

> When over-employment is so high, the balance of power between managers and workers strongly favors the former [who can] fire workers at any moment, on any scale. . . . The unskilled and auxiliary workers . . . are becoming notably dependent on the goodwill of management. But the end of over-employment will force the administration to confront considerable bargaining power of the remaining [skilled, core] workers. That is why managers, while constantly threatening to begin dismissals, will in fact postpone this process as long as possible. In this case managers' legal and economic dominance is supported by the most dependent workers, that is the unskilled.[77]

This quotation graphically illustrates how management has successfully created divisions within the workforce. Undoubtedly, skilled workers are mistaken if they believe that layoffs will somehow skip over skilled workers, even if the burden falls disproportionately on unskilled workers.

From Labor Shortage to Labor Surplus

Indeed, the relative position of both skilled and unskilled workers is adversely affected by the fundamental change in the labor market.[78] Even without large-scale unemployment, much hidden unemployment exists, as many workers are sent on compulsory unpaid vacations when enterprises are short of wage funds. In the middle of 1993, 2.8 million workers were on involuntary vacations, affecting 11.9 percent of all employees in industry; the numbers have remained high years later.[79] In such conditions, enterprises were no longer accepting new employees with open arms; on the contrary, they had closed their gates [priyem] to new workers. At many enterprises the next step has been campaigns against "violators of labor discipline," the alleged do-nothings, truants, and drunks long decried in the literature of the Soviet enterprise. In the past such campaigns involved moral persuasion against violators, or at most fines; enterprises were too labor-hungry to fire workers, who could easily find comparable employment, often at better pay. With enterprises now experiencing a labor surplus rather than a labor shortage, "violators" are simply fired. It is not too hard to imagine the next step being the laying off of auxiliary workers, particularly since this "internal reserve army" is rendered superfluous by the relatively small but growing "reserve army of the unemployed" outside factory gates.[80]

The firing of superfluous workers becomes more probable not when the enterprise is first formally privatized, but after the first shareholders' meeting, when management's position as both controller and de facto owner is more firmly established. According to one study, "Management had little incentive to restructure prior to the first shareholder meeting, because far reaching restructuring programs, which are likely to endanger many work places, are likely to jeopardize management's chances in elections at shareholder meetings where employees are majority shareholders."[81] Managers have proven adept at clearing this hurdle: in the same study, of a sample of 36 enterprises in all but two cases the original directors were appointed as the General Director of the new joint-stock company.[82]

West Siberian: From State Enterprise
to Joint-Stock Company

The discussion in the chapter thus far has appeared somewhat disjointed. A micro-level case study will help illustrate the relationship between enterprise paternalism, the trade union, privatization, and changes in the labor market. For it we will return to West Siberian, one of the two steel enterprises examined earlier in detail. It should be recalled that West Siberian was both a large enterprise and one better positioned than most to survive market competition.

In order to profit from its potential market position, however, the plant would have to restructure—that is, significantly reduce—its immense workforce, which numbered thirty-three thousand in 1991. Yet rather than take such steps to cut costs and boost profits, the plant continued to pour more resources into the "social sphere."[83] In addition to the rather considerable array of goods and services the plant already provided to its employees (as described in detail in chaps. 4 and 5), the plant continued to build still more "social objects," as well as maintain those it had built in the past. Cottages and other housing were under construction, as were indoor swimming pools and sports clubs. Many of the plant's social objects were now formally owned by the city government, but because of the latter's lack of resources, they were fully financed by the steel complex. When asked by a correspondent how life was "under capitalism," the plant's deputy director (and member of the board of directors) complained,

"Formally housing is owned by the municipality. But the plant pays to maintain the housing, and the same goes for social and cultural facilities [*sotskul'tbyt*], and with vacation centers and summer camps for children. . . . In reality, we will not quickly escape from this system, because people are not prepared, both materially and psychologically, for example to pay a thousand times more for an apartment than they pay now."[84]

In fact, the transfer of social services was often occurring in the other direction, from the city to the steel complex: with municipal services deteriorating, the borough could no longer afford to feed students at two local technical schools, so the factory's cafeteria services provided breakfast and dinner to the students.

Further still, the plant was investing considerable resources in activities wholly unrelated to steelmaking: these included an Italian-designed shoe factory (in addition to the shoe-making cooperative that was already in existence) and a furniture factory, along with plans for bottling mineral water, Pepsi, and Fanta, for baking cookies and candy (with Czech technology), for packaging breakfast cereals, and for the construction of a German-designed brewery, all housed on plant grounds. Additionally, the combine was building its own savings bank, which would allow workers to purchase goods at the combine's stores using coupons [*kartochki*].[85]

A good part of the motivation behind these plans was to compensate for the reduced demand for steel products by taking advantage of the lack of low-priced consumer goods. Yet consumer goods production at the steel plant also fit with continued emphasis on paternalism. As workers became increasingly anxious about their future, the administration of the enterprise responded reassuringly that it would take care of all its employees. Workers were to have the first share of the consumer goods produced at the plant. As one former employee recalled, one of director Kustov's favorite slogans was, "Every woman should leave work with a full bag."[86]

But consumer goods production also allowed the plant's administration to claim that, despite the slumping of demand for steel and the large number of employees at the plant, "no one will be left without work." While the number of workers required for these production units was relatively small, plant managers continued to claim that superfluous workers would simply be transferred around the plant rather than laid off, and investment in these new lines of production for the plant was continually justified in these terms.

During the first meeting of shareholders (where he was the only candidate for general director of the joint-stock company), Kustov spoke proudly of the plant's program to create new work spaces. He also expressed concern that the plant's extensive social sphere "not be looked on as a burden." He further explained that while the combine had opted for the first model of privatization, as an open joint-stock company, more than 60 percent of the shares were held by employees of the combine, and other shares were held by connected enterprises, including by workers in social and agricultural facilities largely subordinate to the plant. The director warned that while the controlling share of stock was held by the labor collective, "it might happen like it has at other enterprises" where outsiders gained control, and he admonished workers not to sell their shares to commercial structures or to exchange them for consumer goods.[87]

After presenting his campaign speech, Director Kustov was elected to the Directors' Council, as were all the other nominated candidates. These included four deputy directors, the trade union chair as representative of the labor collective, and a member of the State Property Committee (the state retained one-quarter of the shares). The economic development program presented by the directors was adopted, and the Directors' Council elected Kustov as president of the joint-stock company. Only then was the floor opened up for questions.[88]

Not all employees were happy with this arrangement. While it was proclaimed that everyone was now a part-owner of their enterprise, workers were told that all fifty-five thousand shareholders could not possibly meet at once and that the only way to have one's voice heard was through a proxy. While under the old system at least formally each employee, from the janitor to the director, had one vote, and delegates to meetings of the labor collective were elected from each shop, now one's voice increased or decreased with the amount of shares held. A threshold of one thousand votes was required to be let in the shareholders' meeting, a number impossible for most employees to gather, and angry shareholders were turned away from the doors.[89] One pensioner who was turned away wrote (anonymously) to the plant newspaper to complain: "We were deceived, we have no say." Not surprisingly, despite all the concern among liberal reformers that enterprises had been seized by "collective ownership," workers themselves experienced little sense of ownership: in a survey of workers at the neighboring Kuznetskii Metallurgical Combine, as many as 80 percent responded that they had no sense of ownership in their enterprise, despite being shareholders in the joint-stock company.[90]

Having survived the initial shareholders' meeting that established Kustov as both president and general director of the joint-stock company, he and his subordinates began to set a different tone. The paternalistic rhetoric was maintained, and the plant's management still promised to provide for all those under its wing. Yet within weeks of the first shareholders' meeting, as reported by the plant's newspaper, Kustov pointed to falling real prices for steel and firmly announced that "the combine will no longer feed [*kormit'*] do-nothings," adding further that "we finally need to introduce order in production."[91] A few weeks later at a meeting with representatives of the plant's female workers, Kustov charged that "some are finding time at work for picnicking, for repairing their own cars, and simply doing nothing." He maintained that as a consequence, he had decided in the near future to lay off three thousand of the plant's employees. "It's clear that those first let go should be those who don't exhibit a special zeal for work, who walk around, who drink."[92]

Even before the shareholders' meeting, the plant had taken advantage of changes in the labor market to introduce "a system of individual wage contracts." As explained by one manager, "the more a worker violates the conditions of the contract, the more likely his chances of receiving nothing" and allowing the administration to annul the contract. Unlike before, when enterprises with unsatiable appetites for labor welcomed practically any able-bodied man or woman to work, now "the new person has to demonstrate high professionalism in practice before getting a contract." Positive results, the manager claimed, were already evident. "There is no labor turnover like before, and we don't experience shortages even in those professions in especially short supply, like lathe turner/borer. Productivity has gone up." He cited the example of machine operators of one shop, who, if they worked at last year's pace, would have to work an additional twelve shifts with 150 percent increased output in order to meet the current rate.[93]

Yet the plant administration remained dissatisfied. Within another two weeks the plant newspaper printed a roundtable discussion of the plant's problems with labor discipline. The deputy director of the plant's legal department claimed that "tough measures" were called for and reminded readers that in the collective contract recently adopted, the trade union and the administration signed a joint resolution that made firings more severe:

> If before when someone like a truant was fired, he received practically all his pay, including compensation for unused vacation time. But now all the pay, vacation time included, is taken away with fines. For the month before the sacking, the worker's not paid at all. That is, the person leaves the combine "naked," and more often than not remains in debt to the plant.

Yet the plant's lawyer complained that discipline was not improving: for the first eight months of 1992, there had been 1,460 serious violations at the plant, but for the same period of 1993, there were 1,724, despite the fact that six hundred more workers were fired.[94]

Rather than refuting this depiction of an undisciplined workforce, Pavlenko, the deputy chair of the trade union, joined the discussion by decrying "the wave of drunkenness" that swept the plant in the spring. "If some one is caught drinking at the workplace, it's easy to take care of," since a special statute in the labor code allows for the worker to be fired without the right of appeal. "But if he's caught drinking in the entrance-way after work," the administration was in a more difficult position, since the worker could appeal and was often reinstated.[95]

Reflecting the confused position of the former state trade union at the enterprise, nominally defenders of workers' rights but almost totally dependent on management, Pavlenko complained: "We're running out of measures to take to bring about order. We can't build a prison here. We do whatever is allowed within the law. But repressive measures won't work by themselves, we need to increase production. . . . If production picks up and people are busy, all other problems would be solved."[96]

Indeed, workers at the plant were not "do-nothings" as much as there was often nothing to do. Because of the decline in production levels, people remained idle, and the shops could not fully employ their workers. With such plants overstaffed even during the days when Soviet steel plants churned out tons of steel for a metal-hungry economy, and given the drastic slump in production with largely the same number of employees, workers often played cards or slept on the job.

General Director Kustov's response, at least after the initial shareholders' meeting, was to order "raids" by the personnel department, often during the night shift, aimed at uncovering violations of labor discipline.[97] Elsewhere it was explained that the measure was intended to "improve the organization of labor" by determining each employee's real contribution [*zagruzhennost'*], which would allow the personnel department to draw up plans for layoffs.[98]

But as the deputy trade union chair Pavlenko explained, the plant "is not ready for mass layoffs. Already there is an order for 5 percent reductions on average in the production shops and 10 percent for managerial staff. But these are only the warning signs. The question is, who to lay off, and how? The Labor Code doesn't allow rapid layoffs. We can't fulfill this plan."[99] The legal obstacles to mass layoffs in the Russian Labor Code provide the explanation for the plant's sudden interest in firing "violators of labor discipline." As Pavlenko further explained, "Before we would shame people, lecture them, hang up their pictures, but didn't fire them as a rule, because of the labor shortage. Now there are too many people working, and not enough consumers for steel. So each shop will try to get rid of all violators of labor discipline. With this [Labor Code] statute it is much easier to get rid of people, than by layoffs."[100]

The problem the plant faced with layoffs also provides the best explanation for what would otherwise appear to be a strange turn of events. Though the enterprise trade union was little more than an arm of management, and was searching for ways to discipline and fire its own members, the administration of the West Siberian joint-stock company turned against its compliant union. The first signs of the administration's intentions underscored how little the trade union had changed: Director Kustov and his deputy publicly announced that they were resigning as trade union members.[101] Articles in the plant paper discussed the rights of workers who chose not to belong to the trade union, and workers who wrote in to ask whether the trade unions could withhold vacation trips and workers' compensation from nonmembers were reassured that they could not.

In the past, as noted in a *Trud* article on the subject, Kustov "never passed up an opportunity to proclaim 'The trade union is our greatest support in solving the production and social problems of the collective.'" But now he revealed just how dependent the labor union had been on the goodwill of management by throwing the union off the enterprise grounds. This ejection not only deprived the union of office space, but also prevented union officials from meeting its members during work. Since the combine was so vast that it required its own extensive tram system to ferry workers between shops, the trade union was left with little chance of finding a central location where workers might meet. For good measure, the enterprise automobiles placed at union disposal were taken away and, perhaps most damaging for a union holding little goodwill among its membership, the automatic deduction of union dues from paychecks was canceled. The "social functions" that the union had been most concerned with in the past were now taken over by an enterprise committee established by management.[102]

The proximate cause of the administration's turn against the former state trade union was a conflict over management's proposal to switch from a twelve-hour to an eight-hour work schedule. Since workers had long ago accustomed themselves to the twelve-hour shifts, which allowed them a couple of days off in a row, they raised objections to the proposal. As the trade union chair explained, "We were not opposed to the proposal at first," but simply wanted to consult with workers.[103] But workers remained opposed, and two small shops walked off the job to protest the work changes; the trade union, while attempting to convince the workers to return to work, tried to defend their position before management.[104]

This conflict allowed the administration to take the actions that in all likelihood had already been decided on. Having ordered the trade union off enterprise grounds, management declared the union's attempt to call a meeting of the labor collective to discuss the violation of the collective contract "illegal." Deputy union chair Pavlenko was prevented from meeting with workers at their request, and a union lawyer had his enterprise pass taken away.[105] The union was denied access to the plant newspaper and radio, allowing the administration a virtual monopoly on interpreting the events.

From the perspective of enterprise management, the problem with the trade union was not that it sided with workers over a relatively small question, or that it began arguing with management over certain issues, such as expressing a reluctance to mobilize workers for the factory's annual "potato campaign."[106] Rather, while materially dependent on management, the trade union held significant legal rights that remained from Soviet-era labor laws; under new conditions, these rights could provide a significant check on management. For instance, the system of individual wage contracts violated stipulations in the Labor Code stating that wage issues should be handled in the collective contract signed by the trade union. More importantly, while in the earlier quotation Pavlenko mentioned the legal difficulties of laying off workers under the Labor Code, the real legal obstacle was that such actions required union approval. Before the conflict with management, the union inserted an article in the plant newspaper that sought to convince workers they needed a trade union.[107] "Only a trade union can defend workers from layoffs," the article explained, since the enterprise "can't layoff workers without getting the agreement of the trade union committee. But if there is no trade union, layoffs can take place at management's discretion."[108]

The union took the plant's administration to court, but in spite of its strong legal position, the regional prosecutor asked that the two sides

work things out among themselves. The reaction of the central steelworkers' union illustrates the difficulty of reforming huge union bureaucracies.
While the national union, which under the directorship of Boris Michnik
had declared itself independent of the FNPR and became militant in its
rhetoric, tried to come to aid of the West Siberian union, the regional-level
trade union chair simply arranged a meeting between Kustov and the plant
union chair, where he urged the two to reconcile themselves. The two eventually came to an agreement, with the union ultimately restored to its
offices in the plant, having become somewhat wiser of its dependence on
management and of future conflicts likely in store. But it retained only 25
to 30 percent of its former members. As the union chair confided, "Of
course workers are afraid of layoffs, especially because they now know the
trade union can't defend them. I'm afraid we'll lose if we try [to fight]
again."[109]

While the experience of the West Siberian Metallurgical Combine
provides only a single case study, and the difficulties that workers have
experienced there might not be typical, the case coincides in general out-
line with those of other plants.[110] The case suggests that far from taking
part in "collective ownership," Russian workers are directly experiencing
"nomenklatura privatization"; moreover, workers are being hit hard by
the drastic changes in the labor market, which has swung from a high
demand for labor to a labor surplus in which workers have few cards to
play.[111] Most discouraging from labor's perspective is that the majority of
workers remain effectively unorganized, and until that changes, their situation will likely only get worse.

Nevertheless, workers can express their tremendous grievances in
other ways, short of collective action. For one, as long as even the elements
of formal democracy remain, workers can vote, and given their numbers
and given their anger, their votes are likely to be significant. It is workers'
impact on the political course of post-Communist Russia and Ukraine
that we take up in the next chapter.

CHAPTER 8

Politics and Coal Miners in
Ukraine and Russia

Given the enormous challenges faced by workers in Russia and Ukraine, including a decline in real wages, a rapidly worsening position in the labor market, and threats not only to their jobs but to their industrial communities, how might workers respond? This chapter will examine how the coal miners have replied politically to these challenges, including their participation in the first post-Communist parliamentary elections in each state.

Within the framework of liberal democracy, the primary weapons available to workers are the strike and the ballot. As we have seen, industrial workers outside of mining have thus far proven unable to exercise the strike option and, without independent organization, are unable to nominate labor candidates or form labor parties.

The coal miners of the Donbass and the Kuzbass have proven able both to lead strikes and to create independent political organizations. The mining regions remain the best place to examine workers' political response to the painful economic transformations in Russia and Ukraine. Both regions are overwhelmingly industrial, with coal mining the dominant industry in both cases, and consequently most families, and therefore voters, are working class. With the coal industry still largely controlled by the state in both cases, workers have a direct interest in influencing state policy through the ballot. Here, if anywhere, one would expect to see viable labor parties or politicians aiming appeals specifically to workers. Such was not the case, however. (The Communist Party, so bitterly rejected just a few years ago, is the one political force that has stepped in to fill this void; even it, as we shall see, has largely avoided appealing to workers as a class.)

The starting point for an explanation is the observation that the political space in post-Communist societies has thus far been quite different than those in Western democracies. As Kitschelt has argued, patterns of party competition in post-Communist societies stand in direct contradistinction to those in advanced capitalist democracies. In capitalist democracies, the political "left" typically combines opposition to free-market allocation with support for civil liberties and a strong democratic process, while in post-Communist societies those opposing market allocation also tend to support a more authoritarian political process.[1] For present purposes, this question can be restated more simply: Why is there so little support for a social democratic alternative in post-Communist societies? (On why the Communist Parties of Russia and Ukraine do not fit the social democratic label, we will have more to say at the end of this chapter.) This lack of support is especially puzzling for the miners of Russia and Ukraine, who have demonstrated that, far from being dark and illiterate masses, they understand democratic principles and have fought to implement them, both at the state level and within their enterprise. Moreover, while they supported market allocation as a way of breaking the Soviet state's grip on their economic condition, the values they espoused remained quite workerist and indeed socialist.

I will argue that the ideological legacy of communism has left a blank space on the post-Communist political landscape by discrediting appeals made on a class basis (such as some form of socialism or social democracy). While workers see the world in class terms and remain committed to some of the core ideals of what most others would call socialism (such as workers' control), they lacked a name around which to package their concerns, since the concept of socialism in any variety remains tied to the Soviet system they held in contempt. The failure of the miners' movement, virtually the only independent labor organization in both countries, to articulate an ideological vision for workers distinct from the Soviet system and free-market liberalism, helped pave the way for the success at the ballot box of extreme nationalists and Communists. We will first examine the Ukrainian case, and then the Russian, before returning to the questions posed here at the outset.

Miner Politics in the New Ukraine

In the Donbass, miners employed both the strike and the ballot; in fact, they used a major strike to push through early-term elections for the Ukrainian parliament and president. We will delve into the conflict that led to the strike and then examine how the miners used the political opportunity of the elections they had demanded.

With Ukrainian independence, the Donbass miners became embroiled in a deep regional cleavage, one that overlaps cultural and economic divisions in Ukrainian society: between Russian and Ukrainian speakers and between the industrialized East and the more agricultural West. Ukrainians speaking Russian as a first language tend, for a variety of historical and sociological reasons, to be much less nationalistic then

their Ukrainian-speaking counterparts. These Russian speakers, both ethnic Ukrainians and Russians, are concentrated overwhelmingly in the
industrial East, while Ukrainian speakers predominate in rural areas,
especially in the West. In the Donbass, the number of ethnic Ukrainians
and Russians is approximately the same—51 percent ethnic Ukrainians
and 44 percent Russians, according to the 1989 census—but only 32 percent claim Ukrainian as their mother tongue, as opposed to 66 percent
claiming Russian,[2] and Russian is overwhelmingly the dominant language
in public discourse.

The ties to Russia are not only ethnic: in the heavily industrialized
southeast region of Ukraine, approximately 80 percent of enterprises were
oriented to Russia for either suppliers of inputs or purchasers of their
products.[3] This situation is not surprising, given the fact that almost all
Donbass industry was run by Soviet Union ministries in Moscow rather
than Ukrainian ministries.

These structural and historical factors were further reinforced by the
cultural framework that the Donbass miners continued to use to comprehend their situation. Even after tasting the bitter fruit of free-market pric-
ing for coal, which again underscored their dependence on state subsidies,
the Donbass miners continued to employ their labor theory of value to
argue that they were being exploited. Samofalov of the Kuibyshev mine,
addressing a meeting of miners before their shift, used the following illus-
tration to explain how the exploitation had taken place before and how little had changed since.

> Once the Soviet Union existed. Once clever men worked in our Moth-
> erland's capital city, and each of us received a little something from
> our Motherland's "granaries." All of us worked, poured everything
> into the "granaries," and the clever men divided it into parts. They
> decided themselves how much everyone would get, because no one
> should get rich, no one should "fatten." When the collapse of the
> Union started the "granaries" moved from Moscow to Kiev.

He went on to argue that in the Donbass, "steelworkers, chemical
workers, and so on, all of us create material value," placing it ahead of
other regions, but "if you contribute the lion's share to the budget of
Ukraine, you get only a certain small percentage back to satisfy your
needs, such as day care, pensions, health care. But the Ternopil [agricul-
tural and western] region which produces much less than you do, is given
a big share." These regions "live at our expense." This characterization is
remarkable in that Samofalov and the miners he addressed were vividly
aware of their reliance on state subsidies; yet despite this dependence on

subsidies and the need for state investment, the answer, he and many others argued, was to make the Donbass a free economic zone, as the first step toward a federal Ukraine.[4]

These tensions led to the strike of June 1993. The conflict not only involved miners but also united much of eastern Ukraine—both workers and managers, manual laborers and professionals—against the government in Kiev. The strike began over the latest round of price increases on food and basic consumer items, an action that was exacerbated by many miners not being paid for months. While the work stoppage began spontaneously on June 7 in a single Donetsk mine over these economic issues, the news quickly spread to other mines, and the Donetsk city strike committee put forth political demands: regional independence for the Donbass and a national referendum on (no) faith in the parliament and the president. Within a day all the mines of the Donetskugol coal association had stopped working, and the miners had gathered on the city square.[5]

Workers from other industries showed their support for miners, either by shutting down production or by sending their representatives to the demonstration on the city square. Teachers and medical and cultural workers also took part. By June 11, 150 enterprises in Donetsk province alone had stopped work, including 74 mines. On the city square, speakers argued that government policy was hurting the industrialized region; the phrase "They've squeezed the last juice out of the Donbass" was heard repeatedly. More specifically, demonstrators maintained that the region was not getting its fair share of state revenues and that Kiev's policy on trade meant that goods were not flowing to and from other former Soviet republics, creating losses for industry. If a strike was not sufficient to achieve their goal of regional independence, the miners threatened to call for civil disobedience throughout the region.[6]

The miners and others claimed that their political demands were the most important, and as if to prove their point, they refused to halt the strike after considerable economic concessions were made by the government.[7] Nor did they show much reaction when Efim Zviagilskii, then mayor of Donetsk and the former director of the Zasiad'ko mine where the strike began, was named first vice premier of Ukraine (he was later named acting prime minister).[8] What did end the strike was the decision of the Ukrainian parliament, after three days of discussion, to hold a national referendum on the trust of the population in the parliament and the president.[9]

The strike, which lasted ten days, was considerable in scope. According to the strikers' statistics, more than three hundred enterprises stopped work, and unlike other strikes, workers in other industries took part.[10] The coal miners thus spearheaded the push in the Donbass for regional autonomy and what would amount to early-term elections for the Ukrainian president and parliament. We have noted several reasons for the cleavage between the Donbass in the east and western Ukraine. Not least of these (and despite the region's acknowledged dependence on state subsidies) was the sense of exploitation—that the Donbass is producing more than it is getting back from the state.

It is this sense of exploitation that has led miners and others to call for a free economic zone in the Donbass. If understandable politically, the calls for a free economic zone for the region make little sense economically.[11] Indeed, even when they were calling for an end to the Soviet state, miners in the Donbass understood all too well that they would remain dependent on the state, some state, for survival. As mentioned, the support of the Donbass miners for Ukrainian sovereignty was based largely on the hope that a Ukrainian government with more independence would provide a better deal than the Soviet government in terms of subsidies and support for the mining industry. Most miners and others interviewed in the Donbass held two contradictory viewpoints without particular concern: (1) that the "center" (first Moscow, now Kiev) was exploiting them, and (2) that they were dependent on state subsidies for their survival.

The subsidies were significant: a 550 billion karbovantsi subsidy to Ukrainian coal industry in May–June of 1993 alone; an extrapolation of this rate would mean annual cost of 3,300 billion karbovantsi, or nearly a third of the annual state budget, before counting the wage hikes granted after the July 1993 strike. Many in Ukraine viewed the strike "as the reason for the collapse of the Ukrainian economy."[12] While that appears to be a case of blaming the miners for causing problems to which they were merely responding, it does underscore the pivotal position in which Donbass miners find themselves concerning Ukraine's future. The economic dilemma facing Kiev is either to continue to spend large sums to subsidize unprofitable industries, despite the obvious spur to inflation, or to invest even larger amounts of capital in reconstructing worn-out industries and creating new jobs.[13] An effort to reconstruct the coal industry to help it meet some of Ukraine's energy needs,[14] combined with a measured transition and retraining for coal miners who are laid off, would prove costly in economic terms but may be the only socially and politically viable option. A further option, to employ Thatcher's strategy of direct confrontation with the coalfields, leading to closures and unemployment, would almost certainly be a disaster. Most miners well understand the industry's enormous losses, not only financial but in human lives, and themselves argue that some mines should be closed. But they insist that they be retrained—to build cars, houses, roads, or whatever society needs. Otherwise, as they have already well demonstrated, they are prepared to fight.

Elections in the Donbass

Yet the Donbass miners also had an even more directly political impact on Ukraine. While the miners' demand for a referendum on the confidence of the population in the parliament and the president was subsequently shelved, their demands succeeded in forcing parliament to call preterm elections for both president and parliament. Yet though the action by Donbass workers forced elections, a party that might capture the concerns of workers as a distinct group failed to appear. In fact, the only "Labor Party" in Ukraine was rather transparently organized by enterprise managers from the Donbass.[15] This Labor Party was also tied to members of the Ukrainian government, including Prime Minister Zviagilsky and Deputy Prime Minister Landyk, themselves former managers from the Donbass.

Members of the miners' strike committee in Donetsk ran as candidates for the parliamentary elections, but they failed to articulate a position that appealed to their constituency—industrial workers and their families, who make up the overwhelming majority of the Donbass population. Yurii Boldyrev, former member of the city strike committee and deputy chair of the Donetsk city council, ran as a candidate of the Civic Congress, a pro-Russian party. His platform contained three planks: (1) regional autonomy within a federal Ukraine, (2) both Russian and Ukrainian as state languages, and (3) economic reintegration with Russia.[16]

Mikhail Krylov, cochair of the Donetsk strike committee, also ran as a candidate in the elections. Despite, or perhaps because of, the economy's near collapse and the continued dependence on subsidies to keep the coal industry from ruin, Krylov as candidate continued to push for regional autonomy and the market: "We want to be our own masters and sell our own coal."[17] However, according to one observer, "The strike committee's program differs little from that of the Civic Congress and the Labor Party," certainly limiting their appeal to workers in particular.[18]

Indeed, most commentators predicted that the Labor Party and the Socialist Party of Ukraine would win over the bulk of voters.[19] The latter, one of the two successors to the Communist Party (the other being the Communist Party of Ukraine) and portraying itself as more moderate and social democratic, was said to have gained support from unskilled workers.[20] Yet in the election, it was the Communist Party of Ukraine, little changed in name and program, that won overwhelmingly in the Donbass. After the second round of voting, candidates giving the CPU as their primary affiliation won 36 out of 62 seats; many others elected from the Donbass, while not officially affiliated with the CPU, were likely to support their concerns. The stunning success of the Communists came despite the large number of candidates with various affiliations running in each district.

Why were the Communists in particular so successful? Others, such as the Labor Party, were apparently rejected by their association as both a party of enterprise bosses and a party close to the current government, which was clearly repudiated by Donbass voters.[21] Further, with the economic situation exceedingly dismal, especially with Russia looking vibrant by comparison, the notion of a return to the past clearly had some appeal. It is especially so since the initial support for Ukrainian sovereignty in the Donbass was based almost entirely on the belief that independence from Moscow would leave greater resources at their disposal and create a better standard of living.

Yet there was little or no support for overt Russian nationalists in this center of Russian language and culture, even when Ukrainian nationalists were seen as the main threat to their aspirations. That is in part because ethnic Ukrainians (a distinction kept alive in the region not by language or culture but largely by the Soviet-era passport system) remain a slight majority in the Donbass, even if they are overwhelmingly Russified. Moreover, and partly as a result, Ukrainian nationalists were not attacked for being Ukrainian, but for being nationalists. Well before the Communist Party regained support in the region, many in the Donbass claimed to be antinationalist, employing Soviet-era rhetoric against nationalism, with more than a few equating nationalism with fascism.[22] Given the concerns of reintegration with Russia, regaining the former standard of living, and defeating Ukrainian nationalists, the Communist Party served quite well. On the central issue of regaining former ties with Russia, few could compete with the Communist Party of Ukraine.

Indeed, the CPU called openly for the restoration of the USSR. Moreover, while the head of the CPU in Donetsk oblast offered only mild preelection palliatives such as "basic industries such as coal and energy have to belong to the state,"[23] something few other groups had sought to challenge, the Lugasnk oblast CPU was directly class oriented and populist. There, the party program explained the nation's misery as a product of "the artificial destruction of the planned economy," which caused "a breakdown in production, its subordination to foreign capital and the new local bourgeoisie, and the catastrophic impoverishment of the majority of the population." As a solution to these problems, the party program called for "the (re)introduction of state planning . . . , an end to the politics of price liberalization, and the cessation of the breakup and the transfer of the means of production to the funds of private owners, which inevitably leads to the exploitation of man by man, corruption, robbery, and speculation."[24]

Apparently, an overwhelming number of voters in the industrial Donbass agreed with this analysis. Given the dismal state of the Ukrainian economy, and the fact that by any objective criteria of material well-being the Donbass workers were indeed better off under the old system, this result was perhaps not surprising. Yet it was hard to see how calling for the restoration of the old order presented a realistic solution to Ukraine's economic problems. While Communist parliamentarians have pushed for reintegration with Russia, they have shown little sign of presenting a viable alternative to the economic medicine being prescribed by liberal reformers and international lending agencies.

In July 1994, in the presidential elections forced by the miners' strike a year earlier, Leonid Kuchma, the former manager of a Dnepropetrovsk missile factory, was elected by overwhelming support from eastern Ukraine: in the two-person runoff, he received 82 percent of the votes from the Donbass, while only 4 percent from the strongly Ukrainian nationalist Galician regions.[25] Kuchma's support in the Donbass apparently came from the belief that his rhetoric about restoring ties to Russia signaled a willingness to defend the interests of the industrial east; his tough talk on free markets and the future of unprofitable enterprises appear to have been ignored.[26] Once in office, Kuchma and his Western advisers began to apply liberal economic medicine to the Ukrainian economy.

Yet Kuchma and any government in Kiev faces the same dilemma: in order to halt inflation and stabilize the economy, that government would have to cut subsidies, many of which are aimed at industries in the east. While Kuchma has begun to do just that, quickly using up his capital of goodwill in the Donbass, signs of unrest by miners and others continue to spread. Subsequent reductions in subsidies will lead to bankruptcies and open and widespread unemployment. And if relatively modest price increases were sufficient to bring much of eastern Ukraine to strike and call for the virtual ouster of the previous government and president, then a sudden reduction in subsidies and resulting unemployment will almost certainly do so. Without overcoming this dilemma, the result will likely be continued political crisis, as the Ukrainian economy continues to slide deeper into the morass.

Perhaps more troubling still for the Donbass coal miners, they themselves proved unable to find a viable alternative to the system that both protected and enraged them. Having occupied the square in front of Communist Party headquarters on several occasions, ultimately to demand the breakup of the Soviet state and the removal from power of Party bureaucrats they accused of exploiting workers, the Donbass miners could find no other course than asking that these same people return. And there is little mistaking that these are largely the same people: not only is the party unchanged in name, but the bulk of the Communist deputies come from the familiar triumvirate of regional state officials, collective farm chairs, and factory directors.[27] While the class rhetoric used by these politicians clearly resounded with Donbass voters, miners and others in the region found themselves once again represented by others claiming to act in workers' best interest.

Miners' Politics in Independent Russia

After the fall of the Soviet Union, the miners' movement in Russia was full of contradictions. On the one hand, the miners had achieved almost all of their political demands from the 1991 strike. Their ally Yeltsin was firmly in power, and the miners were well rewarded for the continued political loyalty. Yet, on the other hand, the dramatic economic changes (as outlined in the last chapter) hit the mining regions hard, and support among rank-and-file miners for the political status quo began to evaporate.

After the failed coup attempt, during which Kuzbass miners supported Yeltsin's call for a strike,[28] Yeltsin appointed Kuzbass miner-leaders Kislyuk as governor (or head of the regional administration) and Malykhin as the president's personal representative for the region.[29] And despite all the rhetoric by miners and their allies in favor of the market, the Russian coal industry remained heavily subsidized. While miners were hit along with others by the freeing of consumer prices in January 1992, through their credible strike threat and alliance with Yeltsin they gained a threefold wage increase. Miners in various regions continued to strike quite often with economic demands (aimed at the state), as in March 1993 when strikes erupted in both the Kuzbass and Vorkuta. Yet that same month the Kuzbass workers' committees and NPG supported Yeltsin's call for a referendum on his policies against detractors in the Russian parliament; the support included the threat of a political strike over the issue.[30] To shore up the support of miners before the referendum itself, Yeltsin traveled to the region and promised lower taxes on coal exports, implied that coal miners' wages would be nearly doubled, and ruled out price liberalization for coal.[31]

Yet the Kuzbass miners found themselves in a position much like Poland's Solidarity: they had helped bring a government to power whose policies would create falling living standards and ultimately unemployment for workers. When promises were broken—in conditions of serious economic decline, threats of mine closures, and wages that went unpaid for months—support for Yeltsin began to quickly evaporate among rank-and-file miners. The leaders of the Kuzbass miners' movement—who had backed Yeltsin during his most crucial political standoffs, such as the failed putsch, the April referendum, and the "October events" leading to the shelling of the parliament—tried to square it by denouncing the "government" as opposed to the state, as if a sharp line could be drawn between government policy and the state that appointed the government.[32]

While miners joined liberal reformers to denounce the Communist system they so detested, they had little reason to support liberals now in power and responsible for spiraling prices and falling living standards. The continued support of independent mine leaders for Yeltsin's government during a time of economic upheaval cost them much of the backing from those they were supposed to represent.[33] Survey data in the Kuzbass, while of the population as a whole, show the perceived authority of the workers' committees to have fallen dramatically from 1991 to 1992.[34]

While the rift between the miners and their leaders was widening, others in the Kuzbass increasingly blamed coal miners for their misfortune. The president's unpopular measures were embodied in the region by Governor Kislyuk and President's Representative Malykhin. Moreover, as in the Donbass the material successes the miners gained, especially their high wages, were perceived by others in the region as creating a local inflationary spiral on top of the already high inflation rate.[35] The miners' gains led to a backlash, first among pensioners and others directly dependent on the state budget for their income, which in turn created a base for populist politicians in reaction to the miners' movement. This brings us to the elections.

Elections in the Kuzbass

In the Kuzbass, candidates for the parliamentary elections in December 1993 can be divided roughly into four groups: liberal democrats, authoritarian populists, industrial managers, and labor activists. We will examine the position and relative success of each group subsequently, keeping in mind that, as in the Donbass, the majority of the voters in the Kuzbass are working class.

The relationship of the democrat-intellectuals in the Kuzbass to workers generally and miners in particular was sharply contradictory. On the one hand, members of this political grouping almost universally described how the miners' strike of 1989 awakened their political consciousness. Gennadii Mityakin, Federal Assembly candidate on the Russia's Choice ticket, related his impression upon seeing miners occupying the city square: "It was the most magnificent event in my life, simply colossal. It was the first time in my life that I saw my own people [narod]."[36]

Yet on the other hand, many of these democratic intellectuals were faced with the realization that their economic program was increasingly unpopular in the region. Some explained this fact by referring to the "lumpen consciousness" of the population and consequently of the need for the need for an "intermediate period" of strong presidential rule before Western-style democracy could be implemented.[37] Hence these "democrats" supported shutting down newspapers they did not agree with as well as closing the regional parliament—the most popular political institution in the region. The power of the democrats rested not in the local parliament, but in the governor, who was not elected and very unpopular, yet was the most powerful figure in the region.[38] (Thus the "democrats" held power in the Kuzbass thanks to appointment from above, while the region's most popular figure by far was their political opponent, the "Communist" Aman Tuleev.) Given the dire state of the economy and the fact that their government was in power, the democrats were clearly in a difficult position before the elections.[39]

The authoritarian populists, including many Communists now in the opposition, offered many reasonable positions, including demands that the local government be elected, rather than appointed by the president. They argued further that given the enormous poverty many people were experiencing, liberal reformers had lost touch with the travails of the average citizen. As with the liberals, however, there was no shortage of hypocrisy in their statements. One got a strong sense that their version of populism implied the use of a strong hand, if not outright fascism.[40] In fact, if Zhirinovsky did not exist, he would not have to be invented, because others are waiting to take his place. One such person is Aman Tuleev.

Tuleev is undoubtedly the most popular political figure in the region; as chair of the regional soviet his approval ratings were often between 70 and 80 percent.[41] He has been an opponent of Yeltsin since long before it was popular: he ran against Yeltsin for the Russian presidency in 1991. Tuleev supported the workers' committees after the initial miners' strikes but soon turned against them once they adopted an anticommunist stance. While arguing that he is a true friend of the rank-and-file miner,[42] he has become a bitter opponent of the Kuzbass miners' movement, claiming that the miners had been co-opted by outside political forces.

Tuleev's opponents claim that he openly sympathized with the coup attempt in August 1991 before it failed.[43] He was a Russian people's deputy, where he allied himself with other forces opposed to Yeltsin. Even as a candidate for the federal assembly, after supporters of the parliament had suffered a bloody defeat, Tuleev refused to soften his rhetoric: he proudly wore his people's deputy pin and campaigned openly against Yeltsin's actions in September and October, which he compared to Hitler's putsch. He continues to support the idea of a Siberian republic (or *guberniia*) as a solution to the problems of the Kuzbass.

Without question Tuleev has charismatic appeal. As the author waited for a 7:00 p.m. meeting (after his typical day of campaigning before enterprise labor collectives), Tuleev swept open the door and strode boldly into the room, while his underlings scurried around him like mice. Once he settled in for an interview, lipstick was visible on his collar. Whether speaking to a single person or to a television audience, Tuleev is a captivating speaker: he beats his chest and pulls his hair for emphasis, and he addresses his listeners in a direct language usually suited to intimates talking around a kitchen table.[44]

Yet Tuleev's popularity is only partly attributable to charisma. Part Soviet regional boss and part pork barrel politician, Tuleev is able to deliver for his constituency. During times of crisis, he flies to Moscow, works the hallways and offices, and returns with something tangible for the Kuzbass, which is popularly referred to as "Tuleev's money." As chair of the region's parliament, he directed his goodwill toward his natural constituency—those most vulnerable to market reforms, such as pensioners and others directly dependent on the state budget. Several informants reported that at the end of regular parliamentary sessions, such as the one where he pushed through a motion to let pensioners ride public transportation for free, people lined up to kiss his hands.

While both Tuleev and Zhirinovsky were successful in the Kuzbass in 1993, Tuleev's brand of populism is not based on Russian nationalism, nor could it be, given that he is half Tatar and half Kazakh.[45] In general, nationalism (either in terms of relations with non-Russian minorities or in terms of Russia's lost standing in world politics) rarely surfaced as an issue during the 1993 campaign in the Kuzbass. While nationalism may well resonate in the Kuzbass, as elsewhere in Russia—and Zhirinovsky's bloc won convincingly in the Kuzbass—it was able to do so because the soil was fertile.

Among those themes that were raised successfully in the Kuzbass campaign was the sense of chaos and anarchy [*bezvlastie*]. With bitter irony, the region's citizens pointed to the city of Prokop'evsk as a symbol of disorder. Prokop'evsk is a mining town that literally sits on top of one of the richest coal veins in Russia, yet the city's boilers fail to provide sufficient heat during the Siberian winter, so that people wear coats and hats in school and at home. Related to this sense of chaos was the concern with crime. But crime had additional meaning to people in the Kuzbass beyond the fear of personal safety and the security of property. Rather, there was an overwhelming concern with economic crime, the sense that others were taking advantage of a chaotic situation to enrich themselves.

Most important, and hardly surprising given the conditions, the campaign's biggest issue was the economy. Politicians and citizens alike spoke at length about declining living standards, the number of citizens now below the poverty level, inflation, and the threat of impending unemployment. Miners and other workers at state enterprises were most concerned with their pay being detained for months at a time, which not only made life difficult in itself but, given the rate of inflation, greatly discounted their wages in real terms. Miners in the region threatened to strike and stopped work at several mines over this issue in the month leading to the elections.

This returns us to the question of labor. Given these concerns, where did workers fit in this political schema, and how did they influence the campaign and the election outcome? Again, this is not a theoretical question for the Kuzbass. While the region represents only 2 percent of the Russian population, it produces almost 40 percent of Russia's coal as well as 14 percent of its steel.[46] Moreover, the region's coal miners not only have significant numbers but, unlike most workers in Russia, also have independent organizations and represent a real social force in the region. Further still, the miners have been heavily involved in politics: they have been active in several campaigns, from the elections to the regional and Russian parliaments in 1990, where they sent a number of miners and like-minded supporters into office, to the presidential campaign of 1991 and beyond.

Certainly the most rational electoral strategy would be one appealing to the bulk of the voters—the working class. Moreover, a rational electoral strategy would seem to be one combining support for democracy (giving workers the right to organize) with economic and social guarantees for workers and others—in short, some form of social democracy. That was in fact what most miner leaders described as their political and social goals. But when discussion turned to concrete political action, the language was not subtle, but rather Manichean—well after the failed coup and the end of the Soviet Union, in an independent Russia holding democratic elections while undergoing both large-scale privatization and economic decline, it was still a question of "us" versus "them." For these labor leaders, brought to power on the strength of the miners' strikes, "they" were the "Communists" while "we" were the "democrats."

Among leaders of the miners' movement, there was little consensus on whom to back within the democratic camp. Leaders of the Independent Miners Union (the NPG) allied themselves with Anatoly Sobchak's list (RDDR). As Vyacheslav Sharipov, the chair of the Kuzbass NPG, explained, Sobchak's Russian Movement for Democratic Reform was concerned with workers' issues, such as jobs, and was in favor of a "social partnership"—the corporatist structure of labor agreements that some trade unions in Russia have proposed.

While NPG leaders were supporting RDDR, members of the Kuzbass Council of Workers' Committees, the other regional miners' organization, found themselves much closer to Yeltsin, Gaidar, and Russia's Choice. Aleksandr Aslanidi, once a top leader of the Workers' Committee Council and executive director of *Nasha Gazeta,* the newspaper founded by the miners' movement, ran as an independent candidate for the federal assembly but campaigned on a platform of support for Yeltsin's constitution, the West as a political and economic model for Russia, and continuation of the current reform policies.[47] His campaign was considered to be so close to that of Russia's Choice that a meeting of democratic candidates for the federal assembly was held in the hopes of persuading some of the lesser-known candidates to withdraw. The meeting was held in the Council of Workers' Committees offices and chaired by the council head Golikov.

This divergence within the Kuzbass miners' movement—with one group supporting Sobchak's list, the other much closer to Russia's Choice—led to a local scandal during the campaign. With miners still owed back wages, often for the last several months, a strike threat emerged in several Russian mining regions, as miners rather transparently took advantage of the campaign period to extract concessions from the government. It was a game for both sides, however, as Gaidar made well-publicized trips to both the Kuzbass and Vorkuta, formally as government minister and negotiator, but clearly as candidate proving his ability to undo social tensions. Just prior to Gaidar's visit, and as part of its negotiating tactics, Sharipov issued a statement in the name of the NPG and the Workers' Committee Council that included a threat to not vote for party lists that included government officials if the government did not make certain concessions. While a seemingly rational bargaining tactic, Sharipov had a conflict of interest in such a stance, since he was one of the top candidates on the RDDR party list. More important, Golikov, Aslanidi, and other miner leaders considered that such a statement was extremely dangerous, in that it could play into the hands of their opponents—the Communists. Golikov issued sharp statements in the local press and television denouncing Sharipov's position and claiming that the miners' organizations had agreed to no so such position.[48]

This inability to agree on distancing themselves from the government, even as a bargaining tactic, illustrates the difficult position in which the Kuzbass miners found themselves on the eve of the parliamentary elections. The miners' movement had originally allied itself with Yeltsin in the hopes of improving the material position of miners. Yet while miners had been rewarded for their position by continued subsidies and wage hikes, problems such as delays in getting their wages, unpaid vacations, and threats of mine closures—not to mention the overall economic hardship in Russia—meant that dissatisfaction among rank-and-file miners was very near the boiling point.[49] Given these conditions, backing the status quo was certainly not a winning electoral strategy.

Candidates backed by the miners lost every election in the Kuzbass, with one important exception. Tuleev easily came in first among the eight candidates for the upper house, with an overwhelming 80 percent of the vote.[50] Moreover, his coattails were long: his protégé Burkov won the Duma seat from the city of Kemerovo, and his ally Medikov won the seat from Novokuznetsk. A third seat was won by Galina Parshinsteva, the deputy chief of the Anzhersk Department of Social Defense, while the last seat was won by Nina Volkova, head of the state retail store system in Prokop'evsk. Volkova included among her ideological allies Travkin's Democratic Party of Russia, the Civic Union, and Vladimir Zhirinovsky.[51]

The overwhelming victory by those labeled "Communists" by their opponents stands in contrast to the winner of the second seat in the upper house, that of Aleksandr Aslanidi, erstwhile leader of the miners' movement. Yet Aslanidi clearly did not win because of an effective campaign. In fact, his campaign was clearly disorganized: at the outset, Aslanidi conceded that he had virtually little idea as to how to run his campaign, and entire days were wasted in the logistics of speaking before a single audience of two hundred, or in one case fifty, voters.

Nor did Aslanidi win on the strength of his platform. When presenting his views in front of his natural constituency—coal miners—Aslanidi's message was not well received, to say the least. At one such presentation, he described a trip to Austria, which he claimed had opened his eyes to the much greater living standards in the West. After pushing Yeltsin's proposed constitution, he spoke of the need for further market reform (and even defended Gaidar) in front of miners who had not been paid in months.

Aslanidi's speech was cut short several times by angry remarks, such as that politicians cannot be trusted, that the miners were tired of being lied to, and that anyone who had obtained the chance to travel abroad was suspect. They also made clear their dissatisfaction with a reform that not only failed to give visible results, but had created tremendous hardship and promised more. Yet Aslanidi, one of the chief leaders of a miners' movement that had helped bring an end to the Soviet Union, now stood before his potential constituents as a defender of the status quo.[52]

Aslanidi's success resulted not from strong support from miners or from his platform, but rather from the newspaper he helped run. *Nasha Gazeta,* established in 1990 in the wake of the first miners' strikes, was now the biggest paper in the Kuzbass, though the reasons for its success are partly controversial: its opponents claim that the former paper of the regional Communist Party committee, *Kuzbass,* was forced to survive under harsh conditions, pointing to the ten days that it was closed in September 1993. These same people claim that *Nasha Gazeta* has received favorable credits and other concessions from Yeltsin's government.[53] Yet probably the major reason for its being the most widely read paper in the Kuzbass is that the paper provided free subscriptions to the region's pensioners. (While a questionable move in economic terms, it was nothing less than a brainstorm, because rather than being a profit-making venture, *Nasha Gazeta* is quite plainly a political paper. This paper with the largest circulation in the region has no pretensions to objectivity; its content could best be compared with such American opinion weeklies as the *Nation* or *National Review.*)

The newspaper literally ran Aslanidi's campaign from start to finish: with Aslanidi himself as executive editor, the paper financed the campaign through loans and published pagelong articles that were little more than campaign ads, while the editor in chief was his campaign manager and the paper's journalists were his campaign workers.[54]

One example concerning the region's media illustrates the ideological bind in which the miners found themselves. A delegation of Vorkuta miners arrived in the Kuzbass to seek support for their strike, which was aimed not only at gaining back wages but also at putting pressure on the government for a comprehensive program for the coal industry. Like the Kuzbass's Sharipov, they argued that the miners should threaten to withhold votes from government candidates during the election campaign unless the government agreed to their demands. At a press conference, one of the Vorkuta miners suggested supporting someone besides Gaidar, some "third people" between the Communists and the free marketeers. His statement was cut short by the chief correspondent from Kuzbass television, who shouted, "What 'third people'!? Name names, I want to hear names," before going on to suggest that the only possible alternative were those imprisoned after the defense of the White House. The correspondent, also the program's nightly newscaster, succeeded in displaying his interjection several times on local television, without bothering to show the Vorkuta miners' response to his interjection.[55]

Labor and Social Democracy

Was there a third choice, real or potential, for the voters of the Donbass and the Kuzbass? Above all, what of industrial workers in both regions, who had led one of the strongest anticommunist movements in the history of the Soviet Union and yet were directly threatened by the liberals' economic reform program? Why were labor leaders unable to propose an alternative to the neocommunist populists and the liberal free marketers?

We have already suggested some explanations for why Communist politicians in particular were so successful in the Donbass. As for the Kuzbass, why were worker-activists from Russia's most heavily subsidized industry allied with the radical reformers? A partial explanation has already been provided: The miners had been rewarded by Yeltsin, through greatly increased subsidies, despite his government's declarative tight monetary policy. Moreover, in some sense the miners had come to power—in Kislyuk, the region's governor, and Malykhin, the president's personal representative for the Kuzbass.

This argument is insufficient, however. Overwhelming evidence had been accumulating that the policy of the preelection government was leading directly to mine closures, and this process might occur quickly, especially if the government party won. Rumors were circulating of the World Bank proposal calling for the rapid closure of many Russian coal mines, and even government officials were openly hinting that if they won the elections, they would have to face down labor, especially its most organized sector—the coal miners.[56]

Rather, in both the Donbass and the Kuzbass, there were other, broader factors at work— in particular the ideological legacy of the Soviet experience. In both cases miner-activists remained mired in the old fight against communism. This was especially true in the Kuzbass. As they had during their struggle to end Communist Party hegemony, the leaders of the Kuzbass miners' movement clung to a univariate worldview—it was still a struggle of "us" against "them," or communism versus democracy. They were thus using an old political map to plot strategy in an increasingly complex world.

The complexities included the fact that their erstwhile allies in the anticommunist struggle—the liberals—were now implementing a program that threatened the miners' very livelihood. Indeed, workers face a class predicament—the threat of unemployment, plant closures, and deindustrialization more generally. While individual workers have different exit options, owing to differences in age and skill, the future of entire industrial communities is at stake, giving workers strong common interests.

Miners in both regions implicitly used class rhetoric and concepts from the Soviet era, even when they were fighting against communism. In pushing for the market, they used a labor theory of value, through which they argued they were being exploited by the nomenklatura even while being heavily subsidized. They continue to use such concepts today, arguing that the old nomenklatura is exploiting them still, perhaps even more, as new entrepreneurs. In this way the coal miners understand their social situation in class terms. But the leaders of the miners' movement are unable to acknowledge these notions and to organize them into a viable ideological package, since the language of class is seen as the language of the enemy.[57]

Moreover, for the miner-activists, the experience of communism had discredited the notion of "socialism" in any sense of the term. Even when faced with a challenge as a class, and while using class concepts to comprehend their situation, the Soviet experience has taken the idea of socialism, or even social democracy, off the miners' political agenda. That has left the leaders of the largest independent workers' movement in Russia and Ukraine not only without an alternative to capitalism, but also without an alternative within capitalism. With their leaders thus immunized against class-based ideologies, workers and their dissatisfactions are left available for the appeals of authoritarian populism and nationalism.[58]

Further still, the experience of the Communist Party has meant that parties are associated by workers as something alien to them, as a vehicle for intellectuals and others to steer the lower classes in one direction or another.[59] This perception allowed the one party that has significant organizing experience—the Communist Party—to make significant inroads.

Indeed, in the 1995 Russian parliamentary elections, the results were more of the same, though the Communists gained at the expense of extreme nationalists. Some have argued that this shift occurred precisely because the ideology of the Communist Party of the Russian Federation was itself more nationalist than socialist.[60] Certainly the success of the Communists did not come from working class appeals. While a portion of Ukraine's Communists used militant working class rhetoric, in Russia the Communist Party walked away from its former claim as defender of working class interests above all and instead appealed to the elderly and the disenfranchised generally, as well as to sentiments of nostalgia and patriotism. In fact, the language of class was largely dropped altogether, replaced by that of social harmony imposed by a strong state.[61]

(Tuleev himself joined the Communists, receiving the third position on the national party-list, his charisma balancing the decidedly uncharismatic Zyuganov. Given Tuleev's popularity in the Kuzbass, the CPRF won just short of 50 percent of the region's votes in the 1995 elections. Tuleev even ran for president in 1996, but as a "reserve" candidate to Zyuganov, and his name was often mentioned as a potential prime minister in the event of a Zyuganov victory.)

But the Communists' successes, and the votes they received from workers, were merely by default—workers were offered little alternative. Sergeev, the national leader of the miners' NPG, joined the "left-center" but still pro-Yeltsin Rybkin bloc; the trade union federation FNPR joined with industrialists to form a "Union of Labor," repeating Ukraine's experience where factory directors organized "labor" parties.[62] In the elections, both these parties were trounced.

As a result, workers were left with no alternative vision and no institutional channel to express their grievances in the political realm. And if the foregoing was true for the organized coal miners, the situation is even worse for the majority of workers who remain effectively unorganized. Moreover, the absence of strong social democratic parties or parties closely allied with and appealing to labor is noticeable throughout the former Soviet Union and Eastern Europe.[63]

The stark political choices that workers and others faced in the elections led to significant cynicism about democracy. In the Kuzbass, the most popular choice leading up to the election was clearly "We don't believe in anyone." As one miner yelled at Aslanidi during a campaign stop, "We can elect people, but we'll always be suppressed from above." Without genuine representation for labor, workers are available for the appeals of nationalists and others claiming to defend their rights. In the absence of a party genuinely allied with labor, workers in Russia and Ukraine were faced with the dilemma of choosing between going forward to free-market liberalism or backward to rule by the Communist Party nomenklatura. Given their especially dire situation, workers in Ukraine's Donbass have elected to go back. In the Kuzbass, miner leaders supported the liberals while their rank and file voted for Tuleev and Zhirinovsky. In each case, votes were cast cynically, as workers were not deceived, and in the process the concept of democracy was devalued.[64]

Tuleev and the Communists offer a return to paternalism; they sing a familiar refrain—in return for support and quiescence, they will provide tangible rewards. These are the sort of bosses the miners rebelled against when they had opportunity to do so, suggesting that they would prefer an alternative to paternalistic protection and domination.

In the absence of an alternative, miners and other workers in Russia may have well have found their "third way" in extreme nationalists. According to a survey, after the 1993 election, Zhirinovsky was supported above all by blue-collar workers earning average or above-average wages in state-owned industrial enterprises.[65] He also won more votes in the Kuzbass than in other industrial regions, such as the Urals. Workers in the Northern Steel Combine, where Vorkuta miners ship their coking coal, have openly allied with extreme nationalist groups, revealing that other workers may not have to strike and independently organize before choosing this political path.[66] According to one source, the miners' NPG—once among Yeltsin's strongest backers—in Chelyabinsk and Vorkuta "have begun to call for Zhirinovsky or 'someone like him' because he is strong and will set the country on a straight path."[67] While Zhirinovsky's star has dimmed, in the 1995 elections, the little-known Trudovaya Rossia (Working Russia), a party perhaps best described as workerist-stalinist-fascist, came in sixth place out of a large number of parties, just a fraction of a percentage point short of entering parliament.

Why might the miners have made such a dramatic switch from Yeltsin to Zhirinovsky and Tuleev? Certainly, voters in the Donbass and Kuzbass have followed those in Lithuania, Poland, and Hungary in expressing their dissatisfaction with unbridled economic liberalization. But while voters in the latter states supported reformed Communists now representing a moderate, democratic left, voters in the Donbass and Kuzbass backed the most radical candidates available. Indeed, the Communist Party of Ukraine, Tuleev, and Zhirinovsky appear to have little in common other than the promise of a strong hand to end economic disorder and political chaos. While miners everywhere are given to radicalism, the direction their radicalism takes is undetermined—there is no guarantee they will end up supporting the democratic left. More pessimistically, the coal miners might simply be the avant garde of Russian and Ukrainian politics—they were one of the first social groups to actively support perestroika, but when they became dissatisfied, they turned against Gorbachev and became one of the first groups to demand an end to the Soviet Union. Now that post-Soviet liberalism has failed to deliver, they appear ready to turn elsewhere, perhaps anywhere.

CHAPTER 9

Workers, Politics, and the Post-Communist Transformations

We have attempted to answer two related sets of questions. First, why did steelworkers remain at the mills? Or somewhat more broadly, why have most workers in the former Soviet Union remained quiescent, despite being hit hard by economic disintegration and declining standards of living? Why, well after the downfall of the Soviet Union and the Communist Party that once dominated them, do the same trade unions, largely scorned by their constituency, still hold a virtual monopoly on workers' representation? In short, the legacy of the coal miners notwithstanding, the question has been not why there has been so much labor unrest in the former Soviet republics, but why there has been so little.

The second set of questions has concerned the coal miners themselves, the first group of workers to lead mass strikes and create an independent workers' movement in the Soviet Union in more than sixty years. How did the miners, a core part of the proletariat in the original socialist state, evolve from leading a "purely economic strike" supporting "perestroika from below" to leading a "purely political strike" aimed at forcing Gorbachev to resign, transferring power to the republics, and removing the Communist Party from its position of hegemony, all in less than two years? Moreover, why did the coal miners, working in the country's most heavily subsidized industry, lead a movement not against economic reform but rather demanding the rapid introduction of the market? Further still, and just as dramatically, how did the miners, now disillusioned with liberalism, shift once again to support the return of Communists they had chastised as well as extreme nationalists, even fascists? Why was it so difficult for the miners to craft something resembling a social democratic alternative, as workers' movements in the West had done for so long?

We will examine conclusions to these questions on three broad levels. First, we will explore why the experience of the coal miners and steelworkers has been so contrary to the expectations and assumptions of scholars of Soviet society, and how the perspective advanced here differs from those previous conceptions. Second, the radically different trajectories of steelworkers and coal miners have required different tools of analysis, which raises questions about the ability of two dominant methods of social analysis—rational choice and cultural perspectives—to explain a political movement in its entirety. Third, the actions and experiences of workers continue to shape Russia and Ukraine and have much to say about the potentials for the post-Communist transformations in those societies.

The preceding chapters have called into question some of the conceptions that Sovietologists have used to explain the lack of labor unrest in Soviet society. The totalitarian perspective suggested that the domination of the Communist Party prevented political expression by workers and other social groups. The inverse of the totalitarianism, "civil society," the concept that so predominated in the early post-Communist euphoria, was confidently predicted to flourish in the new environment of freedom. Yet the downfall of the Communist Party, and indeed of the Soviet Union itself, has not led, outside of coal mining, to strikes, to the formation of alternative trade unions, or, more broadly, to a thriving civil society. We have seen how, beyond the Party and the state, many Soviet-era institutions, such as the industrial enterprise, continue to strongly influence the direction of post-Soviet societies. Moreover, independent trade unions, led by the miners' NPG, are perhaps the largest non-Communist social organizations in Russia and Ukraine—a fact that speaks more to the scantiness of civil society than the strength of the independent unions.

If the concepts of totalitarianism and civil society have fallen short, neither has the more popular explanation for labor peace in the post-Stalinist Soviet Union, that of the "social contract" between workers and the regime, been able to account for the case of the coal miners and steelworkers. First, whereas the social contract view noted the correlation between labor peace and the distribution of goods and services throughout Soviet society that appeared to favor workers, at a lower level of analysis we have found that the distribution of many of these goods and services was the source of considerable conflict and even bitterness. Second, whereas the social contract approach saw political elites making conscious policy decisions to favor blue-collar workers (through full employment, roughly egalitarian wages, and the toleration of slack work rules) in return for at least passive political support, here it has been argued that many of these same "policies" were the outcome of the shortage economy rather than conscious decisions of planners and elites.

Moreover, the assumption, held by many social scientists inside and out of the Soviet Union—namely, that Soviet industrial workers supported the status quo and were an obstacle to reform—has not held up against the demands made by the coal miners, or even those of steelworkers who did not strike. Arguably, this assumption was based on the notion that, with the lessening of overt repression, "social peace" must be explained by voluntary compliance and legitimacy: In short, if workers had wanted to strike, they could have.

In contrast, the perspective advanced here has argued that workers in the (now former) Soviet Union have had a strong interest in changing the status quo but have (thus far) been unable to overcome the obstacles lying between individual interest and collective action. As we have seen, the worker in state socialist society has been in a position of dependence, not simply as an individual dependent on the state, but as a working person dependent on the place of work—the industrial enterprise—as the provider of one's basic life needs. Such a nexus of interdependencies can be a powerful disincentive to collective action, particularly when the distribution of goods and services takes place largely at the discretion of management, and alternatives are few.

But the same "economics of shortage" that made the worker dependent on the enterprise also made the enterprise dependent on the worker: thus the dependence has not been top-down, but two-way, or "mutual." Workers used the labor shortage to improve their own situation and fight the capriciousness of managers; managers used the shortage in housing, social services, and consumer goods to tie workers to their workplace. As each side exercised its strengths, it inadvertently strengthened the other: when workers used their "exit" option, they not only created further demand for labor, but also drove management to gather more resources to tie remaining workers to the enterprise. As managers gathered more resources, and distributed them in ways many workers found unjust, they drove still others to leave for work elsewhere.

Workers in Soviet state enterprises have been caught in a collective action problem: The selective incentives that managers have used to prevent workers from acting individually were also used to prevent workers from acting collectively. However, the distribution of goods and services has been highly uneven between industries, depending on the preferences of planners and the ability to barter one's product. As we have seen, coal miners, while highly paid in rubles, received far fewer in-kind benefits than steelworkers, who conversely received lower wages. Compensation with high levels of in-kind benefits created greater dependence since wages could be saved and could be more easily replaced in a new job (not hard to find in a labor-short economy), while losing one's place in line for housing after years of waiting could have been a severe blow. Coal mines that were able, through the initiative of either miners or managers, to barter coal for consumer goods and services were more likely to avoid further rounds of workers' collective action.[1]

Yet the analytical tools used to explain the first set of questions—how certain groups were or were not able to overcome the obstacles to collective action—have been less helpful in explaining an equally important group of questions: How did the Russian and Ukrainian coal miners, once mobilized, transform their objectives from supporting perestroika from below and demanding more from the state to actively supporting the dissolution of the Soviet Union and the introduction of the market? As one moves from individual actors to political movements, the individual-level approach of collective action theories has been less helpful. Moreover, such rational actor analysis assumes preferences as given and is indifferent to the content of a movement's protest, which in this case is the very question one must ask. And that was no small question for the Soviet coal miners. While it is perhaps not too hard to explain why the miners began raising political demands, one must ask why the miners first mobilized not in the conservative direction so many scholars had predicted, but rather in support of liberal and even market reforms.

We have found this radicalization to be best explained first by the institutions of the Soviet political economy, and second, and more importantly, by the cultural and ideological concepts generated by those institutions. Part of the answer stemmed from the state's very visible role in the economy, where the state was not only an abstract entity whose officials were housed in a distant capital, but the state was also present at work every day, embodied in the boss.[2] Yet in terms of the miners' radicalization, what was important was not only structures but how they were perceived.[3] Described as "a state within a state," the Soviet enterprise reflected the distribution of power and privileges in the larger society, with a paternalistic management granting privileges to some but not others, creating obvious disparities between men and women, between the skilled and unskilled, between those in production and those servicing them. Having fought successfully against injustice within the enterprise, as the miners had done, it was a short step to fight against the injustice of the state: It was the state, after all, rather than the market, that determined how much was taken away (through state orders at fixed prices) and how much was returned (in wages and goods).

More important still, the miners interpreted their position through the categories of the once-dominant ideology. Turning that ideology around, they contended that they were being exploited by a parasitic state. Further, miners seized upon the newly emerging dominant ideology of liberalism to argue for a market system, but one, in their articulation, that met the needs of coal miners. Thus, the miners' call for the market stemmed from a sense of exploitation, which was derived in turn from a labor theory of value: Since miners worked hard to produce a material good, they should receive an appropriately decent standard of living. Viewed this way, demands that seemed contradictory were not really so; miners could call for the market, on the one hand, and demand the closing of service and trade cooperatives, on the other.

In *The Radiant Past,* Burawoy and Lukacs demonstrate quite well how the discrepancy between Marxist-Leninist ideology and the reality of everyday experience led workers to a negative class consciousness, one of criticizing state socialism for not living up to its promises.[4] Yet Hungarian steelworkers, like their counterparts in Russia and Ukraine, failed to mobilize and thus to find an opportunity to create an alternative vision. For the coal miners examined here, the ideological concepts of the past not only illuminated the shortcomings of the old system, they also shaped their critical response to it, in both a positive and a negative sense—the miners in fact wanted a society that lived up to the promises of the Russian revolution, but they were unable to name their goal socialism.

At the center of both questions we have examined—the quiescence of steelworkers, the radicalization of coal miners—lies the battle over surplus and its redistribution.[5] Steelworkers struggled against management's powers of paternalistic redistribution within the enterprise, while the miners took on the state's powers to do the same. Thus, surplus and its redistribution are not only at the core of many critical models of Soviet-style socialism, but are also central for how the protagonists themselves—in this case coal miners and steelworkers—perceived the system, their place within it, and the need to transform it.

In this way the "market" resonated among coal miners because it was a dagger aimed at the very heart of the system of paternalistic redistribution. Miners envisioned a market system as self-organized, worker-controlled enterprises, trading more or less as equals; they had no experience to tell them that the coercion of redistributors could be easily replaced by the coercion of market forces.

The miners' producerist ethic—that producers of wealth should be intrinsically valued and should control the wealth they produced—may not seem all that different from that of workers elsewhere. In the United States, a producerist rhetoric pervaded workers' organizations in the 1890s, but by the 1930s, at a time of intense labor organizing, the notion of the worker as a unique producer of wealth was replaced by the notion of worker as a citizen entitled to equal rights.[6] In Italy, a workerist ethic predominated in the workers' milieu well into the 1970s.[7] The cultural framework constructed by the coal miners discussed here is distinct in that the miners' framework contained both normative and cognitive elements. It was not only that justice meant the right to control and dispose of their product; it was also that miners created an understanding of the free market that entailed just this. They believed, in the absence of experience to suggest otherwise, that the liberal economic order and their own notions of social justice coincided, and they acted accordingly. When their own experience told them that the free market not only violated their idea of justice but threatened their very existence as miners, they had already helped bring about the end of the Soviet system, and they proved unable to reorient themselves to the new tasks of finding new allies and crafting a new vision.

But it was not only the ultimately mistaken notion of the market as a new utopia for coal miners that sealed their fate. Given the materialist bent of their thinking, the miners jeopardized the goal of creating a broader movement. If the sense of being exploited led miners to resent managers, it also led to the resentment of bookkeepers and other "nonproductive" workers, often women, who lived no better, and usually worse, than the miners themselves. Indeed, gender divisions were one significant difference between coal and steel: Miners abandoned the nongender-specific *tovarishchi* (comrades) to call themselves *muzhiki* (guys), and the NPG's insistence on organizing only core, male, production workers only reinforced this division. Only belatedly did miners reach out to help organize striking workers in traditionally "female" professions, such as teachers and medical workers. If the miners' NPG gained short-term solidarity by focusing on underground miners, they lessened the chance to combine with other disaffected workers to create a more powerful and lasting movement.[8]

And if resentment of the state's virtually unlimited powers of (re)distribution led them to attack the military-industrial complex and the privileges of the nomenklatura, it also led to attacks by the miners on such basic forms of state assistance as social security. The miners could sound at once both "radical" in calling for workers' ownership and control of the coal mines and "conservative" in demanding that "their" wealth not subsidize others, whether bosses or lower-paid workers. The two notions were not so incompatible: In deciding that the miners should take care of their own, they were only beginning to struggle with ideas of how profitable mines under workers' control might help support unprofitable ones, let alone pensioners or the unemployed.

We have presented two separate modes of explanation for the two different questions posed at the outset: a rational and structural explanation for why steelworkers did not act collectively along with the miners, and an ideological explanation for why miners' demands changed so dramatically over time. As such, we have stood on the periphery of the two predominant approaches to contemporary social theory: rational choice analysis, dominant in economics and political science, and poststructural theory, dominant in the humanities. The attempt to employ elements of two disparate approaches has run the risk of alienating proponents of both.[9] The separate explanations used here have, in part, been the result of an artificial separation and the product of simplifying assumptions in the hopes of parsimonious explanations. Certainly cultural and ideological factors were present in the conflicts within the steel mills, for example, as steelworkers fought for social justice in the intraenterprise distribution of benefits. And the Kuzbass miners, at least, hoped that the market would allow them to exploit their position of having control over (what they hoped would be) a valuable resource.

The modest goal of this work has been to demonstrate that neither of these approaches is sufficient to explain what can be considered a single phenomenon—the miners' dramatic radicalization while other workers remained quiescent. Here we have found rational actors seeking their interests, but with ideological interpretations of what those interests were and how they might be achieved.[10]

Rational and structural explanations, when appropriate, typically provide the most parsimonious explanation for social phenomena; on this basis, one could argue, those are the analytical tools that should be reached for first. When do ideological and cultural factors move to the fore of social explanation? Precisely at critical junctures of the sort that the Soviet miners found themselves. For mostly material and structural reasons, the ancien regime proved untenable; as the cracks in its edifice became more and more pronounced, the ideological mortar began to break as well. Not only was the political and economic system no longer viable, but the entire idea of it was consciously rejected. But with what should it be replaced? With a society in such flux, with old institutions collapsing before new ones can arise, with virtually every dimension of people's lives subject to renegotiation, it is extremely difficult, if not impossible, to grasp where one's material interests lie (let alone to find channels for their adequate political expression). At this point, during the struggle over alternatives, culture and ideology are not simply the product of material and institutional forces, but a causal factor in their transformation and reconstruction. With, for example, no direct experience of such crucial concepts such as the "market," shortcuts are necessary, involving borrowing from one's own cultural understandings to make sense of proposed alternatives. Because new ideas appear much more readily than new political and economic institutions, the struggle over alternatives is in no small part an ideological struggle.

That a cultural explanation will not suffice is clear from the case of the miners and steelworkers, both working in the same communities, often from the same families, interacting with one another and even at times swapping professions. While the everyday practices of miners may have helped them develop special cultural tools, such as stronger solidarity, to cope with the unique demands of their work, one would be hard-pressed to develop an argument based on cultural differences alone to explain why steelworkers did not join their fellow coal miners in striking and organizing in the course of the next several years.

Structural explanations, on the other hand, have a rather difficult time accounting for how the miners seemed to act contrary to their material interests—in demanding the market for an industry so heavily dependent on state subsidies—and for how the miners' avowed goals changed so dramatically— from allying with reformers, even liberal-democrats at one time, and then backing nationalists and communists the next. A rational choice explanation for the miners' actions would be insufficient information: They did not know what the market entailed, and their dramatic shifts in demands reflected a process of learning; after several iterations they are sure to find where their interests truly lie.[11] Such an argument stretches the usefulness of the rational choice approach, since it loses its most attractive feature—parsimony. While miners and others might get it "right" in the long term, the short term is often decisive. To say that the miners helped bring down the Soviet regime and put free marketers in power, all because of insufficient information, is to say not much at all.[12]

Structural/rational arguments can account for why miners tend to be militant throughout the world, but they fail to account for their actions once mobilized. Compare, for example, the cases of coal miners in the Soviet Union and neighboring Romania. In Romania, miners mobilized initially on behalf of the decaying state-socialist regime to crush the skulls of students and liberal reformers, while in the Soviet Union miners organized themselves with the avowed goal of achieving many of the same aims sought by the Romanian intellectuals.[13]

What then of Poland, where workers united across sectors to oppose state socialism and build a formidable movement? There are a number of factors, cultural, historical, and structural, that have been used to explain the rise of Solidarity.[14] Admittedly, the model of "mutual dependence" proposed here cannot on its own explain why, for example, workers struck in Poland but not in neighboring Hungary, and a complete answer for all these cases lies beyond the scope of the present study.[15] Further, still other factors would have to be brought in to explain why in Polish society workers were able to unite with certain sectors of the intelligentsia to make their movement even more formidable, something Soviet workers have failed to do.[16] Yet Poland remains the exception; even there, the working class has failed to meet the challenge posed by the transformation to capitalism.

What are the implications of this study for the post-Communist transformations in Russia, Ukraine, and elsewhere? This discussion suggests that the Soviet experience has bequeathed both institutional and ideological legacies to the post-Soviet states; each will be considered in turn. As David Stark has argued, many economists and political scientists have seen the dramatic changes in this part of the world as the collapse of all that went before.[17] Economists have seen an institutional vacuum, where society will readily obey the laws of neoclassical economics, while political scientists have tended to view the collapse of the Communist Party as leading to utter chaos. Both of these perspectives have missed important institutions that have survived the collapse of communism and are likely to have a significant effect on the course of political and economic transformation.

The concept of mutual dependence of the worker and the enterprise points to several institutions now influencing the economic and political development of the former Soviet Union. The Soviet institution of distributing social services through the workplace, for example, continues to affect the transformation to capitalism.[18] While, in Russia at least, large numbers of industrial enterprises are now formally privatized, they do not yet face hard budget constraints, including bankruptcies. One of the major obstacles to doing so remains the absence of viable substitutes for the vital services supplied by enterprises to a large part, perhaps a majority, of the population. Small entrepreneurs, even if they existed in larger numbers than at present, would have to charge prices beyond the reach of their potential customers. Local governments, which have long and unsuccessfully battled industrial enterprises and state ministries for control of such communal services, simply do not have the resources to run them: The meager resources they do have come primarily from taxes on the very enterprises threatened with bankruptcy. To cut subsidies to these enterprises, forcing many to close, would not simply deprive their workers of wages and benefits (which could be replaced temporarily at least by unemployment payments), but of access to housing, health care, child care, and important sources of food and consumer goods as well. The de facto privatization—and the closure of unprofitable enterprises—will be most difficult in the many Soviet-style "company towns," where one or more enterprises provide virtually all social services to the urban population.

Further, the system of enterprise distribution also explains the continued domination of the once-official trade unions throughout the former Soviet Union. Because the trade unions remain the distributors of such goods as housing, automobiles, and televisions, as well as pensions and sick pay, workers have been fearful of signing a declaration stating they wish to leave the old trade union.[19] Thus, the once-official trade unions, having survived the collapse of the Communist Party and the state and even while generally detested by their constituency, hold a virtual monopoly on workers' representation and are attempting to form corporatist bargains in their name with the state.[20] On the enterprise level, these trade unions are dependent on management for the continued supply of goods and services to distribute to their constituents; thus they can never be independent advocates of workers' interests against management. On the state level, the unions are dependent on the government for the right to distribute social security funds and to continue to retain their vast property holdings; thus they can never be independent advocates of workers' rights against the state.[21] Until the state(s), the enterprises, and these once-state trade unions find an alternative mechanism for performing the social-welfare functions bestowed on the trade unions, they will continue to flourish, with the likely outcome that industrial workers will remain without an independent voice to represent their interests during this period of wrenching social transformation.

Moreover, this enterprise dependence helps explain the continued dominance not only of the old trade unions, but also of state industrial managers. The dissolution of the Soviet Union and the collapse of the central allocation economy has affected the paternalism of state enterprises in contradictory ways. Some enterprises, deep in debt and unable to obtain sufficient credits, simply have abandoned many of the former services (such as vacation centers) supplied to workers, who are now left to fend for themselves. But many other enterprises, such as those in the coal and steel industries examined here, actually have increased their provision of goods and services in the face of continued shortage, spiraling prices, and the inability of local governments to provide additional services.

Why might managers continue to expend valuable resources on procuring goods and services for the workforce, especially when market pressures are increasing and the threat of unemployment is replacing the labor shortage? Walder, in a revision of his earlier thesis, argues that in China, despite considerable market reform and high unemployment, the position of state enterprise manager remains as much a political position as an economic one. The enterprise itself compromises a "socio-political community," with considerable pressure from below. Not only must managers be concerned with maximizing profits, but "also for enhancing employee income and for delivering a wide range of other benefits and services to their employees."[22]

This enterprise dependence becomes all the more important during the privatization process. The ability of enterprise managers to maintain political control of the enterprise explains why most directors prefer privatization plans that give large numbers of shares to the labor collective;

far from leading to direct worker ownership, managers clearly believe that this is the best way for them to remain in command.[23] Indeed, the industrial enterprise as social institution accounts for a striking paradox in the post-Soviet transformations: while the economy is producing only one-half of what it used to, levels of employment have long afterward remained virtually unchanged. While often producing little to nothing and often not being paid (giving new meaning the Soviet-era aphorism "We pretend to work and they pretend to pay us,") workers still get access to enterprise services, are credited with work time towards their pension, and perhaps most importantly, compromise the "labor collectives" through which old managers of state enterprises become new directors of privatized joint-stock companies.

Given workers' dependence on the enterprise, "employee ownership" through the purchase of majority shares in joint-stock companies, while giving workers de jure control of the enterprise, will remain a formality much as did the Gorbachev-era law on electing enterprise managers. (Yet just as the coal miners' strikes transformed the enterprise election law into a source of real power for themselves, enterprises experiencing strikes under such an ownership system could result in de facto workers' control.)[24]

Yet in the longer term, the future of enterprise dependence is limited, even if it is difficult to determine when the longer term might arrive.[25] Unemployment, even if not yet widespread, removes one of the main reasons why enterprises supplied workers with goods and services in the first place—to attract and retain skilled workers in a taut labor market. At the same time, unemployment and the uncertainties of a market economy are already creating new obstacles to, as well as opportunities for, workers' mobilization.

What of the ideological legacies of the Soviet experience suggested by the miners' movement, particularly as they relate to the political and economic future of the former Soviet republics? As for the political sphere, the miners' experience with self-organization would appear to give some faint hope for Russia and Ukraine. As part of the social group often derided by intellectuals as "the dark masses" or even "cattle," miners turned out to have a very powerful understanding of democracy. The ritualistic elections of the Soviet era were not as meaningless as has been thought: The miners appropriated the formal democratic rituals of the old system and infused them with new meaning and substance. After observing many meetings of miners, one image stands out: that of a miner, with coal dust still visible under his eyes, pounding the table and shouting that a motion could not be voted on without a quorum. This desire for democracy is driven by a hatred of bureaucracy and hierarchy, a hatred so strong that it often contradicts the goal of building a sustainable labor movement, as miners quickly recalled representatives whenever they perceived a swollen ego or a loss of empathy with the rank and file.

Yet this desire for democratic accountability extends primarily to the miners' immediate institutions rather than to democratic politics in the formal sense, since in addition to a hatred of bureaucracy, the old regime has left many miners with a strong dislike for political parties of any stripe, often seen as alien to the working class. Moreover, even the democratic tendencies within the miners' movement are conditional: many mines, as we have seen, having (if temporarily) solved their economic problems, have returned to the paternalism of the past.

But the implications of the miners' movement for economic transformation are even more complex. Miners very early on began calling for economic independence from the state, and indeed for market reform, as they discerned that Moscow was continuing to take away more than it was giving back. They explicitly rejected the only economic system that they had ever experienced, but with what to replace it? A new utopia of the market was being proposed by liberal reformers, but what would this utopia entail, what would it look like? Since the miners had never experienced the market, they created their understanding of it: They reached into their cultural tool kit, pulled out mental templates, and grafted their own ideas of utopia onto that being proposed by liberal reformers. The result: a market based on a labor theory of value, not on supply and demand, and capitalism based on workers' control and ownership, not on outside corporate control. These ideas were the product of Soviet institutions, including another formal democratic ritual the miners had appropriated: that of electing managers. Indeed, outliving such institutions, the rhetoric and the practices of the Soviet era provided workers with the notion that they were capable of running their own enterprises. This idea has become clear in the struggle over privatization, as it has hardly occurred to many workers that anyone other than the employees should control their workplace.[26]

However, the miners lacked an ideological foundation upon which to organize themselves toward the goal of workers' control. If the miners employed cultural notions from the Soviet era, they did so without acknowledging them, for they explicitly rejected the Soviet system. Indeed, while the miners used class concepts to interpret their situation, they proved unable to craft an ideological framework based on class, since the language of class was rejected as something of the failed past. The ironic tragedy for workers in post-Communist societies is that just when class antagonisms have, in all likelihood, grown more pronounced than any they have experienced, the explicit use of class-based ideologies has become taboo.

Indeed, for most workers, the Communist experience has taken the idea of socialism, or even social democracy, off the political agenda. That has left workers not only without an alternative to capitalism, but even without an alternative within capitalism. In the absence of class-based appeals, workers and their dissatisfactions are available for the appeals of authoritarian populists and nationalists. While Communists have returned through the back door, even they have abandoned appeals to workers as a class, and appeal instead to the many disenfranchised and to a strong nation united across class lines. If warmly embraced by the elderly, by workers they are merely tolerated, because no one else has offered an alternative.

Liberalism has certainly exhausted its appeal in the eyes of coal miners. With the raising of coal and freight prices and the reduction of subsidies to the industry, coal miners in the Kuzbass—like their counterparts in the Donbass—now appreciate that reliance on the market will mean a large measure of unemployment, especially difficult for mining communities with little else to offer. Miners have shifted the focus of their struggle back to the state, in order to bargain for their social and economic future. Unlike steelworkers, and most every other sector of the working class in the former Soviet republics, miners are organized and ready for the coming battle that unemployment is sure to bring.

Indeed, the case of coal miners and steelworkers points to both the possibilities and the limits for the transformations in the now former Soviet Union and, by extension, the once state socialist societies of Eastern Europe. The Russian and Ukrainian coal miners have shown the possibilities for self-organization, as they acted collectively to increase their voice in decisions affecting their lives and in so doing pressed for the creation of an economic system they believed to be beneficial to their interests. Steelworkers, on the other hand, have reflected the limits of the post-Communist transitions, as they have remained dependent on the enterprise even as their major strength—the labor shortage—shades into unemployment, leaving workers (and others) still seeking individual-level solutions to their dilemmas.

If the goal were to build a capitalist economy, as the present Russian and Ukrainian governments intend, the dependence of workers is in many ways positive, since it has thus far prevented a united working class from opposing the inevitable hardships that bankruptcies and unemployment and the constraints of the world market will bring. At the same time, the "company town" arrangements of many once-Soviet cities make the suggestions for the deindustrialization of the Russian and Ukrainian economies appear utopian, as entire communities remain dependent on unprofitable enterprises. Indeed, by taking advantage of the lack of united worker opposition to push through the rapid privatization of state enterprises, government officials might unwittingly end workers' dependency, perhaps creating the possibility for greater workers' collective action.

If the goal is to build democracy, the dependence of workers presents a much greater obstacle. Workers are experiencing profoundly unsettling and painful changes in their lives, without an institutional channel to express their grievances. Without the self-organization of this largest social group in society, and thus the ability for workers to articulate and defend their own interests, the potential is very real that another group—whether populist demagogues or potential dictators with easy solutions to profound hardships—will once again claim to be acting on behalf of the industrial working class.

Karl Polanyi argued in *The Great Transformation* that as market forces become dominant in a society there will be a "double movement"—the first being the market forces themselves, the second the "self-protection of society" in reaction to the first.[27] He wrote in reference to England during the industrial revolution, where the self-protection of society was eventually achieved through social programs for the poor and unemployed and restraints on laissez-faire capitalism. While Polanyi argued that the self-protection of society was inevitable, the direction it took was not: writing during World War II, he had in mind other reactions, in particular the rise of European fascism. Workers have already had a significant impact on the economic and political course of Russia and Ukraine, and they certainly will again. The direction this impact will take, however, is still an open question.

Notes

Introduction

1. Dietrich Rueschemeyer, Evelyne Huber Stephens, and John D. Stephens, *Capitalist Development and Democracy* (Chicago: University of Chicago Press, 1992); Ruth Berins Collier and David Collier, *Shaping the Political Arena* (Princeton: Princeton University Press, 1992).

2. On the comparative case study method see Charles Ragin, *The Comparative Method: Moving Beyond Qualitative and Quantitative Strategies* (Berkeley: University of California Press, 1987); Arend Lijphart, "The Comparable-Cases Strategy in Comparative Research," *Comparative Political Studies* 8, no. 2 (July 1985): 158–77; Lawrence B. Mohr, "The Reliability of the Case Study as a Source of Information," in *Advances in Information Processing in Organizations,* vol. 2 (Greenwich, Conn.: JAI Press, 1985), 65–93.

3. According to Atul Kohli, because rational choice and cultural perspectives are at opposite ends of the methodological spectrum with so little common ground, "the field of comparative political analysis is again embroiled in theoretical controversy," one which has become "deeply divisive." See Atul Kohli, et al., "The Role of Theory in Comparative Politics: A Symposium," *World Politics* 48 (October 1995): 1.

Chapter 1

1. Gordon Marshall, "Some Remarks on the Study of Working Class Consciousness," *Politics and Society* 12, no. 3 (1983). Marshall calls these views "heterogeneity" and "incorporation," respectively; he proposes his own dichotomy of the recent literature, that of "ambivalence" and "instrumentalism."

2. Ibid., 264. For a list of explanations of working-class divisions, see John H. M. Laslett and Seymour Martin Lipset, *Failure of a Dream? Essays in the History of American Socialism,* rev. ed. (Berkeley: University of California Press, 1984).

3. Richard Hyman, *Strikes,* 4th ed. (London: MacMillan, 1989).

4. Clark Kerr and Abraham Siegel, "The Interindustry Propensity to Strike: An International Perspective," in *Labor and Management in Industrial Society,* edited by C. Kerr (Garden City, N.Y.: Doubleday, 1964), 105–47.

5. Ibid., 105, 111. Other publications, most notably Lipset's *Political Man* and Lockwood's "Working Class Images," echoed this thesis. Seymour Martin Lipset,

Political Man: The Social Bases of Politics, enlarged ed. (Baltimore: Johns Hopkins University, 1981); David Lockwood, "Sources of Variation in Working-Class Images of Society," *Sociological Review* 14, no. 1 (November 1966).

6. P. K. Edwards, "A Critique of the Kerr-Siegel Hypothesis of Strikes and the Isolated Mass: A Study in the Falsification of Sociological Knowledge," *Sociological Review* 25 (August 1977): 551–74; Edward Shorter and Charles Tilly, *Strikes in France, 1830–1968* (Cambridge: Cambridge University Press 1974), esp. 287–95; James E. Cronin, "Theories of Strikes: Why Can't They Explain the British Experience?" *Journal of Social History* 12, no. 2 (1978–79); Howard Kimeldorf, *Reds or Rackets?* (Berkeley: University of California Press, 1988), 13–15.

7. Jonathan and Ruth Winterton, *Coal, Crisis and Conflict: The 1984–1985 Miners' Strike in Yorkshire* (New York: St. Martin's Press, 1989), esp. 102–8. For recent support of the isolated community thesis generally, see the discussion in Albert Szymanski, *The Capitalist State and the Politics of Class* (Cambridge, Mass.: Winthrop, 1977), chap. 3.

8. Cronin, "Theories of Strikes," 201. The work that began the renewed interest in the labor process was that of Harry Braverman, *Labor and Monopoly Capital* (New York: Monthly Review Press, 1974). For a useful survey and critique of the literature on the labor process, see Paul Thompson, *The Nature of Work* (London: MacMillan, 1983).

9. Michael Yarrow, "The Labor Process in Coal Mining: The Struggle for Control," in *Case Studies in the Labor Process,* edited by Andrew Zimbalist (New York: Monthly Review Press, 1979), 187; Shorter and Tilly argue that technology is a central determinant of the ability of workers to organize and that for mining in particular, the technological organization of work means that "miners take pride in their professional traditions, and the web of organizations within the pits, both friendship groups and regular unions, gives them a powerful capacity for collective enterprise" (*Strikes in France,* 13).

10. Even the darkness of the mines is said to contribute, as the bright lanterns can give warnings of an approaching foreman, and miners can turn their lanterns off if they wish to take a break and not be seen. Yarrow, "Struggle for Control," 175.

11. In Britain, for instance, miners were not much more strike-prone than other workers before 1920, and from 1957 until the strikes in 1984, their overt protests had decreased markedly (Cronin, "Theories of Strikes," 203). For an alternative to the stereotypical view of militant miners, see R. S. Moore's *Pitmen, Preachers and Politics* (Cambridge: Cambridge University Press, 1974).

12. Cronin, "Theories of Strikes," 206; Shorter and Tilly, *Strikes in France;* Charles Tilly, *From Mobilization to Revolution* (Reading, Mass.: Addison Wesley, 1978).

13. Diane P. Koenker and William G. Rosenberg, *Strikes and Revolution in Russia, 1917* (Princeton: Princeton University Press, 1989), 11, discussing Shorter and Tilly.

14. For classic accounts of the totalitarian model, see Carl J. Friedrich, "The Unique Character of Totalitarian Society," in *Totalitarianism* (Cambridge: Harvard University Press, 1954), 47–60; Zbigniew Brzezinski, *The Permanent Purge*

(Cambridge: Harvard University Press, 1956). The use of the concept of totalitarianism was recently revived in Eastern Europe and the Soviet Union, in part because of its usefulness as a polemic, but also for its depiction of the scope of activity that the state had reserved for itself, hence of the need to develop civil society. See Jacques Rupnik, "Totalitarianism Revisited," in *Civil Society and the State,* edited by J. Keane (London: Verso, 1988).

15. Joseph Godson and Leonard Shapiro, eds., *The Soviet Worker* (London: MacMillan, 1981). See the discussion of alternative views on Soviet industrial relations in Peter Rutland, "Labor Unrest and Movements, 1989 and 1990," *Soviet Economy* 6 (1990): 193–95.

16. This approach was widely accepted in the Sovietological literature. Linda J. Cook, *The Soviet Social Contract and Why It Failed* (Cambridge: Harvard University Press, 1993); Walter Connor, *The Accidental Proletariat* (Princeton: Princeton University Press, 1991); Janine Ludlam, "Reform and the Redefinition of the Social Contract Under Gorbachev," *World Politics* 43, no. 2 (1991): 284–312; Peter Hauslohner, "Gorbachev's Social Contract," *Soviet Economy* 3, no. 1 (1987); George Breslauer, "On the Adaptability of Soviet Welfare-State Authoritarianism," in *The Soviet Polity in the Modern Era,* edited by Erik Hoffman and Robin F. Laird (New York: Aldine, 1984); Seweryn Bialer, *Stalin's Successors: Leadership, Stability and Change in the Soviet Union* (New York: Cambridge University Press, 1980), 158–65; Stephen White, "Economic Performance and Communist Legitimacy," *World Politics* 38, no. 3 (1986): 462–82; Ed A. Hewett, *Reforming the Soviet Economy: Equality Versus Efficiency* (Washington, D.C.: Brookings Institution, 1988), 39–50. The exact characterization of the "social contract" varied widely, from a rigid paternalism in which "it 'pays' to renounce your freedom" to a Durkheimian solidarity where workers are harmoniously incorporated into the dominant value system. See Ferenc Feher, "Paternalism as a Mode of Legitimation in Soviet-Type Societies," in T. H. Rigby and Ferenc Feher, eds., *Political Legitimation in Communist States* (New York: St. Martin's Press, 1982), 64–81; David Lane, *Soviet Labour and the Ethic of Communism: Full Employment and the Labour Process in the Soviet Union* (Brighton, England: Harvester, 1987).

17. Hauslohner, "Gorbachev's Social Contract"; Cook, *Soviet Social Contract.* The view of Soviet intellectuals was first and most eloquently expressed in the works of Tatyana Zaslavskaya.

18. Rutland, "Labor Unrest," 195.

19. Proponents of the social contract thesis failed to recognize its indebtedness to the concept of "moral economy," underscoring again the division that has existed between Sovietology and broader social theory. The moral economy thesis will be addressed subsequently. Moreover, while James Scott is often most closely associated with the moral economy approach, his subsequent argument about the "weapons of the weak" raises questions at least about the Soviet social contract. James C. Scott, *Weapons of the Weak: Everyday Forms of Peasant Resistance* (New Haven: Yale University Press, 1985). In the Soviet enterprise, workers' notorious noncompliance was one indication of the weakness of any social bargain. In fact, it has been argued that this noncompliance—absenteeism, tardiness, withholding of effort—was itself part of a social compact in the Soviet Union (as suggested by

the popular witticism "we pretend to work and they pretend to pay us"). Perhaps more accurately, this inability of the powerful to coerce or bribe the relatively powerless to comply was an indication that there was not much of a social bargain to begin with.

20. Cook (*Soviet Social Contract*) presents this paradox at the very outset of her study, by noting that while Soviet workers were unorganized, they enjoyed social benefits, such as full employment, that remained inaccessible to even the best organized workers in the capitalist world. Yet the subsequent discussion does not explain why Soviet workers would be more powerful than those in the industrialized West. Others refer vaguely to the ideology of the Soviet system and the traditional Russian fear of the *bunt,* or uprising. This study will refer to the impact of the labor shortage and to managers, who were organized and dependent on workers and claimed to be lobbying on the behalf of their "labor collectives." On this last point, see Simon Clarke, "Privatisation and the Development of Capitalism in Russia," in Simon Clarke et al., eds., *What About the Workers? Workers and the Transition to Capitalism in Russia,* edited by Simon Clarke et al. (London: Verso, 1993).

21. It cannot be argued, as might have been done in the case of the first post-Communist government in Poland, that new governments in Russia and Ukraine are legitimate and therefore have political capital to weather such stormy transitions. Governments in both countries have used up any capital they may have had and are mired in political turmoil.

22. Cook, it should be noted, straightforwardly examines how the miners' case runs counter to the assumptions of the social contract approach.

23. See Michael Burawoy and Pavel Krotov, "The Soviet Transition from Socialism to Capitalism: Worker Control and Economic Bargaining in the Wood Industry," in *What About the Workers? Workers and the Transition to Capitalism in Russia,* edited by Simon Clarke et al. (London: Verso, 1993); Michael Burawoy and Janos Lukacs, *The Radiant Past: Ideology and Reality in Hungary's Road to Capitalism* (Chicago: University of Chicago Press, 1992); Michael Burawoy, *The Politics of Production* (London: Verso Press, 1985); David Stark, "Organizational Innovation in Hungary's Emerging Mixed Economy," in *Remaking the Economic Institutions,* edited by David Stark and Victor Nee (Palo Alto: Stanford University Press, 1989); idem, "Rethinking Internal Labor Markets: New Insights from a Comparative Perspective," *American Sociological Review* 51, no. 4 (1986): 492–504. Other versions of the workers' control argument can be found in Donald Filtzer, *Soviet Workers and the Collapse of Perestroika* (Cambridge: Cambridge University Press, 1994); Hillel Ticktin, *Origins of the Crisis in the USSR* (Armonk, N.Y.: M. E. Sharpe, 1992); Vladimir Andrle, *Workers in Stalin's Russia* (New York: St. Martin's Press, 1988).

24. Janos Kornai, *The Economic of Shortage* (Amsterdam: North-Holland Pub. Co., 1980). See the summary of his work in David Stark and Victor Nee, "Toward an Institutional Analysis of State Socialism," in *Remaking the Economic Institutions,* edited by David Stark and Victor Nee (Palo Alto: Stanford University Press, 1989), 16–20.

25. Albert Hirschman, *Exit, Voice and Loyalty* (Cambridge: Harvard Univer-

sity Press, 1970). For a slightly different application of this concept, see Stark and Nee, "Toward an Institutional Analysis"; and, George Bergsten and Russell Bova, "Worker Power under Communism: The Interplay of Exit and Voice," *Comparative Economic Studies* 32 (spring 1990): 42–72.

26. Reinhard Bendix, *Work and Authority in Industry* (Berkeley: University of California Press [1956] 1974).

27. As Kornai argues, "there is a strong tendency under every classical socialist system to narrow down individual consumption of products and services bought directly by households for money, and concurrently to increase the share of collective consumption distributed in kind by the bureaucracy." Janos Kornai, *The Socialist System* (Princeton: Princeton University Press, 1992), 225. It should be noted that such paternalism is not unique to state socialism. The company town of American history and the current Japanese enterprise are but two other examples. There are important differences—for instance, in the Japanese context the employee has access, depending on the wage level, to a range of alternatives through consumer markets. Given the shortages in state socialist economies, such alternatives were greatly limited. See also Andrew Walder, *Communist Neo-Traditionalism: Work and Authority in Chinese Industry* (Berkeley: University of California Press, 1986), 15–17.

28. Clarke has also recently argued that the state enterprise is a social institution. "The enterprise is the basis of the Soviet workers' social existence: most of the things provided through the enterprise cannot be acquired by any other means, so work defines the workers' identity in a much more fundamental way than it does in the capitalist world. In this sense the enterprise really is a 'state within a state.'" Thus social functions of the enterprise, "one of most glorious achievements of socialism," also became a means of controlling workers (Simon Clarke, "The Contradictions of 'State Socialism,'" in *What About the Workers?* 24).

29. Walder, *Communist Neo-Traditionalism,* 12. For an early application of dependence to Soviet workers, see Viktor Zaslavsky, "The Regime and the Working Class in the U.S.S.R.," *Telos* (winter 1979–80).

30. See Andrew Walder, "Factory and Managers in an Era of Reform," *China Quarterly,* no. 118 (June 1989): 242–64, esp. 249–53. It should be noted however, that because of continued unemployment rather than a labor shortage, Chinese workers have not been able to leave one job for another, a major strength of workers in the enterprises examined here. Thus Chinese workers have had neither "exit" nor "voice," though they have used "the weapons of the weak."

31. In rejecting the "workers' control" view, Clarke argues that any control workers exercise is more than countered by the control over workers exercised by managers (Clarke, "Contradictions of State Socialism"). While there is much to his argument, Clarke misses how labor was commodified in the Soviet system, how it became a scarce supply sought by managers, and that individual actions taken by workers and managers in leaving jobs and hoarding labor had an aggregate effect of increasing the demand for labor and, consequently, the relative power of workers. That this did not fully compensate workers for the inability to act collectively is without argument.

32. V. Kalmyk and T. Sil'chenko, "Sotsial'no-ekonomicheskaia obusloven-

nost' otnosheniie k mestu raboty," in *Otnoshenie k Trudu i Tekuchest' Kadrov*, edited by E. Antosenkov and V. Kalmyk (Novosibirsk: n.p., 1970), 92–120.

33. In this way the provision of goods and services by the enterprise forms a distinct version of the internal labor markets found in capitalist firms. See Paul Osterman, ed. *Internal Labor Markets* (Cambridge: MIT Press, 1984); R. Althauser and A. Kalleberg, "Firms, Occupations and the Structure of Labor Markets," in *Sociological Perspectives on Labor Markets*, edited by Ivar Berg (New York: Academic Press, 1981); P. Doeringer and M. J. Piore, *Internal Labor Markets and Manpower Analysis* (Lexington, Mass.: Heath, 1971).

34. Russell Hardin, *Collective Action* (Baltimore: Johns Hopkins University Press, 1982); Michael Taylor, *The Possibility of Cooperation* (Cambridge: Cambridge University Press, 1987).

35. Burawoy, *Politics of Production*, 189.

36. Regarding workers' collective action specifically, see Adam Przeworski, "Marxism and Rational Choice," *Politics and Society* 14, no. 4 (1985); Claus Offe and Helmut Wiesenthal, "Two Logics of Collective Action: Theoretical Notes on Social Class and Organizational Forms," in *Political Power and Social Theory*, vol. 1, edited by Maurice Zeitlin (Greenwich, Conn.: JAI Press, 1980); James Johnson, "Symbolic Action and the Limits of Strategic Rationality: On the Logic of Working-Class Collective Action," in *Political Power and Social Theory*, vol. 7, edited by Maurice Zeitlin (Greenwich, Conn: JAI Press, 1986); Jon Elster, *Ulysses and the Sirens* (Cambridge: Cambridge University Press, 1984); Colin Crouch, *Trade Unions: The Logic of Collective Action* (London: Fontana, 1982).

37. Resource mobilization theory improved on the previous dominant perspective, that of relative deprivation, in which levels of anger or frustration were seen as the main determinants of collective action. T. R. Gurr, *Why Men Rebel* (Princeton: Princeton University Press, 1979). Accounts of resource mobilization theory can be found in Charles Tilly, *From Mobilization to Revolution* (New York: Random House, 1978); W. A. Gamson, *The Strategy of Social Protest* (Homewood, Ill.: Dorsey, 1975); D. McAdam, *Political Process and the Development of Black Insurgency, 1930–1970* (Chicago: University of Chicago Press, 1982); A. Oberschall, *Social Conflict and Social Movements* (Englewood Cliffs, N.J.: Prentice Hall, 1973); Mayer Zald and J. D. McCarthy, eds. *Social Movements in an Organizational Society* (New Brunswick, N.J.: Transaction Books, 1987). The work of Tilly is more useful in the present context since he and his collaborators specifically discuss strikes, workers' movements, and their political protests against the state.

38. As has been argued elsewhere, resource mobilization theory is "most fruitful in analyzing the mobilization process and in emphasizing the role of existing organizations and networks in laying the groundwork for social movement formation." Bert Klandemans, "New Social Movements and Resource Mobilization: The European and the American Approach Revisited," in *Research on Social Movements*, edited by D. Rucht (Boulder, Colo.: Westview Press, 1991).

39. In what follows, the terms *structural Marxist perspectives* and *rational choice perspectives* will at times be used interchangeably. While not denying significant differences between structural Marxists and rational choice theorists, the two provide ultimately the same explanation at different levels: micro-level

"choices" are almost wholly determined by macro-level incentive "structures." The two coexist most closely in the analytical Marxism approach. See Przeworski, "Marxism and Rational Choice"; Elster, *Ulysses and the Sirens;* and John Roemer, *A Future for Socialism* (Cambridge: Cambridge University Press, 1994).

40. For recent strong statements of interests as arising solely through one's position in the economy, see Jeffrey Frieden, *Debt Development and Democracy* (Princeton: Princeton University Press, 1991); and Ronald Rogowski, *Commerce and Coalitions* (Princeton: Princeton University Press, 1989).

41. It is in this sense that resource mobilization approaches are not "theoretically self-sufficient," since they are dependent on other perspectives for a full explanation; see Herbert Kitschelt, "Resource Mobilization Theory: A Critique," in *Research on Social Movements,* edited by D. Rucht (Boulder, Colo.: Westview Press, 1991), 324–25. Alain Touraine, in his account of the Polish Solidarity movement, demonstrates quite vividly how goals and preferences, far from being constant, were formed and reformed in the course of Solidarity's struggle: Alain Touraine et al., *Solidarity: Poland 1980–1981* (Cambridge: Cambridge University Press, 1983).

42. Gabriel Almond and Sidney Verba, *The Civic Culture* (Princeton: Princeton University Press, 1963). For a summary of this literature see Gabriel Almond, "The Study of Political Culture," in *A Discipline Divided* (Newbury Park, Calif.: Sage, 1990); and Ronald Inglehart, "The Renaissance of Political Culture," *American Political Science Review* 82 (1988).

43. See, for example, Jeffrey W. Hahn, "Continuity and Change in Russian Political Culture," *British Journal of Political Science* 21 (October 1991).

44. Gabriel Almond, "Communism and Political Culture Theory," *Comparative Politics* 15 (1983); Stephen White, *Political Culture and Soviet Politics* (London: MacMillan, 1979); Archie Brown, ed., *Political Culture and Communist Studies* (New York: M. F. Sharpe, 1984).

45. Some of the stronger recent statements can be found in Richard Pipes, *Russia Under the Bolshevik Regime* (New York: A. A. Knopf, 1993); and Walter Lacquer, *The Long Road to Freedom* (New York: Scribner's, 1989).

46. Lucian Pye, "Political Science and the Crisis of Authoritarianism," *American Political Science Review* 84 (1990).

47. For a sharp critique of this view, see Michael Burawoy, "The End of Sovietology and the Renaissance of Modernization Theory," *Contemporary Sociology* 21 (November 1992).

48. David Stark, "Path Dependence and Privatization Strategies in East Central Europe," *Eastern European Politics and Society* 6 (1992).

49. There are some exceptions. The new institutionalists in sociology argue that institutions are often slow to change not only due to sunk costs (as other institutional approaches argue) but also because individuals often cannot conceive of alternatives. In one conception, "Institutions do not just constrain options: they establish the very criteria by which people discover their preferences." Paul J. Dimaggio and Walter W. Powell, Introduction to *The New Institutionalism in Organizational Analysis* (Chicago: University of Chicago Press, 1991), 11.

50. Marsha Pripstein Posusney, "Irrational Workers: The Moral Economy of

Labor Protest in Egypt," *World Politics* 46 (October 1993), 85. The classic accounts of this approach are found in James Scott, *The Moral Economy of the Peasant* (New Haven: Yale University Press, 1976); Barrington Moore, Jr., *Injustice* (White Plains, N.Y.: M. E. Sharpe, 1978); E. P. Thompson, "The Moral Economy of the English Crowd in the Eighteenth Century," *Past and Present,* no. 50 (February 1971).

51. Posusney, "Irrational Workers," 85.

52. Craig J. Calhoun, "The Radicalism of Tradition: Community Strength or Venerable Disguise and Borrowed Language?" *American Journal of Sociology* 88, no. 5 (1983).

53. See Roman Laba, *The Roots of Solidarity: A Political Sociology of Poland's Working-Class Democracy* (Princeton: Princeton University Press, 1991); Touraine, *Solidarity;* Michael Kennedy, *Professionals, Power and Solidarity in Poland* (Cambridge: Cambridge University Press, 1991).

54. In this way, the Soviet coal miners were quite like French workers in the first half of the nineteenth century as described by William Sewell, *Work and Revolution in France: The Language of Labor from the Old Regime to 1848* (Cambridge: Cambridge University Press, 1980).

55. David Laitin and Aaron Wildalvsky, "Political Culture and Political Preferences," *American Political Science Review* 82, no. 2 (1988): 589–90.

56. Ann Swidler, "Culture in Action: Symbols and Strategies," *American Sociological Review* 51 (April 1986); Jack A. Goldstone, "Ideology, Cultural Frameworks, and the Process of Revolution," *Theory and Society* 20 (May 1991): 405–53.

57. Following Goldstone, I define *ideologies* as "self-conscious rationales and programs for political (and social) actions," *culture* more broadly as "the sum of the self-conscious and taken-for-granted symbols, meanings, knowledge, and values that are essential for the expression and interpretation of ideologies, statements, and actions." Ibid., 406. Most cultural settings contain a multiplicity of symbols and traditions from which to draw ideologies, and the struggle is over which to select and give emphasis.

58. Sidney Tarrow, *Power in Movement: Social Movements, Collective Action and Politics* (Cambridge: Cambridge University Press, 1994), chap. 7; Tarrow, "Mentalities, Political Culture, and Collective Action Frames," in *Frontiers in Social Movement Theory,* edited by Aldon Morriss and Carol McClurg Mueller (New Haven: Yale University Press, 1992); David Snow and Robert Benford, "Master Frames and Cycles of Protest," in Morris and Mueller; Snow and Benford, "Ideology, Frame Resonance, and Participant Mobilization," *International Social Movement Research* 1, 1988.

59. Tarrow, *Power in Movement,* 123.

60. Ibid., 123, 130.

61. Burawoy, *Politics of Production,* 195–97. The fusion of politics and economics is discussed in Valerie Bunce, "The Political Economy of the Brezhnev Era: The Rise and Fall of Corporatism," *British Journal of Political Science* 13:129–58. For a somewhat similar argument along these lines, see Wlodzimierz Wesolowski, *Classes, Strata and Power* (London: Routledge and Keagan Paul, 1979).

62. Powell and Dimaggio, Introduction to *New Institutionalism.*

63. Simon Clarke and Peter Fairbrother, "The Origins of the Independent Workers' Movement and the 1989 Miners' Strike," and "The Strikes of 1991 and the Collapse of the Soviet System," in Simon Clarke et al., *What About the Workers? Workers and the Transition to Capitalism in Russia* (London: Verso, 1993). Other chapters in this volume are quite illuminating, especially "The Contradictions of 'State Socialism,'" and "Privatisation and the Development of Capitalism in Russia," both by Simon Clarke. But the rather orthodox Marxist approach often employed by the authors can be limiting; for instance, their perspective completely ignores the common if fleeting interests between workers and liberals in breaking the old system and creating democratic space in which new social actors, workers included, could operate.

64. See the discussion in Calhoun, "Radicalism of Tradition," 903–5.

65. Burawoy takes this somewhat closer to the answer, in arguing that workers used the ideals of socialism to judge the regime, and this insight forms the starting point of the argument being made here about the miners' trajectory (Burawoy and Lukacs, *Radiant Past*). But in a subsequent statement, Burawoy chastises Russian miners for a "myopic, self-aggrandizing, superior attitude . . . toward other workers" in contrast to the shipyard workers of Gdansk ("End of Sovietology," 781). In what follows, it will be argued that miners did in fact try to engage other workers in a broader miners' movement, and only when they failed did they create notions of their superiority over other workers. More important, it is unclear what is gained by criticizing workers for failing to live up to an idealized notion of class consciousness.

66. In William Reddy's work, the idea of the market and the social categories imposed by market language and culture crossed the English Channel much more easily and long before market institutions themselves: *The Rise of Market Culture: The Textile Trade and French Society, 1750–1900* (Cambridge: Cambridge University Press, 1984). If ideas moved relatively easily to eighteenth and nineteenth century France, then they certainly did to post-Communist countries in the late twentieth century.

67. As Swidler argues in "Culture in Action," ideologies are crucial in shaping action during "unsettled periods," but the survival of one ideology over another is ultimately dependent on structural conditions.

Chapter 2

1. Mikhail Gorbachev subsequently argued that the coal miners' strike marked the beginning of the end of the Soviet Union. See his *Zhizn' i Reformi* (Moscow: Novosti, 1995), 2 vols. The previously largest strike was that of one hundred thousand textile workers in 1925–26. Chris Ward, *Russia's Cotton Workers and the New Economic Policy* (Cambridge: Cambridge University Press, 1990).

2. Betsy Gidwitz, "Labor Unrest in the Soviet Union," *Problems of Communism* 32 (November–December 1982). Typically such strikes were localized by authorities who rushed to the scene and quickly made economic concessions, while carting off the assumed ringleaders. One form of protest was "mass absenteeism,"

where workers of a shop wouldn't show up for work on a given day to express a particular grievance. See E. Leont'eva, "Obshchestvennyi konflikt," *Voprosy Ekonomiki,* no. 4 (1989): 120–29.

3. Alla Nazimova, "Chelovek: konflikt na proizvodstve," *Politicheskoe Obrazovanie,* no. 10 (1989): 75–80. See also Walter Connor, *The Accidental Proletariat* (Princeton: Princeton University Press, 1991), 213–14. Just prior to the miners' strike, many Soviet sociologists were at a loss to comprehend strikes in the original socialist state. See the roundtable discussion "Zabastovka v SSSR: novaya sotsial'naya realnost'," *Sotsiologicheskie Issledovania,* no. 1 (1989). Of the Soviet sociologists who were actively researching the new wave of strikes, Leonid Gordon, Alla Nazimova, and their colleagues deserve special mention. On this point, see Leont'eva, "Obshchestvennyi konflikt."

4. "Razgovor u barrakady,"*Sotsiologicheskie Issledovania,* no. 6 (1990). The March actions are detailed in a Kemerovo oblast (Kuzbass) party document of early April, reprinted in Leonid Lopatin, compiler, *Rabochee Dvizhenie Kuzbassa: Sbornik Dokumentov i materialov* (Kemerovo, 1993), 39–40. See also Simon Clarke, Peter Fairbrother, and Vadim Borisov, *The Workers' Movement in Russia* (Aldershot, England: Edward Elgar, 1995), 18–21.

5. Viktor Kostyukovskii, *Zarkoe leto 89–ogo: khronika, dokumenty, vpechetleniya ochevidtsa* (Moscow: Sovremennik, 1990), 10. Besides being an eyewitness to the events, Kostyukovskii includes in his account many documents, tape-recorded interviews, and speeches repeated verbatim. Lopatin's compilation (*Rabochee Dvizhenie Kuzbassa*) is also an excellent source of original documents.

6. Kostyukovskii, *Zarkoe leto 89–ogo,* 8; *Moscow News,* no. 32 1989. Kostyukovskii points out that while the massive strike that followed was largely spontaneous, the initial strike was well planned.

7. Kostyukovskii, *Zarkoe leto 89–ogo,* 10. A fairly straightforward account of the strike in the Kuzbass, written by the Kemerovo Regional Party Committee, can be found in Lopatin, *Rabochee Dvizhenie Kuzbassa,* 76–83. The miners seized the political opportunity provided by the recently convened Supreme Soviet. They saw the sharp nationally televised debates as a signal that their own demands might be tolerated and that the Supreme Soviet might provide a forum for their discussion.

8. *Kuzbass,* 15 July 1989, 1. Clarke, Fairbrother, and Borisov (*Workers' Movement*) present an exhaustive account of the strike as it occurred in the Kuzbass coal field. Yet it would appear that the point of this exercise is to claim that the miners, almost from the beginning, were largely controlled by local party and government officials. They argue, "The most conspicuous feature of the July strike is the speed with which the local powers responded to the challenge, and the effectiveness with which they harnessed the miners' strike to their own more modest ambitions" (27). It is certainly curious to label the first spontaneous nationwide collective action in Soviet history "most conspicuous" for its control by the local power elite. The evidence presented to buttress this claim is selective and ambiguous: that some of the demands were also concerns of some segment of local Party officials and managers, that some of the strike leaders were Party members, and that, after the strike, local Party officials claimed to have the situation under control. Certainly the

strike represented a struggle, and the authorities were trying as much as possible to control events, but in this they were only partially successful at best.

9. Kostyukovskii, *Zarkoe leto 89–ogo,* 112.

10. The list of members of the Kuzbass regional strike committee can be found in Lopatin, *Rabochee Dvizhenie Kuzbassa,* 49–50. Clarke, Fairbrother and Borisov (*Workers' Movement,* 40–41, 44) claim, "In the first hours of the strike, the mine managers and local administration . . . began to impose a hierarchical structure on the workers' movement" through the organization of the strike committees. Yet they provide an example of a mine electing as its strike committee head one of the future leaders of the Kuzbass miners' movement—with miners arguing "Sanka won't keep quiet, let's elect him"—and state, "Anyone who did not do his job on the committee was immediately replaced."

11. Elizabeth Teague, "Perestroika and the Soviet Worker," *Government and Opposition* (spring 1990): 199–200.

12. Theodore Friedgut and Lewis Siegelbaum, "Perestroika from Below: The Soviet Miners' Strike and its Aftermath," *New Left Review* (summer 1990): 11. By good fortune, Friedgut and Siegelbaum were in the Donbass just after the strike ended and present a good deal of interesting material and firsthand accounts. While Clarke, Fairbrother and Borisov (*Workers' Movement*) make much of the Communist Party membership and contacts of various strike members, it should be recalled that a large segment of the population, particularly educated males (and the strike leaders were often well educated), were Party members. Their account also greatly exaggerates the unity of Party members and the lines of opposition between the Party and the rest of society that would become prominent only in the months and years following the strike.

13. Kostyukovskii, *Zarkoe leto 89–ogo,* 20–21; Friedgut and Siegelbaum, "Perestroika from Below," 10; Teague, "Perestroika and the Soviet Worker," 199.

14. Friedgut and Siegelbaum, "Perestroika from Below," 10.

15. This was how miners and strike leaders explained their actions to the author in interviews during the 1991 strike, when demonstrations on the square continued. On the importance of such group action for solidarity, see Rick Fantasia, *Cultures of Solidarity: Consciousness, Action and Contemporary American Workers* (Berkeley: University of California Press, 1988).

16. Interview with Y. Komarov, Novokuznetsk, 3 May 1991. See also Clarke, Fairbrother, and Borisov, *Workers' Movement,* 20, note 9.

17. *Argumenty i Fakty,* no. 30 (1989); *Moskovskie Novosti,* no. 31 (1989): 8; David Mandel, "The Rebirth of the Soviet Labor Movement: The Coal Miners' Strike of July 1989," *Politics and Society* (September 1990). Donbass strike leader Boldyrev, later reflecting on the fear of repression, said: "Sure, some of our demands were political. But if we'd understood they were political, we wouldn't have raised them" (interview with Boldyrev, Donetsk, July 1992). The demands of several Kuzbass cities are documented in Lopatin, *Rabochee Dvizhenie Kuzbassa,* 42–47.

18. Kostyukovskii, *Zarkoe leto 89–ogo,* 23. To which the rail worker

responded, "That's what I thought, we shouldn't, but so you know, the rails will be open, but we're with you."

19. Ibid., 57–58; interview on 5 May 1991 by the author with R. Vakhitov, a bus driver who was to become the chair of the Novokuznetsk strike committee. Bus drivers in some other locations had already struck in conjunction with a new pay system.

20. Nina Maksimova, "Zabastovka: shtrikhi k portretu yavleniya," *EKO,* no. 11 (1989): 68; Kostyukovskii, *Zarkoe leto 89–ogo.*

21. Maksimova, "Zabastovka," 69.

22. Kostyukovskii, *Zarkoe leto 89–ogo,* 76–77; Lopatin, *Rabochee Dvizhenie Kuzbassa,* 55.

23. Kostyukovskii, *Zarkoe leto 89–ogo,* 112. The strike leader went on to explain that the sit-down strike is only one of many forms of strikes, such as "Italian, warning, graduated," among others, which he apparently learned from an encyclopedia entry describing the experience of capitalist countries.

24. Maksimova, "Zabastovka," 69.

25. Kostyukovskii, *Zarkoe leto 89–ogo,* 52. While both these examples are from the Kuzbass, in the Donbass such groups as the Democratic Union, the Ukrainian Helsinki Group, Rukh, and representatives of other groups from Moscow, Leningrad, Kiev, and L'vov were all given "a decisive rebuff" (Friedgut and Siegelbaum, "Perestroika from Below," 22).

26. Friedgut and Siegelbaum, "Perestroika from Below," 22. Clarke, Fairbrother, and Borisov (*Workers' Movement*) give a contrasting interpretation, and certainly intellectuals in the role of outside experts helped the miners draw up their demands, though the miners were wary of outside influence, particularly beyond class lines.

27. Maksimova, "Zabastovka," 69–70. The union Independence, supporting "workers' control at production and all levels of power," is clearly as political as any new party. See *Nasha Gazeta,* 13 February 1990. While the miners were at best suspicious of these radical intellectuals, the intellectuals themselves were not without fault: some did not bother to hide their desire to use the strike to push their own agendas. Others clearly patronized the strikers. In the words of one observer, such treatment took place "precisely when the [miners] demonstrated consciousness and self-consciousness, civic activity and a precise understanding of their situation" (Kostyukovskii, *Zarkoe leto 89–ogo,* 52).

28. Peter Rutland, "Labor Unrest," 201.

29. *Komsomolskaya Pravda,* 14 July 1989. See also Teague, "Perestroika and the Soviet Worker," 199; and Valerie Sperling, "Society Organizes Itself: The Coal Miners' Strike Committees," Department of Government, Georgetown University, 21.

30. *Trud,* Aug. 3, 1989, cited in Mandel, "Soviet Labor Movement," 395.

31. Friedgut and Siegelbaum, "Perestroika from Below," 12.

32. Kostyukovskii, *Zarkoe leto 89–ogo,* 113. Dual power (*dvoevlastie*) was, of course, the term used to describe the authority held by the original Soviets alongside the institutions of the old regime in 1917. This willingness to surrender the newly gained authority on the level of the community contrasts sharply with the authority that was seized on the level of the enterprise.

33. Friedgut and Siegelbaum, "Perestroika from Below," 23; *Argumenty i Fakty,* no. 30 (1989): 8; Mandel, "Soviet Labor Movement," 23. Again, Clarke, Fairbrother, and Borisov (*Workers' Movement*) provide a much different perspective, seeming to find the Party's hand in much of what the strike committee's did.

34. Kostyukovskii, *Zarkoe leto 89–ogo,* 38; Friedgut and Siegelbaum, "Perestroika from Below," 10; Rutland, "Labor Unrest," 204.

35. Maksimova, "Zabastovka," 70; Sperling, "Society Organizes Itself," 28–29.

36. Friedgut and Siegelbaum, "Perestroika from Below," 24. The trade union's provision of food is significant in that while the union rarely defended workers' interests, it was involved in distributing benefits to them, a fact with both positive and negative consequences for workers. We will return to this issue in later chapters.

37. Kostyukovskii, *Zarkoe leto 89–ogo,* 8; Friedgut and Siegelbaum, "Perestroika from Below," 26; Maksimova, "Zabastovka," 70. For a firsthand account of the sort of meeting at a steel plant at which the STK is elected, see chapter 3 of this volume.

38. Friedgut and Siegelbaum, "Perestroika from Below," 26; Teague, "Perestroika and the Soviet Worker," 201.

39. Friedgut and Siegelbaum, "Perestroika from Below"; Teague, "Perestroika and the Soviet Worker." After the strike the law was changed, removing the provisions on elections of managers and gutting the responsibilities of the STK.

40. Teague, "Perestroika and the Soviet Worker," 198; Friedgut and Siegelbaum, "Perestroika from Below," 28; Maksimova, "Zabastovka," 70. To be sure, the situation varied from mine to mine, as did the permanency of this arrangement, as we shall see in later chapters.

41. Kerr and Siegel, "Propensity to Strike."

42. *Izvestia,* 14 July 1989, 3; Kostyukovskii, *Zarkoe leto 89–ogo,* 44.

43. We will return to this point in chapter 4.

44. Yarrow, "Labor Process in Coal Mining," 170, 187.

45. On the difference between the labor process in underground and strip mining, with the latter said to be more like road construction, see Yarrow, "Labor Process in Coal Mining," 182, 189. Strip mines and enrichment plants also joined with underground miners in future strikes.

46. Kostyukovskii, *Zarkoe leto 89–ogo,* 39. Evidence that all the strip mines in the Kuzbass were on strike is provided by an interesting anecdote. It seems that seismographs at electric stations had for some time been picking up shocks that could not be accounted for until the strike. When the strike began, the shocks stopped, and when the strike ended, they began again, leading to the conclusion that they were caused by explosions at the strip mines. The explosions were causing shocks because the strip mines were destroying the water table; the land was becoming dehydrated and thus losing its ability to absorb shock. Ibid., 32.

47. "Travma," *Ekonomicheskaya Gazeta,* no. 7 (1989): 17.

48. Such topics were forbidden themes in the Soviet press until the policy of glasnost, and its open discussion may have had a significant impact on the coal miners.

49. *Kuzbass,* 13 July 1989; *Argumenty i Fakty,* no. 30 (1989). The miners' wrath

at these figures was compounded by the wastefulness of the Soviet economy, where between seven and ten million tons of coal were lost each year simply by falling off coal cars, meaning that some miners' lives were lost for nothing (Donald Filtzer, *Soviet Workers and the Collapse of Perestroika,* (Cambridge: Cambridge University Press, 1994) 210). These numbers have not improved with the end of the Soviet Union and the opening to the market: According to Kemerovo Governor Kislyuk, since 1989 the death rate in Kuzbass mines has tripled (Open Media Research Institute Daily Report, September 6, 1995).

50. Kostyukovskii, *Zarkoe leto 89–ogo,* 8.

51. Mandel, "Soviet Labor Movement," 382–83; Kostyukovskii, *Zarkoe leto 89–ogo,* 16; Sperling, "Society Organizes Itself," 8.

52. Judith Thornton, "Soviet Electric Power in the Wake of the Chernobyl Accident," in John P. Hardt and Richard Kaufman, eds. *Gorbachev's Economic Plans,* vol. 1, Joint Economic Committee of Congress (Washington, D.C.: GPO, 1987); David Warner and Louis Kaiser, "Development of the USSR's Eastern Coal Basins," in ibid.; *Soviet Energy Data Resource Handbook,* Government Printing Office, 1990; "Travma."

53. Kostyukovskii, *Zarkoe leto 89–ogo,* 26. The subsidies to the branch were reportedly 5.4 billion rubles in 1988 and 1 billion more in 1989.

54. "Razgovor u barrakady."

55. Rutland, "Labor Unrest," 197.

56. On the usefulness of an institutional approach for understanding state socialist societies, see Stark and Nee, "Institutional Analysis."

57. *Izvestia,* 12 August 1989, cited in Friedgut and Siegelbaum, "Perestroika from Below," 14–15.

58. *Za chest' shakhtera,* 24 July 1989. In fact, the problem with implementing this demand was not the result of bureaucracy, but that the additional pay was to come from self–financing, or savings within each mine.

59. This impression comes not only from the sources cited in this chapter, but from the author's own extensive interviews in the mining regions during the second strike two years later, discussed in chapter 6. This sense of exploitation remained constant throughout; what did change was the strategies the miners employed to overcome it, as we shall see.

60. Michael Burawoy, *Politics of Production: Factory Regimes under Capitalism and Socialism* (London: Verso, 1985).

61. Friedgut and Siegelbaum, "Perestroika from Below," 17. On *podsnezhniki* in other industries, see Filtzer, *Collapse of Perestroika,* 48–49.

62. This resentment extended to the privileges of bosses beyond the enterprise; see the Kemerovo Regional Party Decree following the strike reducing the privileges to party and other leaders, including the opening of stores and hospitals long closed to the general public. Lopatin, *Rabochee Dvizhenie Kuzbassa,* 92.

63. Underscoring one miner's complaint that "we haven't seen perestroika yet," one mine director prior to the strike was rewarding exemplary miners with the title of "Stakhanovites of perestroika." The irony of combining perestroika with Stalinist symbolism was not lost on the miners. They reportedly responded, "There is no perestroika, its wheels are spinning, but still there are 'Stakhanovites

of perestroika.'" Lopatin, *Rabochee Dvizhenie Kuzbassa,* 100. The first miner's complaint is cited in Lewis Sieglebaum, "We Haven't Seen Perestroika Yet: Behind the Soviet Miners' Strike," *Nation* 249, no. 13 (1989).

64. *Stakhanovets,* 10 August 1989. See also *Gornyatskoe Slovo,* 22 July 1989; *Za Chest' Shakhtera,* 29 July 1989.

65. See, for example, Friedgut and Siegelbaum, "Perestroika from Below."

66. Mandel ("Soviet Labor Movement") portrays the miners as defending a significant portion of the status quo, in particular state property and the planning system, against private property and the market. Clarke and Fairbrother ("Origins of Workers' Movement," 134–35) argue that political demands were largely the successful attempt of mine managers to deflect criticism from themselves.

67. For Clarke and Fairbrother ("Origins of Workers' Movement," 134), "the political demands of the miners were substantially influenced by enterprise directors and by the Union government," since the miners' initial demands were "largely parochial grievances, most of which were addressed to mine management," but "enterprise management successfully deflected worker criticism towards the ministerial system and political actors. . . ." This argument is reprised and expanded upon in Clarke, Fairbrother, and Borisov, *Workers' Movement.* It will be asserted here that this argument misses the blurred distinction between politics and economics in the Soviet system, where central political actors were seen as largely responsible for the economic state of affairs of individual enterprises. Indeed, it is hard to see how these demands—which they characterize as involving "pay, living conditions, the shortage of housing, and the money that was taken away . . . to support the bureaucrats"—could be solved by mine managers and local officials (Clarke, Fairbrother, and Borisov, *Workers' Movement,* 49). Ironically, while employing a Marxist framework of analysis, Clarke and Fairbrother wind up arguing for a sharp distinction between politics and economics that the actors themselves did not share. Their argument leads to the conclusion that Soviet coal miners generally were incapable of seeing beyond bread-and-butter issues to demand the transformation of a system they found to be grossly exploitative.

68. "Protokol o soglasovanikh merakh mezhdu regionalnim zabastovachnim komitetom kuzbassa i komissiei TsK KPSS, Soveta Ministrov SSSR, i VTsSPS," Prokop'evsk, 17–18 July 1989, in Lopatin, *Rabochee Dvizhenie Kuzbassa,* 68–75.

69. Twenty rubles a ton was well below the world price of $25 to $49 a ton, or 500 to 980 rubles at the unofficial exchange rate in 1989. Rutland, "Labor Unrest," 203.

70. Kostyukovskii, *Zarkoe leto 89–ogo,* 15. See also *Kuzbass,* 23 August 1989.

71. On the importance of resonance for the potency of a social movement, see the discussion of collective action frames in the first chapter of this book.

72. Filtzer, *Collapse of Perestroika,* 98. Clarke, Fairbrother and Borisov (*Workers' Movement*) are right to note that interests here converged between miners and more ambitious mine directors, and the latter had further interest in deflecting anger away from themselves. Yet given their limited resources, it is difficult to see how the miners' concerns could have remained confined to their individual enterprise; even new managers elected by the miners would face the same limited scope for change.

73. Kostyukovskii, *Zarkoe leto 89–ogo*, 36.

74. Ibid., 63. As well as a sense of exploitation, this speech and others also reflect a disdain for redistribution generally, a point that will be returned to in the following chapters.

75. Ibid., 66.

76. Filtzer, *Collapse of Perestroika*, 95.

77. While there had been nationalist demonstrations in the peripheral republics up to this point, this was the first major collective action in the Slavic center of the Soviet Union, and one made up not by nationalist intellectuals, but by the state's avowed constituency—the working class. Subsequently, the miners were to claim that their action signaled to Eastern Europeans, who would bring down the Berlin Wall some months later, that "There'll be no more tanks." Lopatin, *Rabochee Dvizhenie Kuzbassa*, 404.

Chapter 3

1. Stephen Kotkin, *Steeltown, USSR* (Berkeley: University of California Press, 1991), 257.

2. During industrialization:

> ministries and factories literally tore cities apart, each trying, by fair means or foul, to build "its" houses hard by the factory gates, to create, at any cost, "its" residential district with "its" water supply, "its" sewage system, "its" heating plant, club, small store—in a word everything for itself and nothing for the city.

B. Svetlichnyi, "Urban Development and City Planning," *Arkhitektura SSSR, no. 3* (March 1966): 31, cited in William Taubman, *Governing Soviet Cities: Bureaucratic Politics and Urban Development in the USSR* (New York: Praeger, 1973), 24.

3. Thus in Magnitogorsk, the famed metallurgical combine owned most of the housing in the city (with other enterprises owning almost all the rest) and operated most municipal services, including mass transit. When the mayor appealed to the Ministry of Municipal Services for help in strengthening city-owned services, he was told with a touch of black humor, "Your city is not a city. It is the property of the metallurgical combine," which in turn was subordinated to the Ministry of Ferrous Metallurgy in Moscow. Yet by 1970 this "company town" had a population of 364,000. Cited in Taubman, *Governing Soviet Cities*, 54, 59–60. For a prodigious study of the development of this archetypal Soviet enterprise-town, see Stephen Kotkin, *Magnetic Mountain* (Berkeley: University of California Press, 1995).

4. Henry W. Morton, "The Contemporary Soviet City," in *The Contemporary Soviet City*, edited by Henry W. Morton and R. Stuart (Armonk, N.Y.: M. E. Sharpe, 1984).

5. Wolfgang Teckenberg, "Labour Turnover and Job Satisfaction: Indicators of Industrial Conflict in the USSR?" *Soviet Studies* 30, no. 2 (April 1978): 193.

6. David Powell, "Labor Turnover in the Soviet Union," *Slavic Review* 36, no. 2 (June 1977): 268–85; Morton, "Contemporary Soviet City," 16.

7. Teckenberg, "Labour Turnover," 196.

8. This is doubly so when the state limits differentials in wages, as was the case in state socialist societies.

9. Theodore Friedgut, *Iuzovka and Revolution*, vol. 1 (Princeton: Princeton University Press, 1989).

10. As one study of the Soviet steel industry found, "obsolescent equipment, crowded plant sites, and overloading of support services typify the old, relatively small plants. . . . Reconstruction and modernization of these plants would require such a large investment as to be an inefficient use of capital." Inefficiency notwithstanding, reconstruction has been undertaken at Donetskii, with a continuous billet mill installed in the mid-1970s. Boris Rumer, *Soviet Steel: The Challenge of Industrial Modernization in the USSR* (Ithaca: Cornell University Press, 1989), 64.

11. Cheryl Harris, "Modernization of the Soviet Steel Industry," in "Gorbachev's Economic Plans," vol. 1, study papers submitted to the Joint Economic Committee of Congress, 23 November 1987, U.S. Government Printing Office, Washington, D.C., 1987. This production in old plants with obsolescent equipment is especially characteristic of steelmaking in Ukraine, which comprised about 40 percent of Soviet steelmaking. Rumer, *Soviet Steel,* 15.

12. Rumer, *Soviet Steel,* 54.

13. Ibid., 59, 144.

14. Friedgut, *Iuzovka and Revolution.*

15. Connor, *Accidental Proletariat,* 11.

16. Rumer, *Soviet Steel,* 4.

17. *Kuzbass,* 18 July 1989, 1. Most appeals came from Ukraine, another indication of how dependent the steel industry there was on the Kuzbass for coke, given the lack of adequate-quality coal in the Donbass.

18. Ibid.

19. *Pravda,* 28 October 1989, as quoted in Friedgut and Siegelbaum, "Perestroika from Below." Despite the letter writers' claim that "both you and we are representatives of the working class," three of the four were plant directors.

20. *Ekonomika i Zhizn',* no. 35, August 1990.

21. The propaganda against the strike was quite heavy-handed in such centrally controlled publications as *Pravda, Rabochaya Tribuna,* and *Trud,* as well as in such economically liberal papers as *Ekonomika i Zhizn'.*

22. Oleg Semyenov, interview by author, Novokuznetsk, 3 May 1991.

23. *Pravda,* 27 March 1991; *Rabochaya Tribuna* 30 April 1991.

24. *Metallurg* [hereafter *M*], 26 July 1989. "Specifics of production" refers to the potential damage to blast furnaces if shut down.

25. *M,* 2 August 1989. At an earlier meeting that took place during the miners' strike, which discussed among other problems the sharp labor shortage, working conditions, wages, and the plant's provision of food and housing, the director promised that one hundred apartments would be available soon and that the entire housing problem would be solved by the year 2000.

26. Absent were such important points for the miners as changes in the administration of the enterprises, new elections for trade union and STK representatives, legal status for strike committees, and the reduction of the number of managerial personnel. Instead there were several references to protecting the rights of managers, specialists, and service workers, including the removal of limits on bonuses to these groups. Also included was an urgent demand for the Supreme Soviet to accelerate the adoption of a law governing strikes, a law the miners bitterly opposed. Ibid.

27. *M*, 16 August 1989.

28. *M*, 30 August 1989.

29. *M*, 18 October 1989. As was fairly typical in the Soviet division of labor by gender, the crane operators were women. Indeed, gender divisions were one significant difference between coal and steel: while women were prohibited by law since the Khrushchev era from working underground in mining, roughly one-half of the employees in the two steel mills examined here were women. As was the case throughout the economy, steel professions were often segregated by gender, with many of the typically female positions being peripheral to production, and usually involving lower pay; women also largely filled above-ground and service jobs in the coal industry. Although the maleness of underground coal mining might contribute to the miners' sense of solidarity, the women steelworkers often led what little strike activity there was in these plants; it was clearly not the case that women workers were somehow more passive than men and it is hard to see how gender divisions could be more than a partial factor in the inability of steelworkers to act collectively.

30. Independent journalist for *Kuzbasskie Vedomosti*, author's interview, Novokuznetsk, 5 May 1991. The strikes were well covered in the city paper *Kuznetskii Rabochii* and were mentioned in other plant newspapers, for example, *Za Aluminum*.

31. Women were prominent in this early strike as well. It is worth noting that the workers attempted to solve their conflict in the same way that the Mezhdurechensk miners attempted to solve their grievances before they began the miners' strike: not through their trade union representatives, but by writing to the trade union newspaper *Trud* in Moscow. The grievance, in this case about not getting paid for additional work performed, was passed on to the local prosecutor's office. Many showed up at a planned shop meeting with the prosecutor, but the prosecutor went first to the shop manager's office. The manager's deputy eventually walked out and told the meeting that the money belonged to the plant, not the workers. "So this is how we 'talked things out,'" one worker remarked. *MZ*, 10 March 1989.

32. *MZ*, 15 March 1989.

33. *Kuznetskii Rabochii*, 10 March 1989.

34. Ibid., 30 March 1989.

35. Ibid., 10 March 1989.

36. Ibid., 30 March 1989. These actions coincided with strike warnings at a shop in the nearby Kuznetsk Metallurgical Combine, as well as short strikes at

individual mines. All were documented in a Kemerovo region (Kuzbass) Party Committee report, reprinted in Lopatin, *Rabochee Dvizhenie Kuzbassa,* 39–40.

37. *MZ,* 14 June 1989.

38. *MZ,* 18 July 1989.

39. Ibid.

40. In further evidence that these committees were fundamentally different than those of the miners, Kustov, the director of West Siberian, was present at the negotiations as a "specialist." *MZ,* 21 July 1989.

41. Ibid.

42. Ibid.

43. The composition of the committee can be found in Lopatin, *Rabochee Dvizhenie Kuzbassa,* 108–9. Though there is no direct evidence that only "yes-men" attended the conference and decided the fate of the workers' committees, there is evidence that these meetings are carried out in a less-than-democratic fashion. The author attended a conference in 1991 that was to vote on the collective contract between the administration and workers for the following year at a nine thousand-employee foundry-mechanical factory in Moscow, where some shops had struck and workers had gained at least some political space from the administration. Nonetheless, the trade union chair and the general director dominated the meeting in tandem, only written questions were allowed in response to the collective contract presented by the administration, and when presented with the charge that many of the delegates had been chosen illegally, both the director and the trade union chair answered, "I know nothing about how the delegates were chosen." In this fashion the collective contract for the following year was adopted, a contract that defines not only wages and working conditions but also many of the living conditions (housing, health care, day care, vacations) for the plant's employees.

44. *M,* 19 August 1989.

45. *M,* 18 December 1989. Whether such arguments were persuasive or not, the director was elected a people's deputy.

46. The plant was capable of many such things, he argued. Dwellers of one street had long complained to local government officials about the raw sewage seeping into their courtyards and street, but the problem was not solved until the plant sank sewage pipes and built fifty meters of road. The director claimed this was only one of many such possible projects. *M,* 4 April 1990.

47. *M,* 30 December 1989. In addition, the plant began to provide interest-free loans up to 1,500 rubles to young families with children and provided loans for "individual housing construction," with the debt to be repaid by the plant after twenty years of service. As for the latter, workers who left without good reason had to pay back the loans immediately with full interest, and the same went for those who systematically violated labor and production discipline. *M,* 12 May 1990.

48. *M,* 30 August 1989.

49. Workers resented being sent to do farmwork, and those who stayed were unhappy as well, since they were paid more "so that work doesn't stop, and we have to work longer days. But after all the Siberian summer is short, and you want to do some work on your garden plot, to vacation with your family. . . ." *MZ,* 14 June 1989.

50. *MZ,* 25 August 1989. In an indication of how the administration viewed the provision of food to its workers, a member of the official workers' committee stated, "The rhythm of the work of the complex depends on how public food-stuffs are provided in the cafeterias. And good food is a deposit towards a person's mood and the productivity of his work." *MZ,* 11 October 1989.

51. *MZ,* 7 September 1989.

52. *MZ,* 13 July 1990.

53. *MZ,* 24 October 1990.

54. Ibid. Filtzer (*Collapse of Perestroika,* 58 n. 7) notes a "marked increase in workers' reliance on the workplace" for food and consumer goods during the latter half of perestroika, presumably as goods disappeared from state stores and prices elsewhere soared. "In the late 1980s 51 percent of sewing machines, 51 percent of soft furniture, 42 percent of refrigerators, 32 percent vacuum cleaners were purchased through the closed distribution system at people's place of employment." At Moscow's AZLK auto factory in 1990, sale of consumer goods amounted to more than the total yearly wage fund. David Mandel, *Perestroika and the Soviet People: Rebirth of the Labour Movement* (Montreal: Black Rose, 1991), 157 n. 3.

55. *MZ,* 28 November 1990.

56. *MZ,* 10 February 1989.

57. *MZ,* 7 March 1989.

58. *MZ,* 10 March 1989. The director claimed that, as with many other demands, the length of vacations was set by law (*Goskomtrud*) and thus his hands were tied.

59. *Kuznetskii Rabochii,* 10 March 1989. One problem in sorting out how much different workers are paid is the complex system of bonus payments. In addition to one's average salary, which is set according to one's skill rating level (1–8), there are bonuses for fulfilling and overfulfilling the plan, a yearly "13th month" bonus, a regional coefficient for working in Siberia and in an "ecological zone," payments for "general and special years of service," and other privileges and rights.

60. *MZ,* 11 July 1989.

61. *MZ,* 25 August 1990. Among those also discriminated against in this fashion were workers in the health sector and the children's sector and the workers who maintained the plant's housing and communal services.

62. Those listed as having received the cars were primarily skilled workers. *M,* 23 August 1990.

63. *M,* 26 July 1989.

64. *M,* 18 October 1989.

65. *M,* 25 October 1989.

66. *M,* 16 August 1989.

67. *M,* 23 August 1989. Filtzer (*Soviet Workers,* 47–53) notes that labor shortages only deepened with perestroika's steps toward the market.

68. *M,* 2 June 1989.

69. Ibid.

70. *M,* 29 November 1989.

71. *MZ*, 21 July 1989.

72. *MZ*, 14 June 1989.

73. *MZ*, 11 October 1989.

74. *MZ*, 1 August 1990.

75. *M*, 21 March 1991.

76. *MZ*, 30 November 1990.

77. *M*, 5 August 1989.

78. *M*, 2 June 1990.

79. *M*, 6 June 1990. Their chief concern was that the central government compel local governments to give steelworkers a greater share of housing.

80. *MZ*, 5 July 1989; *MZ*, 12 July 1989.

81. *MZ*, 3 November 1989.

82. Ibid.

83. *MZ*, 11 October 1989. The preferential distribution of enterprise goods and services to favored workers was officially codified in the 1970 USSR Labor Code:

> workers and employees who have successfully and conscientiously performed their duties shall be granted priority and privileges in the areas of social, cultural, housing, and personal services (trips to sanitariums and rest homes, improvement in housing conditions, etc.).

On the other hand, "rolling stones" and "slackers" were deprived of bonuses and promotions, denied passes to rest homes, and moved through the housing line slowly, if at all. Powell, "Labor Turnover," 282.

84. The trade union, he claimed, unlike the STK, which voted to maintain the status quo, voted to keep housing distribution within existing laws. "Today the right to the provision of housing outside the line" is given not by one's belonging to a certain profession, "but exclusively by conscientious work and active participation in the public life of the collective, that allows a worker to be placed in the category of '*peredoviki.*'" *MZ*, 11 October 1989.

85. "Just imagine," remarked the trade union chair for the foundry shop, "that the plant receives, let's say 400 apartments, then it follows that the first 400 in line will receive them. . . ." *MZ*, 23 October 1990.

86. The minuses, according to the trade union chair, were for those workers "who generally have nowhere to live. They live in a different settlement, or the husband and wife stay in different worker dormitories. We have 130 such people in our shop and who will look out for them?" Supporters of the plan cited the example of Krivorozhstal' Steel Complex, which from 1978 to 1985, it was said, had waged a struggle for the establishment of a single line. Ibid.

87. *MZ*, 7 November 1989.

88. *MZ*, 23 November 1989.

89. Ibid.

90. *MZ*, 27 December 1989.

91. In order to hedge bets, the plant's two existing construction units, SMU 1 and 2, continued to build housing. *MZ*, 10 February 1990.

Chapter 4

1. *MZ*, 9 January 1990; 27 July 1990; 22 August 1990.
2. *MZ*, 28 November 1990.
3. *M*, 30 August 1989.
4. They argued the STK "should be like the Supreme Soviet where a deputy is elected from his district, and he is not elected again or confirmed." By analogy, the letter states, "the STK should be direct representatives of the shops and departments," without additional confirmation and that the STK chair should be elected by the entire workforce through secret balloting. *M*, 11 November 1989.
5. Ibid.
6. *MZ*, 15 December 1989.
7. *M*, 29 November 1989; *MZ*, 21 November 1989; *M*, 29 November 1989.
8. *M*, 29 November 1989; *MZ*, 10 February 1989; *MZ*, 1 December 1989.
9. *MZ*, 9 January 1990.
10. The price increases meant that steel plants were unable to fully pay wages, threatening workers with cuts between 25 and 100 rubles a month, as well as sharp drops in funds for housing and child care. Filtzer, *Collapse of Perestroika*, 76, 119.
11. *M*, 17 January 1990.
12. Ibid. While Filtzer notes a resulting number of strike threats in the steel industry, as reported in the central press, these appear to have been either engineered or co-opted by management and the official trade union, with the latter able to claim a victory when the government agreed to partial compensation for the price increases. These concessions proved only temporary, however, with little subsequent protest. Filtzer, *Collapse of Perestroika*, 76, 119, 141.
13. *M*, 7 April 1990.
14. Ibid.
15. As stated in the paper, "The time has come for the factory's journalists to come out from under the rigid 'five-cornered' press of the party committee, the trade union, the administration, the Komsomol—and lately—the STK. The paper should be the organ of the labor collective." *M*, 12 May 1990.
16. *MZ*, 8 July 1990. The plant's official resolution is reprinted in Lopatin, *Rabochee Dvizhenie Kuzbassa*, 312.
17. *MZ*, 27 July 1990.
18. *MZ*, 19 September 1990.
19. *M*, 5 August 1989.
20. *M*, 9 August 1989. Still, the trade union remained partly responsible for maintaining labor discipline. At the meeting where the next collective contract was discussed, the trade union chair chastised the workforce for 699 days of work time lost to workers' absences. *M*, 16 August 1989.
21. *M*, 16 September 1989.
22. *M*, 20 September 1989.
23. *M*, 18 October 1989.
24. *M*, 25 October 1989.
25. Ibid.
26. Ibid.

27. *Kuznetskii Rabochii,* 30 March 1989.

28. *MZ,* 7 June 1989.

29. *MZ,* 11 October 1989.

30. Ibid.

31. *MZ,* 3 July 1990.

32. "And something else. When questions concerning social problems were raised at the conference, in response we heard 'There's no money.' They couldn't even come up with 900,000 rubles to build a sanitarium for people going on pension. . . . I consider that for a complex having such profits, social questions should have significance of the first degree. We earn, and we should distribute the fruits of our labor." *MZ,* 4 July 1990. Here he combines (as do the miners in the following chapters) the idea of traditional trade union bargaining over wages with the syndicalist notion of the right to independently "distribute the fruits of our labor."

33. *MZ,* 6 July 1990.

34. *MZ,* 10 October 1990.

35. *MZ,* 23 October 1990.

36. And this despite the fact that the ministry officials and steel enterprise managers all over the country were speaking out almost daily concerning the dire situation caused by the lack of coking coal and its effect on production and pay. The industry was still reeling from the 1989 coal strike when the 1991 strike began. In some instances, steelworkers stopped working involuntarily, as when the Azovstal' plant sent five thousand workers on unpaid leave. One furnace was shut down at Donetskii for lack of coke, while at other plants blast furnaces, open-hearth furnaces, and rolling mills were shut down, at the risk of extensive damage. Filtzer, *Collapse of Perestroika,* 141–44.

37. *M,* 20 April 1991.

38. Ibid. Filtzer notes there were other isolated strikes in steel plants during the miners' strike, though these were co-opted by the trade union and by management. Filtzer, *Collapse of Perestroika,* 113.

39. *MZ,* 18 July 1989.

40. Oleg Semyenov, interview by author, Novokuznetsk, 6 May 1991. The Kuznetskii plant is several kilometers away from West Siberian and, while thirty years older, has approximately the same number of employees.

41. Vladimir Petrov, interview by author, Novokuznetsk, 6 May 1991.

42. Kotkin, *Steeltown, USSR,* 28. Similarly, the editor of the local newspaper told him, "The most influential workers at the steel plant are taken care of [*prikormleny*], especially in relation to the general Magnitogorsk population. The have better food, lots of meat, and a chance to obtain some of the many spoils that 'fall' the factory's way, from imported cassette players to one of our better domestic-make automobiles. They may not be happy with everything, but why strike?" Ibid., 257–58.

43. Ibid., 258–59.

44. *Kuzbass,* 13 July 1989; *Argumenty i Fakty* no. 30 (1989).

45. Filtzer, *Collapse of Perestroika,* 76 n. 95.

46. Gurr, *Why Men Rebel.*

47. Conversations with steelworkers at Donetskii took place in April 1991. The

workers appeared unconcerned with taking time off from their workday to answer the questions of an uninvited guest, and at least one was clearly drunk. Though reticent to criticize the administration, they had many disparaging comments to make about their trade union—"We have no trade union like you do in your country," one said, unprompted—and, like the Donbass miners, they were very concerned about the economic future of their plant. The impression gained from conversations with steelworkers and the pages of the plant newspapers in Russia and Ukraine closely mirrors that of Burawoy with Hungarian steelworkers: "The class consciousness . . . is of a negative character, opposed to hierarchy, bureaucracy, injustice, inequality and inefficiency. It recognizes the systemic and class origins of pathologies." Michael Burawoy, "Reflections on the Class Consciousness of Hungarian Steelworkers," *Politics and Society* 17, no. 1 (March 1989).

48. In a reflection on this very question, Burawoy produces a complex argument to explain why steelworkers did not follow the example of coal miners. First, as basic goods producers in a supply-constrained economy, miners were privileged by the state, but they lost their privileged position with perestroika. Second, steelworkers were able to avoid a similar decline by shifting their product profile, thus getting higher state purchase prices for their goods. Third, miners, owing to their unique work regime, experienced an exaggerated form of "workers' control" over production, which led them to more greatly experience exploitation by the state ("End of Sovietology," 780–81). Yet this argument breaks down on each point: The steel industry in the former Soviet Union has suffered dramatically during the overall decline in production; changing one's product profile is no longer valid given the lack of state orders and the glut on the steel market; and the miners' political militancy followed and was a product of their strike activity and subsequent organization rather than a precursor to it. This last point will be addressed in the following chapters.

49. In 1989, wages for underground coal miners were generally reported at around 600 rubles per month, while those of steelworkers averaged 350 rubles per month. More precise figures are available for 1987, two years before the first strike, when the average monthly industrial wage was 222 rubles, while the coal industry average was 352 rubles and basic underground mining professions averaged between 400 and 500 rubles. In ferrous metallurgy, the average was 248 rubles. *Trud v SSSR* (Moscow: Financi i Statistiki, 1988), 189–201.

50. Kostyukovskii, *Zarkoe leto 89–ogo*, 62. Mines were further disadvantaged in terms of social infrastructure in two respects. First, because a mine has a definite life span—unlike an industrial factory, which theoretically can be continually modernized—there is less incentive to sink capital in permanent infrastructure such as housing or cultural and educational facilities in a mining settlement. Second, many mining communities are indeed isolated, and while this in itself does not breed radicalism, as the isolated community thesis maintains, it does mean there is less social infrastructure than in a larger city. Indeed, the differences in the living conditions for miners and steelworkers in the Donbass were evident from its initial industrialization over a hundred years ago. See Friedgut, *Iuzovka and Revolution*.

51. Filtzer, *Collapse of Perestroika,* 97–98.

52. The numbers are even worse for Donetsk when the number of marriages,

and thus presumably the number of new housing applicants, is compared with the number of new housing units built; then Donetsk was twenty-fifth out of twenty-eight. Henry Morton, "The Contemporary Soviet City," in H. Morton and R. Stuart, eds., *The Contemporary Soviet City* (Armonk, N.Y.: M. E. Sharpe, 1984).

53. This strategy was conveyed to the author by several miners. See also *MZ*, 7 November 1989. In general, Filtzer argues, high wages and social benefits tended to coincide, though "there were exceptions, in particular coal mining, where the appalling state of housing was one of the main grievances behind the 1989 strikes" (*Collapse of Perestroika*, 76). Yet payment in kind did not always correlate with payment in wages, even within single firms. In one particularly in-depth study, it was found that while skilled workers were better paid than engineering and technical workers (ITRs), housing conditions were better for ITRs—even the lowest-paid engineering worker was less likely to live in a communal apartment than the best-paid skilled worker. With housing an especially scarce commodity, this would have been an especially significant form of compensation. Connor, *Accidental Proletariat*, 114–15.

54. J. H. Westergaard, "The Rediscovery of the Cash Nexus," *The Socialist Register, 1970* (London: Merlin Press), esp. 120–21. Thus miners in Vorkuta, of Russia's Far North, were drawn from other parts of the Soviet Union in the hopes that savings from the high wages would allow them to buy a home and retire in Russia's temperate south. Inflation immediately wiped out those plans and contributed to their militancy. See "In Russia's Far North, Inflation Destroys a Dream," *Moscow Times*, 3 March 1993.

55. Connor, *Accidental Proletariat*, 172.

56. As Filtzer notes, "So long as a worker is still in the housing queue she or he remains dependent on keeping her or his job" (*Collapse of Perestroika*, 76). This is not to say that wages were unimportant to steelworkers, but rather, they represented one component of an overall compensation package. Both steelworkers and miners demanded wage increases.

57. Kerr and Siegel, "Propensity to Strike," 110.

58. Ibid.

59. Katherine Stone, "The Origin of Job Structures in the Steel Industry," *Review of Radical Political Economics* 6, no. 2 (summer 1974): 156.

60. Szymanski, *Politics of Class*, 63; See also Lipset, *Political Man*, 252. For some empirical support, see Richard F. Hamilton, *Affluence and the French Worker in the Fourth Republic* (Princeton: Princeton University Press, 1967), 205–28.

61. Shorter and Tilly, *Strikes in France, 1830–1968*, 15. Marx's comment from "The Eighteenth Brumaire of Louis Bonaparte" is discussed in connection to the collective action problem by Hardin, *Collective Action*, 223.

62. Only a few years ago, approximately one-third of all enterprises in the steel industry produced 90 percent of all pig iron and 70 percent of all steel in the USSR. Rumer, *Soviet Steel*, 4.

63. Interview with Oleg Semyenov.

64. On the creation of a "ripple effect" as a way out of the collective action

problem, see John Chamberlin, "Provisions of Collective Goods as a Function of Group Size," *American Political Science Review* 68 (1974): 707–16.

65. Interview with Oleg Semyenov.

66. Nikolai Sokol, interview with author in Donetsk, 21 April 1991. Sokol, a miner elected to the Donetsk City soviet, was studying strike participation in the Donbass.

67. For more on the Zasiad'ko mine, see Stephen Crowley and Lewis Siegelbaum, "Survival Strategies: The Miners of Donetsk in the Post-Soviet Era," in *Workers of the Donbass Speak: Survival and Identity in the New Ukraine, 1989–1992,* edited by Lewis Siegelbaum and Daniel Walkowitz (Albany: State University of New York Press, 1995).

68. Friedgut and Siegelbaum, "Perestroika from Below," 7. For more on Zviagil'skii, see chapter 8 in this volume.

69. *Verchernyi Donetsk,* 17 April 1991.

70. Ibid. For a somewhat less eccentric and thus more typical example of a mine that struck in 1989, but whose trading contacts held back a strike two years later, see the description of the Kuibyshev mine in Crowley and Siegelbaum, "Survival Strategies." Not surprisingly, striking miners referred to their colleagues at Zasiad'ko, Kuibyshev, and elsewhere as *kolbasniki* (sausage-lovers).

71. Yurii Gerol'd, interview with author in Moscow, 13 February 1991; *Nasha Gazeta,* 20 February 1990.

72. Another remarkable example of a mine in this third category is Vorkuta's Vorgashorskaya mine, which "had by far been the most militant in 1989. However, the mine had since obtained the right to export above-plan coal, and the miners did not want to lose their foreign contracts and the resulting 'barter,'" and were now denounced by their colleagues elsewhere as "strikebreakers." Mandel, *Perestroika and the Soviet People,* 169. Other examples can be found in Filtzer, *Collapse of Perestroika,* 105 n. 108; and *Nasha Gazeta,* 5 June 1990.

73. The Kuzbass miners were both resentful and envious of Gerol'd. That the miners' goal of independence in many ways contradicted the solidarity that gave them strength is a point that will be revisited in the final chapter.

74. There were no cases that I found, neither in central, regional, or local press, nor during field work, where miners broke such a significant contract arrangement to strike.

75. Linda Cook, "Labor's Response to the Soviet Post-Communist Transition" (paper presented at the annual meeting of the American Political Science Association, September 1992).

76. Why were there not more strikes in light industry, where both wages and in-kind benefits are low? One hypothesis is that workers in food and consumer industries were more likely to steal products, such as workers in a meatpacking plant literally bringing home the bacon. Clifford Gaddy, using data from emigre surveys, argues that this was largely not the case ("Pretending to Work and Pretending to Pay: A Hedonic Wage Approach to the Behavior of Soviet Workers and Managers," *Berkeley-Duke Occasional Papers on the Second Economy of the USSR,* Paper no. 24, January 1991). A second argument would point out that these industries are typically filled by female workers, but given the willingness of women

steelworkers to strike in the plants examined here, that argument does not appear convincing. A more compelling explanation is that these industries were less strategically placed to cause economic disruption through striking than coal, steel, and other heavy industry, and that workers in these industries were more threatened by unemployment.

77. The work of economic historian Douglass North makes one cautious in predicting the rapid demise of such institutions, no matter how revolutionary the change in economic structures. See his *Institutions, Institutional Change, and Economic Performance* (Cambridge: Cambridge University Press, 1990).

Chapter 5

1. This meeting was vividly captured in the film *Perestroika from Below* (Past-Time Productions), and excerpts of the transcript are published in Lewis Siegelbaum and Daniel Walkowitz, eds., *Workers of the Donbass Speak: Survival and Identity in the New Ukraine, 1989–1992* (Albany: State University of New York Press, 1995). The complete transcripts were provided by the Donetsk Oral History Interview Project [hereafter DOHIP], headed by Walkowitz and Siegelbaum. The conference took place on 5 August 1989, roughly two weeks after the strike had ended in the Donbass.

2. On the last point, Efimov replied that trips had been given, for instance, to a local coking plant, so that they would accept substandard coal from the mine, and trips were given to other enterprises for spare parts in short supply. This statement led another delegate to retort: "Then why were trips given to the KGB and the local draft board? What kind of spare parts do you get from them?"

3. With the talk of repression, the miner moved to discussing a demand, one made throughout the mining regions after the strike, that would seem trivial to anyone used to the disparities of a market economy: the miners called the separate sauna for managers a "social injustice" and demanded it be shared with everyone.

4. Delegates at earlier meetings at the mine voted to remove the chief economist, two chief engineers, a deputy chief engineer, the chief housing inspector, a shift manager, and the director of the Miner sanatorium. When someone suggested getting rid of the trade union altogether, a strike committee member declared, "I think we have one law only—the workers' meeting decides. The supreme law is the workers' meeting." But debate focused on new candidates for trade union chair. When someone suggested nominating an educated person, another delegate countered that strike committee members were doing fine without much education, while still another retorted, "'They' all had educations, they were all smart and literate, but they made such a mess out of things."

5. The focus here and throughout will be on the two largest coal basins, where the author conducted field research: the Kuzbass in western Siberia of the Russian Republic and the Donbass in eastern Ukraine. The other basins that were significant in the strike movement are Vorkuta (the Pechora basin) in the far north of Russia and Karaganda in northern Kazakhstan.

6. When he visited the Kuzbass some months before the first strike, Prime

Minister Ryzhkov was reportedly reduced to tears on seeing miners' living conditions (Rutland, "Labor Unrest").

7. Ibid., 197.

8. Kostyukovskii, *Zharkoe leto 89–ogo*, 82; *Argumenty i Fakty*, no. 30 (1989); Friedgut and Siegelbaum, "Perestroika from Below," 15.

9. Kostyukovskii, *Zharkoe leto 89–ogo*, 32, 47; V. Andriyanov, "Gornyi udar," *Dialog*, no. 1 (1990): 62. Yet environmental demands also demonstrated how distant market forces were from miners' lives in 1989—they included open-face miners demanding the closure of open-face mines and that the coal town Berezovskii switch to gas from coal to fire the city's boilers. Lopatin, *Rabochee Dvizhenie Kuzbassa*, 47.

10. Rutland, "Labor Unrest," 197.

11. Kostyukovskii, *Zharkoe leto 89–ogo*, 62. The region also produces many industrial goods that were scarce within the region itself because they were commandeered by state authorities for distribution elsewhere. Thus one sharp problem, housing, was caused in no small part by the lack of cement, of which the region makes five million tons a year, most of it distributed elsewhere. Ibid.

12. Ibid., 81.

13. Ibid., 82.

14. The environmental problems of the Donbass are described in *Sotsialisticheskiya Industriya*, 2 August 1988.

15. Adding to the sense of being in another era, the miner (on pension though still in his fifties, the normal retirement age for miners being fifty to fifty-five) showed signs of illiteracy and displayed his political preferences by the two portraits of Stalin that hung on his living room walls.

16. Rutland, "Labor Unrest," 198; Richard M. Levine, "Mineral Industries of the USSR," *Mining Annual Review* (1990); Warner and Kaiser, "Eastern Coal Basins," 534; Filtzer, *Collapse of Perestroika*, 98.

17. Warner and Kaiser, "Eastern Coal Basins"; *Pravda*, 8 July 1989. This argument indicates how the basins were already competing against one another before the strike began. In post-Soviet Russia, transportation costs are of vital significance for the Kuzbass, as we shall see in chapter 7.

18. Friedgut and Siegelbaum, "Perestroika from Below," 29; Rutland, "Labor Unrest," 216.

19. "Razgovor u barrakady," 67–69.

20. Rutland, "Labor Unrest," 207; *Trud*, 18 November 1989, as quoted in Teague, "Perestroika and the Soviet Worker," 202.

21. "Razgovor u barrakady," 68. See also Lopatin, *Rabochee Dvizhenie Kuzbassa*, 201–2.

22. Kostyukovskii, *Zharkoe leto 89–ogo*, 49; *Trud*, 4 August 1989, 5 August 1989.

23. In response to a trade union official who characterized the strike as "purely economic," a miner-activist responded, "Undoubtedly, the strike in itself is political. Sure, in essence our demands carry a social-economic character, but the nomination of worker-leaders into the organs of management and power—this is a political phenomenon. In my opinion, politics and economics are hard to sepa-

rate." "Razgovor u barrakady," 67, 72; *Sobesednik,* no. 49 (December 1989). In the Kuzbass, discussion of the removal of article 6 from the constitution had begun in September. Lopatin, *Rabochee Dvizhenie Kuzbassa,* 115–16, 121.

24. Rutland, "Labor Unrest," 210.

25. Ibid. As mentioned in the last chapter, this radical mine subsequently abstained from the 1991 political strike.

26. "IV Konferentsiya Soyuza Trudyashchikhsya Kuzbassa," 18–19 November 1989, Novokuznetsk, published proceedings.

27. *Nasha Gazeta* [hereafter *NG*], 11 December 1989; 23 January 1990; 13 March 1990.

28. Beginning with their first strike, miners expressed disdain for the official media. During the 1989 strike, the local and central press were said to print "blatant untruths," and the miners grew so angry at the press that they ceremonially tore up newspapers at demonstrations. Once the strike ended, the media focus shifted to discrediting the now powerful strike committees through articles with titles like "Is the Regional Strike Committee Thirsting for Power?" The result was that the miners trusted very few sources of information and even discounted news from their own strike committees when it ran counter to their interests. Maksimova, "Zabastovka," 74; Rutland, "Labor Unrest," 200–201; *Stakhanovets,* 10 August 1989, 5 October 1989.

29. Members of the regional party committee who protested the interference in the workers' movement "of those not of workers' origin" were reminded that Marx, Engels, and Lenin were not proletarians either. *NG,* 11 December 1989; 30 December 1989.

30. *NG,* 20 February 1990; 3 April 1990. As a source of information about the machinations of the workers' movement in the Kuzbass, it must be recognized that *NG* most closely reflects the views of intellectuals who sympathize with the worker-activists rather than the rank and file. Yet it has been surprisingly candid about the shortcomings of the movement, proudly proclaiming its editorial independence even from workers' committees, and at least in its first few years, is a rich source of material. On the confrontations between the regional Party and the paper, see Lopatin, *Rabochee Dvizhenie Kuzbassa,* 273–75, 314–15.

31. *NG,* 11 December 1989; 13 February 1990; and *NG,* 20 December 1989, cited in Clarke, Fairbrother, and Borisov, *Workers' Movement,* 53 n. 52. Kislyuk and Golikov would later become two of the most anticommunist leaders of the miners' movement.

32. A delegation of Kuzbass miners sent to Vorkuta during the latter's political strike returned with a report very critical of the political demands, which they explained by referring to the influence of outside "emissaries." Lopatin, *Rabochee Dvizhenie Kuzbassa,* 190–93. Yet three of the four delegates—Yurii Gerol'd, Anatoly Malykhin, and Yurii Komarov—would soon become every bit as politicized.

33. *NG,* 6 February 1990; 11 December 1989; 13 and 27 March 1990, 5 June 1990.

34. Of the thirty-five, seven were said subsequently to abandon the workers' movement platform. Out of a total of twenty people elected to the Russian Congress of People's Deputies from the region, eleven were nominated by the workers'

committees, though several later changed positions. Lopatin, *Rabochee Dvizhenie Kuzbassa,* 207–13.

35. *NG,* 13 March 1990; 17 and 24 April 1990; 9 October 1990. Rutland, "Labor Unrest," 206.

36. *NG,* 1 May 1990.

37. *NG,* 8 May 1990; interviews by author with Yurii Gerol'd in Moscow, 20 February 1991, and with Yurii Butchenko in Novokuznetsk, 5 May 1991; Rutland, "Labor Unrest," 215. Survey data provided to author by Viktor Komarovskii, who conducted the survey. See also V. V. Komarovskii and E. B. Gruzdeva, *Shakhterskoe Dvizhenie* (Moscow: Institute of Problems of Employment and Ministry of Labour, 1992).

38. *NG,* 1 May 1990.

39. Komarovskii survey data; "Razgovor u barrakady," 70, 68; "Pervyi S'ezd Shakhterov SSSR," 11–15 June 1990, collected materials, Donetsk, part 2, 31.

40. *NG,* 10 April 1990; "Pervyi S'ezd Shakhterov SSSR," part 1, 46; *NG,* 25 September 1990.

41. *NG,* 12 June 1990.

42. "Pervyi S'ezd Shakhterov SSSR," part 2, 55, 51–52, 64.

43. Komarovskii survey data.

44. "Pervyi S'ezd Shakhterov SSSR," part 2, 39, 41.

45. Ibid., part 2, 44, 46.

46. Ibid., part 1, 75.

47. Ibid., part 2, 34.

48. Ibid., part 2, 47.

49. Ibid., part 2, 86, 45.

50. Ibid., part 2, 39, 53.

51. Ibid., part 2, 51, 63, 53.

52. Ibid., part 2, 48.

53. Komarovskii survey data; "Pervyi S'ezd Shakhterov SSSR," part 1, 77.

54. "Pervyi S'ezd Shakhterov SSSR," part 1, 48.

55. Ibid., part 1, 48, 56–62.

56. Ibid., part 1, 41, 69, 98.

57. Ibid., part 1, 32, 96; Komarovskii survey data.

58. *NG,* 28 August 1990, October 9 1990; see also *NG,* 25 September 1990.

59. Shchadov was ready to oblige. He had wanted a hand in the running of the first congress: he sent telegrams to mine directors and trade union officials before the first congress stating that the timing was wrong, that it should be held in Moscow rather than Donetsk, and that the elections of delegates to the congress should be considered void; to which a *Nasha Gazeta* correspondent replied, "Only in our country would the employer dictate to the employees how their independent congress should be run" (*NG,* 5 June 1990). Nevertheless, the coal ministry helped finance the first congress.

60. This account of the second congress is taken from *NG,* 30 October 1990 and 6 November 1990, and interviews with several participants.

61. *NG,* 6 November 1990.

62. Miners in several mines began in July 1990 to demand the removal of Com-

munist Party committees from their enterprise. Lopatin, *Rabochee Dvizhenie Kuzbassa,* 312–13; Clarke, Fairbrother, and Borisov, *Workers' Movement,* 97 n. 35.

63. *NG,* 12 June 1990, 5 June 1990, 28 August 1990, 25 September 1990. The problem was recognized as critical in a resolution of the Fifth Conference of Workers' Committees of the Kuzbass in September 1990: "The regional committee of the Communist Party, by means of unpublicized decrees about the organization of recalls [of workers' committee members] and commentary on certain leaders of the workers' movement, has sought to pull apart the workers' committees. They have partially succeeded, the more so since [the committees] themselves have made a series of tactical mistakes. As a result many committees at enterprises and even in cities have become empty. The link between the council of workers' committees of the Kuzbass and the labor collectives has become weak." The conference appealed "to all labor collectives with the call to renew the workers' committees in the enterprises and in the cities so that they will become one of the guarantees of political stability in the region." *NG,* 9 October 1990.

64. *NG,* 14 August 1990.

65. "Razgovor u barrakady," 75, 69; Rutland, "Labor Unrest," 212. In discussing the workers' committees, Clarke and Fairbrother note the "substantial turnover" in the committees (Clarke, Fairbrother, and Borisov, *Workers' Movement,* 81 n. 1) but later claim of the committees, "Nominally all members were elected from below, but in practice anybody who wanted to serve on a committee could secure election, provided they could get release from work . . ." (83 n. 9). Yet it was the difficulty in obtaining a "release from work" which accounted for the tremendous turnover. To serve on a committee, either you had to be on a pension or have your collective vote for you to be "freed from production," which meant that your salary was paid from the mine's wage fund, something working miners did not take lightly. Delegated miners had to report back to their collectives to account for their time spent and could be easily recalled by stopping their pay. In one case, Anatoly Malykhin, having just achieved nationwide notoriety as a hunger striker who addressed the Congress of People's Deputies during the 1991 political strike, had to return to his mine in Novokuznetsk before conferring with Kuzbass strike leaders, in order to account for himself and to have his mandate renewed.

66. In Russia, the calls for alternatives were being led by the liberal reformers allied around Yeltsin. Yeltsin himself recognized the power of coal miners to push for change in ways that liberal intellectuals could not, and he courted their support. Miner leaders in the Kuzbass, perceiving common interests, joined this alliance for radical political change. On meetings and agreements between Yeltsin and worker committee leaders, see Lopatin, *Rabochee Dvizhenie Kuzbassa,* documents 283–85, 318.

67. *NG,* 22 May 1990, "Pervyi S'ezd Shakhterov SSSR," part 2, 76; part 1, 92.

68. When asked if everyone agreed with the demands, Golikov responded, "We can't move forward until everyone agrees. . . . On one point of the demands we had to have two breaks until a consensus was reached . . . No one said no to the strike," suggesting that the decision to strike was widely supported, but the direction it

should take—political or economic—was more complicated. *NG,* 3 July 1990; 10 July 1990.

69. *NG,* 17 July 1990; Rutland, "Labor Unrest," 218; Lopatin, *Rabochee Dvizhenie Kuzbassa,* 318–23, 329–33.

70. *NG,* 17 July 1990.

71. The first committee member stated that if the miners had a real trade union, they wouldn't have to go to the capital and ask for food. "But for now, we must go." Still another committee member stated that the link between the city and the regional workers' committees was weak, and that while they used to go to the regular weekly meetings, in the last three months they had gone only two or three times. *NG,* 8 January 1991. The weakness of the workers' committees just prior to the 1991 strike was discussed candidly by committee leaders themselves. Lopatin, *Rabochee Dvizhenie Kuzbassa,* 406, 407.

72. *Komsomolskaya Pravda,* 6 November 1990. To this Golikov responded, "We would go. If we could see that there are forces, which were capable of expressing our interests. If we were sure, that that process was irreversible . . ." *NG,* 13 November 1990.

Chapter 6

1. The account of the strike is based on media reports and the author's observations in Moscow and the coal regions and interviews with participants.

2. TASS, 3 January 1991, reprinted in United States Foreign Broadcast Information Service Daily Report [hereafter FBIS], 1 March 1991.

3. In part because of the directors' actions, the Ukrainian government granted an increase in the wholesale price of coal of 2.2 times, and a 6.9 percent increase in wages. They also agreed in principle to take the republican coal industry under the wing of the Ukrainian government. *Komsomolskaya Pravda,* 24 January 1991.

4. TASS, 27 February 1991, reprinted in FBIS, 1 March 1991.

5. This last demand would give more power to the republic. It is worth noting that ethnicity played little role here: most of the miners in the Karaganda fields are Russians or ethnic Germans.

6. They also demanded that the Russian government (led by Boris Yeltsin) be granted greater access to the mass media. According to the Prokop'evsk city strike committee, where these demands were said to first arise: "As long as there's no freedom in Russia, the center will exploit and order around the Russian people. Everything earned by us will be taken away by the center and distributed just like it always was." Lopatin, *Rabochee Dvizhenie Kuzbassa,* 399–400.

7. Ibid., 408–17; *Pravda,* 4 March 1991; TASS, 6 March 1991, in FBIS, 6 March 1991.

8. Radio Kiev, 11 March 1991, in FBIS, 12 March 1991. While Yeltsin was actively courting the support of striking miners in Russia in his bid for independence, Kravchuk actively opposed both the economic demands of the Donbass and the nationalist and political demands in western Ukraine. *Pravda,* 1 March 1991.

9. On the growth of the political strike in the Kuzbass, see the documents in Lopatin, *Rabochee Dvizhenie Kuzbassa,* 418–22, 425.

10. *Pravda,* 15 March 1991. This last demand is a curious one given that the Donbass miners knew that they were being greatly subsidized by the state. This point will be returned to subsequently.

11. The strike committees numbers, though no doubt inflated, can be found in Lopatin, *Rabochee Dvizhenie Kuzbassa,* 426, 429, 443–44. Beyond the horizontal contracts discussed in chapter 4, a selective incentive argument can help explain the difference in participation between the two major strikes. While Donbass miners struck in 1989 to insure that the economic benefits given to Kuzbass miners applied to them, the political demands that predominated in the 1991 strike were certainly less "divisible" and, if achieved, would apply to striking and nonstriking mines alike.

12. Ibid., 453. In Karaganda the regional court ruled that the strike could not be termed illegal since it was a political strike, and the law concerned only economic strikes. In Pavlograd the miners argued that this was the same strike as in 1989, which they claimed had only been suspended and thus was legal. In Tula miners threatened to flood their mine if any legal sanctions were applied against them. Central Radio, in FBIS, 4 April 1991; TASS, in FBIS, 20 March 1991; Radio Rossii, in FBIS, 26 March 1991.

13. Interview with miner from the mine Sotsialisticheskii Donbass, Donetsk, 21 April 1991; Radio Mayak, in FBIS, 4 April 1991.

14. *Pravda,* 26 March 1991.

15. *Pravda,* 4 April 1991; Radio Mayak and Central Television, in FBIS, 4 April 1991. It seems that Gorbachev was getting squeezed from both sides. Just prior to his concessions, he received a telegram from Communist Party leaders in the Kuzbass in language that foreshadowed the putsch later that year: "Silence on the miners' political strike . . . is impermissible. It will lead to the further exacerbation of the political and economic situation . . . , to the collapse of state structures . . . , to chaos and anarchy. We demand . . . that you take decisive steps, adopt emergency and immediate measures, directed at halting the breakdown of the economy, stabilizing the situation, and securing law and order. Further delay is criminal. . . . Otherwise we will be forced to seek your resignation from the position of General Secretary of the Communist Party." Lopatin, *Rabochee Dvizhenie Kuzbassa,* 439–40.

16. *Izvestia,* 5 April 1991; *Pravda,* 5 April 1991.

17. Thus the Mezhdurechensk city strike committee declared that the "exorbitant jump in prices" meant that Gorbachev "is not only continuing the policy of exploiting all workers, but has begun the stage of *super-exploitation,*" while the "Bolshevik" mine, living up to its name, decried the increase by demanding "Land to the peasants, factories to the workers, mines to the miners—in deed, not in words!" Lopatin, *Rabochee Dvizhenie Kuzbassa,* 447, 448 (original emphasis).

18. Ibid., 440; Radio Mayak, 3 April 1991, in FBIS, 4 April 1991. According to a correspondent for Radio Moscow reporting from the Donbass, the economic strike that started on March 1 had completely changed: "It has turned into a political strike; now only political demands are heard." FBIS, 12 April 1991. The

author's research in the Donbass in April 1991 also found miners consumed with political concerns.

19. *Sovietskaya Rossiya,* 28 March 1991; *Pravda,* 28 March 1991; FBIS, 28 and 29 March 1991. The strike was said to affect, due to the loss of steel, the construction and auto industries. Much of this sort of reporting was propaganda aimed against the strike.

20. FBIS, 25 March 1991.

21. *Pravda,* 29 March 1991, 8 April 1991; TASS, in FBIS, 13 March 1991, 9 April 1991; Radio Kiev, in FBIS, 14 March 1991; Central Television, in FBIS, 15 April 1991.

22. *Neues Deutschland,* 8 April 1991, translated in FBIS, 12 April 1991; *Izvestia,* 21 March 1991. The Kuzbass Strike Committee Council thanked all those who had given the strikers material support, "but now more important for us is support through the action of an *all-union political strike."* Lopatin, *Rabochee Dvizhenie Kuzbassa,* 452 (original emphasis). According to a Makeevka strike committee member, "We thought that the workers of other branches, who are being robbed by the state in the same manner, would support us, but nothing of the kind happened. . . . We have understood that we won't achieve anything until we consolidate our forces." Mandel, *Perestroika and the Soviet People,* 193.

23. In one case, an entrepreneur who had organized a children's pony ride outside a Moscow Metro (subway) station set up a collection box for donations to the miners' strike fund.

24. Radio Rossii, in FBIS, 16 April 1991.

25. Their chief demand was to be permitted to sell a certain amount of their product independently. *Trud,* 28 March 1991.

26. *Izvestia,* 23 March 1991, 28 March 1991.

27. AFP in FBIS, 28 March 1991.

28. *Pravda,* 20 April 1991.

29. Indeed, the author declined an invitation to attend a conference of worker-activists in Minsk on the weekend before the strike, on the grounds that there was little activity there. The conference suggests that despite the largely reported spontaneous nature of the strike, there were leaders ready to assist in its organization, which helps explain how the demands quickly escalated from protests against price increases to more political concerns.

30. The strike primarily hit metal-intensive industries, which were largely without steel due to the miners' strike and the decline in interrepublican trade. With the breakup of the Soviet Union, Belarus was left with a large number of steel-consuming enterprises but very little steel of its own. See "What Happened in Belorussia?" *Izvestia,* 15 April 1991; Filtzer, *Collapse of Perestroika,* 110–13. Despite the sharp increases in prices on April 1, other than in Minsk there were none of the spontaneous uprisings that were long assumed by observers of the Soviet Union to be the inevitable reaction to price increases.

31. Radio Mayak, in FBIS, 26 April 1991.

32. Mandel, *Perestroika and the Soviet People,* 187.

33. Ibid., 188. Writing soon after the strike, Mandel argued, "For the mines,

the transfer boils down to greater autonomy and, in particular, the retention of a greater part of their revenues" (192).

34. In a sign that many miners saw themselves, and not managers, in control, several mines continued to strike because workers wanted to elect new directors, despite the nullification of the enterprise election law. Mandel, *Perestroika and the Soviet People,* 195.

35. At strike committee meetings attended by the author in the Kuzbass, the decision to end the strike was made only after very sharp debate. Strike committee members were so distrustful of the Soviet government that they refused to call for an end to the strike even after their own elected chair, Vyacheslav Golikov, read the text of the government agreement verbatim over the phone from Moscow. They insisted that only when they could see a copy with the prime minister's signature would they go to their collectives and recommend a vote to end the strike. Even then, they insisted as insurance that the strike had not been stopped (*prekrashchat'*) but only suspended (*priostanovit'*).

36. The coal industry in each republic was transferred to republican jurisdiction.

37. All-Union Radio, in FBIS, 19 March 1991.

38. Goskomstat figures reported by Radio Moscow, 13 May 1991, in FBIS, 14 May 1991.

39. They continue: "This is not simply an academic question, because the political orientation of the working class may again prove decisive in the next phase of political development in the former Soviet Union" (Clarke and Fairbrother, "Strikes of 1991," 162). While accusing the miner-leaders of acting like Bolsheviks, Clarke and Fairbrother cling to the Leninist notion that the miners were incapable on their own of presenting anything other than bread-and-butter demands. If that is indeed the case, it is hard to see how, on their own, they will prove decisive in the next phase of political development.

40. Ibid.

41. On the importance of the international market for coal as an explanation for miners' motivations, see Cook, *Soviet Social Contract,* esp. 157.

42. Filtzer, *Collapse of Perestroika,* 81, 108; see also 120–22. Likewise Leonid Gordon finds among Kuzbass activists "a certain unsteadiness and flimsy character of [their] consciousness, and the existence of discrepant and not completely assimilated elements." "Russian Workers and Democracy," *International Journal of Sociology* (Winter 1993/94): 9. From a Marxist perspective, Filtzer interprets the miners' stance as based on a "naive and idealized" conception of capitalism, while from a liberal perspective, Gordon sees the legacy of socialist thinking among miners as a product of "ideological stereotypes" and the support for capitalism based on "common sense" (Filtzer, *Collapse of Perestroika,*; Gordon, *Russian Workers and Democracy,* 39).

43. This conclusion and the following discussion are based largely on a series of open-ended interviews with miners in Moscow and the coal regions during the 1991 strike. The author's arrival in Donbass and Kuzbass was serendipitous to the strike and found miners with a lot of time on their hands to answer questions from

a pesky American researcher. In order to acknowledge both the tension and the congruence in views between miners and the leaders of the miners' movement, the interviewees will be labeled as follows: regional leader, mine-level activist, rank-and-file miner.

44. The following comes from the author's transcript of the meeting of representatives of the workers' committees, the NPG, and the Confederation of Labor, Moscow, 12–14 February 1991. The representatives were both regional leaders and mine-level activists.

45. Two years later the miners had still failed to create a coordinating organ. One delegate complained to the meeting that only three representatives were left on the government commission responsible for overseeing the fulfillment of Decree No. 608 and that several regions had no representative at all. Despite all the organization building discussed in chapter 4, the 1991 strike was coordinated, if at all, by an ad hoc group of miners from hotel rooms in Moscow. On the ad hoc interregional coordinating committee, see Lopatin, *Rabochee Dvizhenie Kuzbassa,* 428–29.

46. Even among the gathered representatives, the discussion sometimes reached the absurd. "Let's strike, they're not fulfilling the demands, we'll sort it out later," argued one, which led to the reply, "If we followed that principle, we would have struck a hundred times already." Author's transcript.

47. Interview with Mikhail Krylov (regional leader), in Donetsk, 1 July 1992.

48. Many such concessions granted by the state actually required that the individual enterprise come up with additional money for their implementation.

49. Interview with Pavel Shushpanov (regional leader), in Moscow, 14 February 1992. The February meeting ended with a resolution calling for negotiations on the tariff agreement and preparation for an all-union strike. Lopatin, *Rabochee Dvizhenie Kuzbassa,* 391–92.

50. Author's transcript. While the miners had previously forced a change in the government (*pravitelstvo*), they now focused their attentions on the state (*gosurdarstvo*). Gorbachev's popularity was further hampered at the time by a recent presidential decree implementing a 5 percent sales tax; the text of the decree was displayed prominently by every cash register in the country and soon became known as the "presidential tax."

51. Ibid. The fund for social development paid for miners' housing, day care and cultural centers, vacations, and so forth.

52. *Trud,* 4 January 1991, as translated in FBIS, 17 January 1991. This made it difficult for the independent trade union to confine itself to economic issues, as many leaders said it should. Other organizations—regional strike committee councils, the Confederation of Labor—were supposed to "dirty themselves" with politics.

53. "Vremya," in FBIS, 1 March 1991.

54. TASS, in FBIS, 5 March 1991.

55. *Rabochaya Tribuna,* 26 March 1991. The image of sausage was often used to ridicule economic demands: while miners who did not strike were called *kolbasniki* (sausage-lovers), those who struck with only economic demands were said to be striking "for sausage."

56. Interview with October miners (mine-level activists), in Donetsk, 21 April 1991.

57. Interview with Samofalov (mine-level activist), published in Lewis Siegelbaum and Daniel Walkowitz, "'We'll Remain in This Cesspool for a Long Time': The Miners of Donetsk Speak Out," *Oral History Review* 20, nos. 1–2 (spring-fall 1992).

58. To be sure, this was not a labor theory of value in the strict sense of calculating the value of all products on the basis of past and present labor. Rather, it had to do with their own product, which was valuable because they had invested their labor in it and it was needed by the national economy, independently of the price it brought on the market.

59. Author's transcript. This labor theory of value was evident from the beginning of the miners' movement and explains what some commentators found contradictory about the demands of the 1989 strike—support for independence for their mines (for the market), while denouncing cooperatives (against the market). See Mandel, "Soviet Labor Movement." Rather than mere selfishness, the miners maintained that they produced a material value, while the cooperatives merely distributed what others produced.

60. Author's transcript.

61. Interview with October miners (mine-level activists); interview with Rostov miners (mine-level activists), in Moscow, 29 March 1991.

62. Interview with striking miners (rank and file), in Donetsk, 18 April 1991. The remark about foremen was exaggerated since several had joined and become leaders of the miners' movement.

63. Interview with October miners (mine-level activists).

64. Interview with October miners (rank and file), in Donetsk, 25 June 1992. It is interesting to note that the remark about smashing the system was made well after the downfall of the Soviet Union.

65. Samofalov, "Miners Speak Out." Likewise, in the neighboring October mine one year later, miners were outraged when they discovered that the director was getting as much as 50,000 rubles a month while miners were being paid 15,000–20,000. See Crowley and Siegelbaum, "Survival Strategies," 27.

66. Interview with striking miners (rank and file), in Donetsk.

67. Ibid.

68. Thus there was anger not only because their labor was being exploited, but that now the wealth of country was being exploited, too. Interview with Rostov miners (mine-level activists).

69. Payment according to labor was of course Lenin's definition of socialism.

70. Interview with Yurii Komarov (regional leader), in Novokuznetsk, 3 May 1991.

71. Interview with Rostov miners (mine-level activists).

72. Samofalov, "Miners Speak Out."

73. Mikhail Krylov (regional leader), in Siegelbaum and Walkowitz, *Workers of the Donbass Speak,* 120.

74. To which his workmate responded:

I read somewhere in *Komsomolka* that in 1989 or '90 the air force alone used 3 times more fuel than civilian planes. How are we going to live well? We can't fly, we can't drive, no one can harvest bread, there's not enough fuel, but these planes fly. Who are they protecting us from? Do you want to attack us?

Interview with Badaevskaya miners (rank and file), Novokuznetsk, 4 May 1991.

75. She continued, "The principle of our society was to rob someone to make them a slave, to give them the minimum necessary for survival, without the right to demand anything more." Interview with Olga Samofalova (factory-level activist), Donetsk, 17 June 1992.

76. Crowley and Siegelbaum, "Survival Strategies."

77. *Komsomolskaya Pravda,* 9 April 1991.

78. Radio Rossii, in FBIS, 25 March 1991.

79. *Pravda,* 18 April 1991. This promise was never fulfilled.

80. Interview with Rostov miners (mine-level activists).

81. Interview with Anatoly Malykhin (regional leader), Novokuznetsk, 2 May 1991.

82. Meeting of the Novokuznetsk city strike committee, 6 May 1991, author's transcript. As one account put it, the concessions to end the 1991 strike "were made to miners, not as wage-labourers, but as *de facto* managers, if not owners, of their mines." It was "implicit in the very conditions of their transfer to republican jurisdiction (it was the miners who will decide how to spend the additional revenues left with the enterprise, its form of management and ownership)." Mandel, *Perestroika and the Soviet People,* 156, 194–95 (original emphasis). These promises were not realized, as we shall see.

83. Interview with Rostov miners (mine-level activists).

84. "But in general let them, up top, think about what form of property there should be," he continued. "For people it's all the same, they need someone to pay them. And who will pay them—whether an entrepreneur or the state—doesn't have any significance." Interview with October miners (mine-level activists), 1991. For miners in the Kuzbass, who from a position of strength had many more options from which to choose, such questions were very significant, and they considered themselves good enough economists to tackle them, or if not, they hired those who were.

85. Interview with Krylov (regional leader). The common assumption, in the Donbass as in the Kuzbass, was that privatization of state property meant a transfer to worker ownership; in the Kuzbass it was seen as profitable and a good idea, while in the Donbass it was not feasible.

86. Samofalov, "Miners Speak Out."

87. Interview with Valery Samofalov, in Donetsk, 24 June 1992.

88. These issues are discussed in detail in Crowley, "Between Class and Nation: Worker Politics in the New Ukraine," *Communist and Post-Communist Studies* 28, no. 1 (March 1995).

89. See chapter 1.

90. Thus, as one Donetsk miner told the author in explaining what economic changes were needed, "There should be an owner, but we have no owner. The type

of owner, who is for the people, and not for himself. Like your businessmen." Interview with striking miner, (rank and file), Donetsk, 18 April 1991.

91. "The miners' leaders who favour full enterprise autonomy under the market mean by this 'the free economic entrepreneurship of the mine collectives.' Miners typically talk of their 'right to dispose freely of their product.'" Mandel, *Perestroika and the Soviet People,* 195. For evidence that this tendency goes beyond mining to other industries in Russia, see Clarke, "Privatization."

92. Especially as employed by Tilly, *From Mobilization to Revolution.*

93. See chapter 5.

94. The difference in the exploitation of the Donbass was that it occurred over a much longer period than in the Kuzbass, beginning with imperial Russia. Thus the Donbass coal fields were more fully exploited in the sense that they are almost worked out, leaving the miners with few resources.

Chapter 7

1. This instrumental approach to a sovereign Ukraine, based not on nationalism in the Russian-speaking Donbass but on calculations of economic and political power, was nonetheless combined with the full embrace of the symbols of Ukrainian nationhood, such as the Ukrainian flag and the trident.

2. He added, however, "But we don't completely trust the Ukrainian government either." Interview with October miners, Donetsk, 21 April 1991.

3. Siegelbaum and Walkowitz, *Workers of the Donbass Speak,* 120.

4. Interview with Yurii Makarov, in Donetsk, 24 June 1992.

5. Ukraine's advantages included raw materials, large size, location near Europe with access to the sea, skilled workforce, and high level of industrialization. Leslie Dienes, "Energy, Minerals, and Economic Policy" and other articles in *The Ukrainian Economy,* edited by I. S. Koropeckyj (Cambridge: Harvard University Press, 1992). As for the level of industrialization, by the 1960s, production in Ukraine's coal-metallurgical-heavy machinery complex exceeded that of any country in Western Europe.

6. David Marples, *Ukraine under Perestroika: Ecology, Economics and the Workers' Revolt* (New York: St. Martin's Press, 1991).

7. Jay Mitchell, "Macroeconomic Perspective of the Ukrainian Economy," paper presented at the conference "Challenges of Transition for Ukraine's Economy," Washington, D.C., September 1993, 6–7; *Ukrainian Weekly,* 24 October 1993; *Financial Times,* 22 December 1993; Chrystyna Lapychak, "Back on Track," *Transition,* 15 March 1995.

8. In a measure of the impact of inflation on different social groups, consumer baskets (based on the monthly Ukrainian Army ration) were used to assess changes in purchasing power. In November 1992, the average wage in the state sector was 2 to 3 times that needed to purchase the basket, while in the mining industry it was 10 times and in the retail sector only 1. By March 1993 those factors had fallen to 1 for state employees, 2 for miners, and 0.5 for retail workers. In late June 1993, following the miners' strike, the miners had pushed their factor to 5, while

the average wage had fallen to 0.6 and in retail to 0.3. Simon Johnson and Oleg Ustenko, "The Road to Hyperinflation: Economic Independence in Ukraine, 1991–93," paper presented at the conference "First Steps Toward Economic Independence: New States of the Postcommunist World," Stockholm, August 1993.

9. Lapychak, "Back on Track."

10. In no small part due to pressure from the miners and industrialists of the Donbass, Fokin was later removed and replaced by the former factory director Kuchma from nearby Dnepropetrovsk (later elected Ukraine's president). Following the sequence of the miners' battle with the Soviet government (where they first forced Prime Minister Ryzhkov's resignation, then focused on President Gorbachev), Donbass miners then turned their wrath on Ukrainian President Kravchuk.

11. As in Russian coal mining regions, the increases in miners' wages led to an inflationary spiral within the Donbass, on top of the already high general inflation. The wage structure was further distorted when peripheral and service workers in the coal industry were given wage increases along with the more militant underground workers. Thus, striking doctors in the Donbass could argue that a professor of surgery's pay was one-quarter that of a janitor in a coal mine office, and drivers in the coal industry could get paid three to four times more for the same work as drivers in other industries.

12. He added that it was unthinkable to close the twenty-one mines in the city, since half the population—around half a million people—were connected with the mining industry. Interview with Viktor Bychkov, 18 June 1992.

13. Ibid.

14. The subject was brought up by Makarov in defense of the miners' relatively high wages:

> Thirty-two people were killed at the Yuzhno-Donbasskaya mine last year; the other day in Krasnodon sixty-two people were killed, and two are still missing. And by the way, three people were killed yesterday at the Moushke-tovskaya mine. So the miners have paid for their wages with their blood.

Interview with Yurii Makarov, in Donetsk, 24 June 1992.

15. Ibid.

16. Interview with Yurii Boldyrev, 1 July 1992.

17. Interview with Mikhail Krylov, 3 July 1992.

18. Peter Rutland, *Business Elites and Russian Economic Policy* (London: Royal Institute of International Affairs, 1992), 41–42.

19. Ibid.; Lopatin, *Rabochee Dvizhenie Kuzbassa,* 550–58, 565. Despite the unprecedented price increases for which the public was ill prepared, 1992 was a year of relative labor peace compared to 1991. Strikes by workers paid directly from the state budget (such as teachers and medical workers) accounted for some 90 percent of all strikes in the first quarter of 1992. Linda Cook, "Russia's Labor Relations: Consolidation or Disintegration?" in *Russia's Future: Consolidation or Disintegration,* edited by Douglas W. Blum (Boulder, Colo.: Westview Press, 1994), 73.

20. *Megapolis-Express,* 24 February 1993, 15.

21. *Izvestia,* 8 May 1993, cited in *RFE/RL Daily Report,* 11 May 1993. By early 1996, the coal industry remained second only to agriculture in state subsidies.

22. The decree, entitled "Concerning Measures for Stabilizing the Situation in the Coal Industry," also gave the industry more incentive to export. *RFE/RL Daily Report,* 22 June 1993.

23. *RFE/RL Daily Report,* 23 and 24 June 1993. As one Russian newspaper warned in its headline, "Coal prices are let go. So are miners." *Megapolis Express,* 30 June 1993.

24. Komersant no. 25, 21–27 June 1993, as translated in *Current Digest of the Post-Soviet Press* 45, no. 26 (1993).

25. *RFE/RL Daily Report,* 24 June 1993.

26. Ibid., 20 and 29 July 1993.

27. Ibid., 29 October 1993 and 15 November 1993.

28. The World Bank proposal spoke of the need to move much more quickly than the British government in closing down the coal industry, though the number of colliers in Britain declined from 500,000 in 1960 to 30,000 thirty years later, with, it should be recalled, considerable social and political turmoil. As to the latter point, the World Bank mentioned only briefly in its comprehensive initial draft that "To attempt mine closures without adequate preparation may result in extensive labor unrest." Such were the heady days of the international lending agencies in Russia before the sobering results of the 1993 elections. The final report, scheduled for publication shortly after the elections, was substantially revised to avoid "social distress and political tension" and published a year later. Though the scale and speed of the proposed layoffs were the same, the final proposal was subtitled, "Putting People First." "Russian Federation: Restructuring the Coal Industry: Putting People First," World Bank Report No. 13187–RU, 2 volumes, 12 December 1994.

29. Ibid., original emphasis, 13. The reason for the drastic reductions in the Kuzbass, about half of the total reductions for the Russian coal industry as a whole, was said to be the cost of freight transport.

30. On this point also see Simon Clarke and Peter Fairbrother, "After the Coup: The Workers' Movement in the Transition to a Market Economy," in *What About the Workers? Workers and the Transition to Capitalism in Russia,* edited by Simon Clarke et al. (London: Verson, 1993), 175.

31. This was certainly the case in December 1993 at the Dmitrova mine in Novokuznetsk, one of the first slated for closure, where miners seemed little concerned with the possibility of losing their jobs. Indeed, while miner leaders agreed with the need of closures in some cases, if provisions were made for new jobs and resettlement, the miners of Dmitrova, which had little economic prospect in any case, responded overwhelmingly in a survey that they preferred to continue working in their present positions to being given new jobs. Data provided by Konstantin Burnishev.

32. At the Derzhinsky mine in Prokop'evsk in December 1993, several miners summed up their situation thusly: "Everything is as it was" [*Kak vso bylo, tak vso est'*].

33. One of the NPG's basic demands was for an hourly wage rather than piece rate payments. Miners would avoid medical checkups because the discovery of silicosis meant lower-paying surface work. Filtzer, *Collapse of Perestroika,* 21.

34. Michael Bernstam and Thomas McCurdy, "Subsidies and Employment in the Russian Coal Industry," report published by Partners in Economic Reform, Moscow, 1994, 2–14, 15.

35. Rusugol is the Russian Coal Company that is the successor to the Coal Ministry. In a case typical of the post-Soviet era, Rusugol is part state ministry, distributing subsidies from Moscow throughout the coal fields, and part private corporation, seeking diamond and gold concessions and other profit-making enterprises unrelated to the coal industry.

36. Mines in Inta, which produce primarily energy coal, are paid on time by the government to prevent the shutting down of power plants, while mines in nearby Vorkuta, many of which produce coking coal, often go unpaid for several months. Strikes in Vorkuta over unpaid wages have failed to gain support in Inta, leading to considerable acrimony between miners within the region.

37. Interview by author with Vladimir Aksenov, in Novokuznetsk, December 1993.

38. Interview by author with Petr Bizyukov, in Kemerovo, November 1993. This was true even before the collapse of the Soviet Union. According to a regional people's deputy from Vorkuta in February 1991, "Barter is a noose around the neck of the labour movement. Management doses it out in small portions, like bones: Fight over it and don't bark . . . They have bought the working class with this barter." (cited in Mandel, *Perestroika and the Soviet People,* 162).

39. Rutland, *Business Elites,* 44.

40. In a study of several enterprises in the military industry, which has been especially hard-hit by the withdrawal of state subsidies, "The social safety net that is supposed to be administered by the central government is perceived as a failure by enterprises, which still feel obligated to pick up the slack." This holds true even for enterprises running in the red. The study concluded that these enterprise managers want to continue running most of their social facilities, with the general exception of housing, the most expensive item, though even here enterprises were moving ahead with new construction. Tova Perlmutter, "Reorganization of Social Services," in *Defense Industry Restructuring in Russia: Case Studies and Analysis,* edited by David Bernstein (Stanford: Center of International Security and Arms Control, December 1994), 186–88.

41. Simon Clarke, Peter Fairbrother, Vadim Borisov, and Petr Bizyukov, "The Privatization of Industrial Enterprises in Russia: Four Case Studies," *Europe-Asia Studies* 46, no. 2 (1994): 179–214.

42. Rutland, *Business Elites,* 44. In the coal industry, all enterprises, no matter how profitable, receive subsidies for social infrastructure, providing yet another example of how the Soviet welfare state was, and to a large degree still is, administered through the workplace. Bernstam and McCurdy, "Subsidies and Employment in the Russian Coal Industry."

43. This point is well made by Clarke, "Contradictions of State Socialism" and "Privatization."

44. For a more detailed account of these two cases, see Crowley and Siegelbaum, "Survival Strategies."

45. See chapter 5.

46. Interview with October NPG members, 25 June 1992.

47. The importance of directors appears to be especially crucial in the uncertain climate of institutional breakdown. This importance is exemplified in such cases as the Zasyadko mine (see chap. 4), and the cases of economically successful enterprises combined with increased paternalism described in Clarke et al., "Privatization of Industrial Enterprises."

48. Cook, "Russia's Labor Relations," 71.

49. Ibid. On the centrality of labor pacts for the success of economic liberalization, see Adam Przeworski, *Markets and Democracy: Political and Economic Reforms in Eastern Europe and Latin America* (Cambridge: Cambridge University Press, 1991), 180–87.

50. While the FNPR has threatened strikes, it has never actually called out workers, and it is unlikely that it could do so. On this point see Cook, "Russia's Labor Relations," 75.

51. Clarke and Fairbrother, "After the Coup," 184.

52. Ibid. Thus, while the rhetoric of the official unions is often against the government, the unions are "absolutely dependent on the government for retaining their power, privileges, and wealth. The government only had to hint at removing" these privileges for the unions to knuckle under. Clarke, Fairbrother, and Borisov, *Workers' Movement*, 406.

53. Ibid., 194, 195.

54. On the NPG's strike-proneness, see Cook, "Russia's Labor Relations."

55. On the reasons for the limited success of sectoral unions, see Clarke and Fairbrother, "After the Coup," 189.

56. According to one mine's official trade union chair, "At first the NPG . . . pushed aside health issues, daily life concerns, and all the rest. But now the NPG takes care of everything up to trade and the distribution of foodstuffs—that is, those things for which the NPG leaders always cursed us." *Pozitsiia,* 6–12 May 1992, p. 1. Yet given the union's militance, if only on bread-and-butter issues, it is surely an overstatement to assert that "The NPG was reproducing the traditional forms of Soviet trade unionism with a vengeance." Clarke and Fairbrother, "After the Coup," 181.

57. Interview with Krylov.

58. Clarke, Fairbrother, and Borisov, *Workers' Movement,* 134–35, 141–42.

59. Interview with October miners, July 1992. In this way the workerist mentality described here could move fairly easily from arguing that workers as a class should enjoy the fruits of their labor to arguing that workers as individuals should.

60. L. A. Gordon, E. B. Gruzdeva, and V. V. Komarovskii, *Shakhtery–92: Sotsialnoe soznanie i sotsialnnii oblik rabochei elity v poslesotsialisticheskoi Rossii* (Moscow: Progress-Kompleks, 1992), translated as Leonid Gordon, "Russian Workers and Democracy," *International Journal of Sociology* (winter 1993–94): 3–99.

61. Gordon, "Russian Workers and Democracy," 36.

62. Ibid., 38.

63. Ibid., 44.

64. The social upheavals might include "struggle against the emergent bourgeoisie, Sacco and Vanzetti and the electric chair—anything you can think of," even "civil war." Ibid., 41.

65. Ibid., 46. As Gordon notes, no doubt with some understatement, it "seems that the time when the majority would accept the domination of private property in large industries as something natural has not yet come" (47). Indeed, even among these "worker elite," the new order was hardly "natural." Turning to the subject of the recent liberalization of prices, Gordon reported that "Pavel R." argued bluntly, "The government should be made to pass a law stipulating imprisonment for price increases, as was done in 1937. The prices will immediately go down and everything will be normal" (51).

66. Clarke and Fairbrother, "After the Coup," 198.

67. Vladimir Gimpelson, "Why Is There No Mass Unemployment," unpublished document.

68. Clarke, Fairbrother, and Borisov, Workers' Movement, 164.

69. V. Polterovich, "Ekonomitcheskaya reforma 1992 goda: bitva pravitelstva s trudovymi kollektivami," Ekonomika i matematicheskiye metody, no. 4 (1993).

70. Cited by Gimpelson, "No Mass Unemployment," who also cites twelve indepth interviews he conducted with managers between October 1992 and May 1993 as supporting the survey data.

71. This situation is discussed in K. Pistor, "Privatization and Corporate Governance in Russia: An Empirical Study" (paper presented at the Workshop on Russian Economic Reform, Stanford University, 22–23 November 1993). On earlier Labor Collective meetings, see chapters 3 and 4.

72. Gimpelson, "No Mass Unemployment"; Clarke, "Privatization," 217.

73. Pistor, "Privatization and Corporate Governance."

74. Gimpelson, "No Mass Unemployment"; Clarke, "Privatization."

75. Izvestia, 7 December 1993.

76. Clarke, "Contradictions of State Socialism," 22.

77. Document from the executive committee of the NPG, "Novoye rabochee i profsoyuznoye dvizheniye," no. 1, Russko-Amerikanski Fond Profsoyuznykh issledovaniya i obutcheniya, 1993, cited in Gimpelson, "No Mass Unemployment."

78. Clarke argues that the impact of labor shortage on workers' relative power within the enterprise has been exaggerated. See Clarke, "Contradictions of State Socialism." But from the workers' perspective, the change from facing great demand for one's labor to facing the threat of unemployment, with all the consequent changes in one's relative power, is certainly the most dramatic they face.

79. The average duration was eighteen days per employee. Gimpelson, "No Mass Unemployment."

80. The phrase of "internal reserve army" for auxiliary workers is Clarke's ("Contradictions of State Socialism," 20–23). Women, who disproportionately find themselves among those "peripheral" to production, are also often the first to be let go. This practice is often justified on the assumption that a male breadwin-

ner remains, and that the woman's labor is needed at home. Thus, the division of workers along gender lines precedes the division of workers into core and auxiliary.

81. Pistor, "Privatization and Corporate Governance," 17.

82. Ibid., 14. Both of the exceptions involved other managers acting to prevent an outside takeover supported by the director. She also notes that the board (or *council* in Russian) of directors is usually subordinate to the director.

83. Though the plant was now declared a joint-stock company, it continued to mobilize workers from all of its subdivisions for planting, weeding, and the harvesting of potatoes and vegetables from the state farm subordinate to the plant. These campaigns were organized by the plant's trade union. *MZ*, 4 September 1993.

84. When asked why he started the conversation with such a topic, the deputy director responded because this was absurd for a joint-stock company since it ate so heavily into profits. He cited the cost of maintaining housing alone at 16 billion rubles a year. *Kuznetskii Rabochii*, 11 November 93. Pistor's survey of enterprises also found formal ownership of social objects by the municipality, with continued funding by enterprises.

85. The only problem the plant was facing in the carrying out of these schemes was a shortage of construction workers for the building projects, "despite the high pay." *MZ*, 4 September 1993.

86. Interview with L. Reginskaya, in Novokuznetsk, December 1993. In further indication of the plant's paternalist bent and following a time-honored tradition, the directorship (the director and two deputies) in the second quarter of 1993 listened to the concerns and requests of 439 people during "personal reception hours," while shop bosses received an additional 609 over the same period. The majority came with questions about the distribution of consumer goods, the rendering of aid after a fire or robbery, or to ask for a loan. *MZ*, 14 September 1993.

87. *MZ*, 7 August 1993.

88. Ibid.

89. *MZ*, 14 September 1993.

90. Data provided by Lyuba Reginskaya.

91. *MZ*, 31 August 1993.

92. Having shown the stick, Kustov went on to discuss the plans for expanding the plant's social infrastructure that would presumably benefit those employees who made the cut. *MZ*, 4 September 1993.

93. *MZ*, 7 August 1993.

94. In an indication that something of a moral economy still existed, the only violators of discipline who were not fired were those with five or more children. The head of the blast furnace shop claimed that in the first eight months of 1993, there were 131 violators of labor discipline, of whom 129 were fired, the 2 exceptions being those with large families. *MZ*, 18 September 1993.

95. Why a trade union official should be concerned with firing workers for drinking after work was a question left unasked.

96. The participant at the roundtable most sympathetic to the side of workers was a representative of the city's police department. He argued that the statistics on

increases in labor violations were flawed, since only now was the plant showing a strong interest in counting and documenting the violations. Another article claimed that since "everybody knows the reality of forthcoming layoffs," the number of "violations" had decreased somewhat. *MZ*, 18 September 1993.

97. Ibid.

98. *MZ*, 14 September 1993.

99. *MZ*, 18 September 1993.

100. Ibid.

101. Underscoring as well the cozy relationship between union and management, the deputy director claimed unique authority in explaining his decision to leave the trade union: before being promoted to management, he was the combine's trade union chair. "I Am Leaving the Trade Union," *MZ*, 23 October 1993. After a few months, of the seven hundred managers who had been trade union members, only thirty-five remained.

102. *Trud*, 30 November 1993. As regional paper *Kuzbass* noted (25 November 1993), "As a rule in these battles between the trade union and the enterprise, it is the top managers who are the initiators," suggesting this was not an isolated incident, even within the Kuzbass.

103. Interview by author with S. Skripnichenko, in Novokuznetsk, 9 December 1993.

104. Ibid.

105. *Trud*, 30 November 1993; *Kuzbass*, 25 November 1993.

106. This explanation was given to the author by trade union chair Skripnichenko.

107. According to the chair, after the conflict many workers asked why they should pay union dues when management now handled "social questions." Interview with Skripnichenko.

108. Likewise, the article maintained, only through a collective contract signed by the trade union could workers influence wages. "Unfortunately, many workers naively imagine the future under the new form of property, because they don't know the law." *MZ*, 17 August 1993.

109. Interview with Skripnichenko. Most other enterprise trade unions had not even tried to fight. In a discussion at the neighboring Kuznetskii Metallurgical Complex of how the "pocket trade union" at West Siberian was punished for trying to become involved in work-related issues, one Kuznetskii worker replied, "Our trade union hasn't even tried to stick its head out of the pocket. It's too warm and cozy there." Interview with Kuznetskii workers, 10 December 1993.

110. Filtzer, *Collapse of Perestroika*, 220.

111. In response to what one observer has called "an open, deliberate, massive offensive against workers' living standards" by the Russian government, workers, especially miners, have staged hunger strikes, blocked railways, and issued bomb threats, but few groups of workers have successfully carried out large-scale collective actions. David Mandel, "The Russian Labour Movement and Politics," *Labour Focus on Eastern Europe*, no. 52 (autumn 1995): 41, 50.

Chapter 8

1. Herbert Kitshelt, "The Formation of Party Systems in East Central Europe," *Politics and Society* 20, no.1 (March 1992), esp. 16–27.

2. Andrew Wilson, "The Growing Challenge to Kiev from the Donbass," *RFE/RL Research Report* 2, no. 33 (20 August 1993): 8.

3. *Zhizn'*, 15 June 1993. Thus in Ukraine ethnic and national issues, such the question of Ukrainian as the state language, overlap with class and economic concerns, in particular whether state support and subsidies should be geared toward agriculture or toward industry. These conflicts coincide on the crucial issues of state building, economic reform, and policy toward Russia: Ukrainian nationalists and western Ukrainians favor building a strong independent state above all, while those working in industry and eastern Ukrainians generally favor strong trade and other contacts with Russia, and they are not willing to suffer economic hardship, even temporarily, for the sake of a strong Ukraine.

4. 25 June 1992, DOHIP. Samofalov's address was prompted by his return from a picket of the parliament in Kiev, attended by miners and other workers from the Donbass, where these demands were advanced.

5. *Vechernii Donetsk,* 6 June 1993; *Zhizn'* (Donetsk), 6 June 1993.

6. *Vechernii Donetsk*, 11 June 1993. The demands for regional independence and a referendum had reportedly been worked out at a meeting of Donbass miners at Novogrodovka in May; there Ukraine's policies on taxation, banking, and customs came under heavy condemnation. *Zhizn'*, 11 June 1993; *KAS-KOR Digest* (Moscow) 3, no. 6 (June 1993).

7. *Zhizn'*, 30 June 1993.

8. See chapter 4 for discussion of the Zasiad'ko mine.

9. *Vechernii Donetsk,* 12, 15, 16, 18 June 1993. On the very high level of distrust in Kravchuk and the parliament in the region as compared with that of other regions in Ukraine, see Kathleen Mihalisko, "Ukrainians and Their Leaders at a Time of Crisis," *RFE/RL Research Report* 2, no. 31 (30 July 1993).

10. One reason the strike was so successful was that, in contrast to previous miners' strikes, managers and local governments were not opposed to but openly supported the miners' demands. While the strike was started spontaneously by coal miners, directors wholeheartedly supported the demands—aimed at Kiev and not management. Coal directors and other industrialists, in fact, refused to open talks with Kiev on economic questions until the strikers' political demands were met. *Zhizn'*, 12, 15 June 1993; *Vechernii Donetsk,* 12, 18 June 1993. Yet there is little evidence that this was a "director's strike" in the sense of being planned and controlled by enterprise directors, as some accounts characterized the events. *New York Times,* 17 July 1993.

11. The more convincing definitions describe the plan for a "free economic zone" in terms of greater autonomy for the region. Illyushenko, the head of the Donetsk coal trust Donetskugol', defines the goal as allowing the region to form its own budget, to direct the policy of regional banks, and to negotiate economic agreements with neighboring regions in Russia. *Zhizn'*, 30 June 1993.

12. *Segodnya,* 23 March 1994, as translated in *CDSP* 46, no. 12 (1994).

13. *Moscow News,* 18 June 1993.

14. Ukrainian coal would seem to be one answer for the country's energy needs, of which Ukraine at present can meet only 30 percent. Yet thermal stations now rely on oil and gas more than coal; Donbass coal is costly, and in the present economic and political conditions, production is unreliable. David Marples, "Ukraine, Belarus, and the Energy Dilemma," *RFE/RL Research Report* 2, no. 27 (2 July 1993). Production has declined to such an extent that Ukraine has had to stop exporting coal to nearby Bulgaria, despite the drastic need for hard currency. In fact, despite having the Soviet Union's largest coal basin, Ukraine produced only 70 percent of the coal it consumed before the collapse of the Union. David Marples, "Turmoil in the Donbass: The Economic Realities," *Report on the USSR* (12 October 1990), 15. Coal presently accounts for 34 percent of Ukraine's fuel consumption.

15. The party is often derided as the "party of the red directors." On the formation of the Labor Party and its platform, see *Pervaya Linaya,* 5 and 11 January 1993; *Vechernii Donetsk,* 23 and 30 December 1992.

16. Monika Jung, "The Donbass Factor in the Ukrainian Elections," *RFE/RL Research Report,* no. 12 (25 March 1994).

17. Ibid. This suggests that Krylov, as leader of the Donbass miners, continued to argue for both market allocation and workers' control over their product.

18. Ibid. Their ability to appeal to workers as a group was further weakened when both the independent miners and the once-official unions nominated separate slates of candidates.

19. Ibid.; Jarolsaw Maryniuk, "Demographics of Party Support in Ukraine," *RFE/RL Research Report,* reprinted in *The Ukrainian Weekly,* 26 December 1993 and 2 January 1994.

20. Maryniuk, "Demographics of Party Support."

21. Dominique Arel and Andrew Wilson, "The Ukrainian Parliamentary Elections," *RFE/RL Research Report* 3, no. 26 (1 July 1994).

22. In their study of Kuzbass miner activists, Gordon, Gruzdeva and Komarovskii note that "on the ethnic question, the direct rejection of state socialist ideology [on other questions] by worker activists is replaced by the preservation and purification of the international values it proclaimed." *Shakhteri–92,* 48.

23. Jung, "Donbass Factor."

24. "Election Program of the Luhansk Oblast Organization of the Communist Party of Ukraine," *Vybor: gazeta sotsialisticheskoi orientatsii* (Luhansk), no. 16 (1994), cited in Arel and Wilson, "Ukrainian Parliamentary Elections."

25. David Marples, "Ukraine After the Presidential Election," *RFE/RL Research Report* 3, no. 31 (12 August 1994).

26. Dominique Arel and Andrew Wilson, "Ukraine under Kuchma: Back to 'Eurasia'?" *RFE/RL Research Report* 3, no. 32 (19 August 1994).

27. Arel and Wilson, "Ukrainian Parliamentary Elections," 14.

28. The Kuzbass was one of few places outside of Moscow and Leningrad to mobilize during the failed putsch, when some forty-one mines went on strike after the announcement of the coup attempt in August 1991. See Lopatin, *Rabochee*

Dvizhenie Kuzbassa, 498–520. While Clarke and Fairbrother ("After the Coup") see that as a modest turnout and evidence of the miners' conditional support for "liberal reformers," it appears to be a case of seeing the glass as half empty. They also claim, without providing any evidence, that many of the mines that did strike did so at the prodding of mine directors. Why mine directors in the Kuzbass would (successfully) convince their workers to strike against the coup while managers in most every other industry and region did not do so is not explained.

29. Lopatin, *Rabochee Dvizhenie Kuzbassa.*

30. FBIS, 3 and 15 March 1993.

31. *RFE/RL Daily Report,* 12 April 1993. He subsequently broke the promise of no price increases for coal when he attempted to liberalize coal prices three months later.

32. Thus Golikov, a strong Yeltsin supporter, blamed Yeltsin's Prime Minister Chernomyrdin for the coal industry's problems. "We've asked every government for a plan for the development of the coal industry, including the number of mines that need to be closed. We've still gotten no answer. Chernomyrdin refuses to talk with the miners. Well so did Ryzhkov, Pavlov, Gorbachev. I don't need to remind you where they are now." *Pulse,* news program of Kuzbass Television/Radio, 21 November 1993.

33. Certainly it was here, with the liberal government in place, that the miner-leaders became detached from their constituency, rather than earlier when the Communist Party remained in power, as Clarke and Fairbrother ("Strikes of 1991") claim.

34. In the 1991 survey, 25 percent of Kuzbass residents said the authority of the workers' committees had risen, 27 percent said the committees' authority had declined, and 10 percent said it had no authority; by 1992, only 5 percent said its authority had risen, while 36 percent said it had declined and 29 percent said it had no authority. Likewise, by 1992 workers' committee leader Golikov proved to be very unpopular among Kuzbass residents: 61 percent disapproved of him, while only 7.4 percent approved. Data provided by the Kuzbass Center for the Study of Public Opinion at Kemerovo State University.

35. Prices in coal regions were sometimes 50 percent more than in surrounding regions. Clarke and Fairbrother, "After the Coup," 186–87.

36. He continued, "I said to myself, 'Here are the real people [*Vot on narod*].'" Interview by author with Gennadii Mityakin in Kemerovo, 26 November 1993. Many other political actors dated their political awakening to the first miners' strike, speaking of what they had done "after the strike."

37. Vladimir Lebedev, a candidate on the RDDR party list, made this point most strongly, though in his political views he was moderate relative to other liberals. Interview by author in Kemerov, 25 November 1993. One candidate, Bella Denisenko, a former people's deputy in the Russian parliament and the acknowledged leader of Russia's Choice in the Kuzbass, had risen to national political prominence by joining with three Kuzbass miners in a 1991 hunger strike but now candidly expressed a readiness to jettison her former partners since they were not willing to swallow the bitter pill of further shock therapy and mine closures. Interview by author in Novokuznetsk, 9 December 1994.

38. According to a survey done in November 1992 by the Kuzbass Center for the Study of Public Opinion, the regional soviet received a positive rating of 26, while the Congress of People's Deputies, the Supreme Soviet, and the president all received negative ratings. Mikhail Kislyuk, the head of the regional administration, received a rating of negative 44.

39. Nevertheless, Russia's Choice, the bloc most closely associated with the liberals, fielded candidates in every race in the Kuzbass.

40. To the extent that anti-Semitic sentiments are related to fascism in Russia and elsewhere, an extreme form was presented by Vladislav Streligov, the former deputy chair of the Kuzbass soviet and a close ally of Tuleev, at the end of an extended conversation on Kuzbass politics. Apparently dropping his guard, he conveyed his view of the world as one controlled by a conspiracy of Jewish bankers. Interview with author in Novokuznetsk, 8 December 1993. Anti-Semitic statements, if not in this extreme form, were not the sole property of this political wing, however. Mityakin, the Russia's Choice candidate for the federal assembly, explained his quite strained relationship with Governor Kislyuk by referring to the latter's ambitious nature as a product of his being a Jew. (Kislyuk, for his part, referred to himself as Orthodox when a visitor inquired about a Roman Catholic Madonna statue in his office.)

41. Data provided by the Kuzbass Center for the Study of Public Opinion at Kemerovo State University.

42. According to one longtime political observer in the region, Tuleev did not win many votes in miners' districts during his presidential bid in 1991. Leonid Lopatin, interview by author, in Kemerovo, 29 November 1993.

43. Tuleev flew to Moscow to meet the coup leaders, later returning to Kemerovo, saying he supported the coup's goals, but found the means unconstitutional. Lopatin, *Rabochee Dvizhenie Kuzbassa,* 503–6, 511–13.

44. Tuleev claims to be studying for an advanced degree in psychology, in order to "better relate to the people." Interview with author, in Kemerovo, 29 November 1993.

45. Though the Georgian Stalin successfully employed Russian nationalism, Tuleev's physical features clearly mark him as an ethnic "other." While Tuleev is addressed in public as Aman Gumirovich, his name officially appeared on the ballot as Aman-Gel'dy Moldagasyevich.

46. AVISTA data base.

47. As Aslanidi explained during his campaign, ". . . namely the market and democracy allow people to live better and more free than we lived under 'developed socialism.' There, in market conditions, people who work—I've seen them myself—are unfettered, smiling, free. There are unemployed—yes, there are serious problems, and society there sympathizes and takes care of these problems. But what is important is something else: there every person who is not working *dreams* of becoming a working person—there's a powerful stimulus for progress!" *NG,* 23 November 1993 (original emphasis).

48. According to Golikov, "Such a statement against one part of the democratic wing during an election campaign is extremely destructive. . . . We have more serious opponents, with whom we must fight." *NG,* 25 November 1993.

49. Such a level of dissatisfaction was probably true for workers throughout Russia. *Izvestia* argued before the election that a social explosion was possible at any moment in any region. *Izvestia*, 26 November 1993. On the tension in the mining regions, see also *Izvestia*, 24 and 30 November 1993.

50. By percentage of valid votes cast.

51. One interesting part of the Russian elections was the fate of candidates from the industrial elite, who, despite their enormous resources, did quite poorly. In the Kuzbass, Yurii Malyshev, Russia's top coal boss (as head of Rusugol) lost his bid for the upper house, despite being responsible for the distribution of coal subsidies throughout Russia, a point of no small importance for the Kuzbass. For all his efforts at spreading largesse throughout the region, Malyshev was derided as playing "the good uncle" as well as being a member of the Nomenklatura. Another coal boss, A. Botalov, lost despite being opposed by two female candidates with similar platforms—both emphasizing "social protection" for the population. For more on this question, see Stephen Crowley, "The Kuzbass: Liberals, Populists and Labor," in *Russia's Protodemocracy in Action: Perspectives on the Election of 1993*, edited by Timothy Colton and Jerry Hough (Washington, D.C.: Brookings Institution Press, 1997).

52. Aslanidi's performance as a candidate before miners' collectives strongly contrasts with his leading of a meeting of Kuzbass miners' representatives two years earlier (also attended by the author) that voted to end a two-month strike aimed at gaining Russia sovereignty. Aslanidi has become more soft-spoken and reflective in a workers' environment that often chooses dynamic and even gruff leaders.

53. The paper had gradually shifted from being a chronicle of the workers' movement to an organ of the liberal political wing of the Kuzbass. See Clarke, Fairbrother and Borisov, *Workers' Movement.*

54. Journalists from the paper attended Aslanidi's campaign functions as agents of the candidate, introducing him with a rousing speech before sitting down to report on the event as a correspondent for the paper. *Nasha Gazeta* journalists also ran press conferences for the candidate, sitting on the other end of the microphones from their colleagues at other papers.

55. Author's transcript.

56. For example, the *RFE/RL Daily Report* cites an AFP story which argued, "In private . . . members of the Russian government are saying that, in the new year, the Yeltsin leadership will have to follow the example of Thatcherite Britain and face down a challenge from organized labor. They say that the only industries in which independent unions are strong enough to mount a sustained strike are coal mining and defense production and that the government could defeat a strike in either. This is because coal stocks are high following the general fall in production. . . ." Elizabeth Teague, "Gaidar Warns Insolvent Firms," *RFE/RL Daily Report*, 15 November 1993. Such plans were evidently put aside when the government parties were defeated in the polls.

57. David Ost, "Labor, Class and Democracy: Shaping Political Antagonisms in Post-Communist Society," in *Markets, States, and Democracy: The Political*

Economy of Post-Communist Transformation, edited by Beverly Crawford (Boulder, CO: Westview Press, 1995).

58. Beverly Crawford suggests the metaphor of workers being allergic to class-based appeals; I have here changed it to workers being immunized by the experience of communism. Beverly Crawford, "Markets, States, and Democracy: A Framework for Analysis of the Political Economy of Post-Communist Transformation," in *Markets, States, and Democracy.*

59. Gordon and his colleagues, reporting on their in-depth interviewing of miner-activists, note that while the respondents all agree that, as one puts it, "without a political wing, the workers' movement can't make it," the idea of a workers' party is almost never mentioned. The authors conclude that the possibility "seems to be subconsciously rejected by the workers." Gordon, Gruzdeva, and Komarovskii, *Shakteri–92,* 57.

60. Veljko Vujacic, "Gennadiy Zyuganov and the 'Third Road,'" *Post-Soviet Affairs* 12, no. 2 (April–June 1996); David Remnick, "Hammer, Sickle, and Book," *New York Review of Books* 43, no. 9 (23 May 1996).

61. Vujacic, "Gennadiy Zyuganov."

62. Boris Kagarlitsky, "Russian Trade Unions and the 1995 Elections," *Labour Focus on Eastern Europe,* no. 52 (autumn 1995).

63. Is social democracy a real alternative for post-Communist workers? Or is it simply to be expected that miners and others will support authoritarian and paternalistic solutions to their dilemma, since they are positioned to be likely "losers" in a market economy? Strictly speaking, social democracy in the Western European sense is an unlikely prospect in the short term, since there is no expanding pie to redistribute, and a capitalist economy is not already in place. Yet social democracy in the postcommunist context might be one in which labor actively participates in making political decisions. While labor will never have the resources of the state or industrial managers, it may have the power to veto some of their decisions. Both the authoritarian populists and the liberals would prefer that labor not actively participate in the political process, the former because their positions would be challenged and the latter because a docile labor force would be more competitive in the world economy. A negotiated solution would in some sense involve the working class negotiating its own demise. Yet the terms—including new jobs, retraining, the pace of deindustrialization and the strength of the social safety net—are important and would at least be partly of workers' own choosing. It would not be a utopia, to be sure, but workers well understand the bind they are in. Though the costs to the state of such a negotiated solution would be high, the alternative might be quite a bit starker. For empirical support of social democratic attitudes in Russia, see Robert Brym, "Reevaluating Mass Support for Political and Economic Change in Russia," *Europe-Asia Studies,* 48, no. 5 (July 1996).

64. As Clarke, Fairbrother, and Borisov conclude, "In the absence of a workers' movement through which workers can articulate their anger, through which they can have some hope of changing the system in ways that can improve their own lives, they will vote for populist demagogues. Not in hope, nor in expectation, but in frustration and despair" (*Workers' Movement,* 411).

65. The survey was conducted by VTsIOM. "Who Voted for LDPR," *Izvestia,* 30 December 1993.

66. An independent trade union at the steel combine has turned to the fascist organization Russian National Unity to defend workers' interests. According to Russian researchers, the ground for this alliance was paved by privatization: "Conducted almost exclusively for the benefit of the [enterprise] directors' corps and local administrations, it in effect made workers into serfs of the factory bosses." Further, "directors' accounts in foreign banks are growing fat, mansions are springing up, and the workers are watching as property that until quite recently they believed to belong to 'all the people' melts away." Indeed, Russian National Unity appeals directly to class interests, in proposing "that enterprises be transferred to the ownership of the labor collectives without compensation and that workers' control be introduced at production facilities." Moreover, it intends to defend these interests not only with rhetoric, but by force: where the fascists have intervened, enterprises have been seized, directors have been barred from their plants, and their houses have burned down. "Fascists Who Speak the Truth: Red-Brown Hues in the Russian Workers Movement," *Novya Ezhedevnaya Gazeta;* translated in *Current Digest of the Post-Soviet Press* 94, no. 19 (1994): 5–6; "Northern Steel as a Bulwark of Russian Fascism," *Izvestia,* 11 May 1994, as translated in *Current Digest of the Post-Soviet Press* 66, no. 19 (1994); Kirill Buketov, "Russian Fascism and Russian Fascists," document distributed on-line by KAS-KOR, Moscow, 20 November 1994.

67. Mary Louise Vitelli, director of Partners in Economic Reform, Russia.

Chapter 9

1. For evidence of a strong relationship between paternalism and labor quiescence in coal communities in the United States, see John Gaventa, *Power and Powerlessness: Quiescence and Rebellion in an Appalachian Valley* (Urbana: University of Illinois Press, 1980).

2. Burawoy, *Politics of Production,* 195–97.

3. For example, when miners first engaged the Soviet state during their first strike, they showed signs of seeing it as omnipotent—they called for state and Communist Party officials to come from Moscow to personally sign the many promises conceded to the miners, and they did not question the government's concessions, no matter how lavish. The miners of 1989 believed that the Soviet state was a powerful institution capable of fulfilling their demands; that it proved unwilling or incapable, especially with a signed document as proof of its failure, led to rapid disillusionment with the state, first as a body to be appealed to with grievances and later as an entity that served any purpose at all.

4. Burawoy and Lukacs, *Radiant Past.*

5. Thus a focus on the "point of production" and shop-floor relations is not sufficient. Burawoy, *Politics of Production*; Filtzer, *Collapse of Perestroika.* Equally, if not more, important are the enterprises as communities, and their ties to the larger political economy, that had so much to do with how workers and their

families not only worked, but lived their lives. Indeed, it was through concerns not only with the politics of production, but the control of the distribution of their product throughout society that drove the miners' militance.

6. Michael Kazin, *The Populist Persuasion* (New York: Basic Books, 1995).

7. Sidney Tarrow, "Mentalities," 192–96; and Tarrow, *Democracy and Disorder: Protest and Politics in Italy, 1965–1975* (Oxford: Oxford University Press, 1989).

8. With the first waves of unemployment falling most heavily in women, they were certainly among the most disaffected workers. See Judith Shapiro, "The Industrial Labour Force," in *Soviet Women and Perestroika,* edited by Mary Buckley (Cambridge: Cambridge University Press, 1992); Filtzer, *Collapse of Perestroika,* 163–80.

9. By the phrase "standing on the periphery," I intend to acknowledge that no attempt has been made to fully employ either paradigm, for example by using game theory or in-depth textual analysis. This limitation reflects both the author's own shortcomings and the prejudice that, in this case at least, not much explanatory power would be gained through such methods.

10. As Peter Evans quite reasonably put it: "One must combine conventional political economic analysis, which focuses on how people get what they want, with cultural approaches, which help us understand the nature of the preferences themselves." "The Role of Theory in Comparative Politics," 9.

11. At the very least, one would need to significantly broaden the perspective of orthodox economics in order to make sense of this case. As Peter Murrell argues, defending his evolutionary approach, "The behavior of economic agents [in the evolutionary view] is a product of both present incentives and of the historical and social processes that have shaped these agents. Since this is especially so for perceptions of the world and for information acquisition, problems of incomplete information and of learning are especially important in times of great change. . . . [E]conomic agents accumulate knowledge in a learning-by-doing process that is shaped by their historical experience." Murrell, "What is Shock Therapy: What Did it Do in Poland and Russia?" *Post-Soviet Affairs* 9, no. 3 (1993): 119.

12. Likewise, the argument by many structural Marxists is that not only are interests clearly defined and we can know them, but any action deviating from these interests must be explained by outside intervention and influence—in this case manipulation by Communist Party elites and liberal intellectuals. This is essentially the argument Clarke and his collaborators give for the paradox posed by the miners' actions in *What About the Workers?; The Workers' Movement in Russia.*

13. *New York Times,* 15 June 1990. Romanian miners also dramatically changed their actions and demands over time.

14. Laba, *Roots of Solidarity*; David Ost, *Solidarity and the Politics of Anti-Politics* (Philadelphia: Temple University Press, 1990); Jadwiga Staniszkis, *Poland's Self-Limiting Revolution* (Princeton: Princeton University Press, 1984); Touraine et al., *Solidarity: Poland, 1980–81.* While Polish workers, unlike Soviet coal miners, were able to unite across industries, there was a remarkable similarity in the demands of Polish workers and Soviet miners, including the use of the labor theory

of value. See Laba, *Roots of Solidarity*; Maurice Glasman, "The Great Deformation: Polanyi, Poland and the Terrors of Planned Spontaneity," *New Left Review*, no. 205 (May–June 1994).

15. The dependence of the worker and the state enterprise is a product of the shortage economy, itself a result of economic centralization. Thus, where the economy has been more greatly centralized, such as the former Soviet republics, one would expect this mutual dependence to be stronger than in a relatively less centralized economy, such as Hungary or Poland. Moreover, shortages, especially in the consumer sector, were alleviated to a greater extent in some Eastern European societies through private farming, the toleration of petty entrepreneurship, and the shorter legacy of Communist Party rule.

16. Kennedy, *Professionals, Power and Solidarity*.

17. David Stark, "From System Identity to Organizational Diversity: Analyzing Social Change in Eastern Europe," *Contemporary Sociology* (1992): 299.

18. One clear analogy with the steel enterprises discussed here are the company towns of early capitalism. Yet ironically, while enterprise dependence in the former Soviet Union appears to be a case of a bloated welfare state, it was the establishment of the welfare state in capitalist societies that finally ended workers' near-total dependence on the employer. By guaranteeing the provision of a minimum standard of living, regardless of one's work performance, the welfare state ended the employers' direct control over the reproduction of the labor force. See Burawoy, *Politics of Production,* 125–26.

19. To call such items "selective incentives" is misleading in at least two respects: they were originally intended not to retain members in the trade union, but workers in the enterprise, and they have become the primary service these organizations provide. On "selective incentives" as applied to trade union membership, see Mancur Olson, *The Logic of Collective Action: Public Goods and the Theory of Groups* (Cambridge: Harvard University Press, 1977), and the critical discussion in Colin Crouch, *Trade Unions: The Logic of Collective Action* (London: Fontana, 1982).

20. On the corporatist bent of these trade unions, see Cook, "Labor's Response."

21. See also Clarke, Fairbrother, and Borisov, *Workers' Movement,* chapter 7; David Mandel, "The Russian Labour Movement and Politics," *Labour Focus on Eastern Europe,* no. 52 (autumn 1995).

22. See Walder, "Factory and Managers," esp. 249–53. In the former Soviet Union, such positions have become even more directly political: As noted earlier, director Sledenev of the Donetskii steel plant was elected to the Ukrainian Supreme Soviet on the basis of his position at the plant, joining many other industrialists to form powerful blocs in the Ukrainian and Russian parliaments. Efim Zviagil'skii, director of the paternalistic Zasiad'ko mine, was elected member of parliament and mayor of Donetsk and was appointed acting prime minister of Ukraine for close to a year (before fleeing the country on charges of using his office to enrich himself). These political positions are often used to seek contacts, both foreign and domestic, for furthering the economic base on which their power rests.

23. On this point see also Clarke, "Privatization."

24. Indeed, as the miners' experience shows, the ability of managers to control such institutions is not absolute. Thus, managers must delicately attempt to maintain a paternalism that insures their continued control without provoking concerted action by workers that might remove them from office.

25. The work of economic historian Douglass North makes one cautious in predicting the rapid demise of such institutions, no matter how revolutionary the change in economic structures or even property rights. See North, *Institutions*.

26. See also Clarke, "Privatization."

27. Karl Polanyi, *The Great Transformation* (Boston: Beacon Press, [1944] 1957).

Selected Bibliography

Almond, Gabriel. "Communism and Political Culture Theory." *Comparative Politics* 15 (1983).

Almond. Gabriel. "The Study of Political Culture." In *A Discipline Divided*, edited by Gabriel Almond. Newbury Park, Calif.: Sage, 1990.

Almond, Gabriel, and Sidney Verba. *The Civic Culture*. Princeton: Princeton University Press, 1963.

Althauser, R., and A. Kalleberg. "Firms, Occupations and the Structure of Labor Markets." In *Sociological Perspectives on Labor Markets*, edited by Ivar Berg. New York: Academic Press,1981.

Andriyanov, V. "Gornyi udar," *Dialog,* no. 1 (1990).

Andrle, Vladimir. *Workers in Stalin's Russia*. New York: St. Martin's Press, 1988.

Arel, Dominique, and Andrew Wilson. "Ukraine Under Kuchma: Back to 'Eurasia'?" *RFE/RL Research Report* 3, no. 32 (19 August 1994).

Arel, Dominique, and Andrew Wilson. "The Ukrainian Parliamentary Elections." *RFE/RL Research Report* 3, no. 26 (1 July 1994).

Bendix, Reinhard. *Work and Authority in Industry*. Berkeley: University of California Press, 1956.

Bergsten, George, and Russell Bova. "Worker Power under Communism: The Interplay of Exit and Voice." *Comparative Economic Studies* 32, no.1 (spring 1990).

Bernstein, David, ed. *Defense Industry Restructuring in Russia: Case Studies and Analysis*. Stanford: Center of International Security and Arms Control, December 1994.

Bialer, Seweryn. *Stalin's Successors: Leadership, Stability and Change in the Soviet Union*. New York: Cambridge University Press, 1980.

Braverman, Harry. *Labor and Monopoly Capital*. New York: Monthly Review Press, 1974.

Brecher, J. "Uncovering the Hidden History of the American Workplace." *Review of Radical Political Economics*, no. 4 (1979).

Breslauer, George. "On the Adaptability of Soviet Welfare-State Authoritarianism." In *The Soviet Polity in the Modern Era,* edited by Erik Hoffman and Robin F. Laird. New York: Aldine, 1984.

Brown, Archie, ed. *Political Culture and Communist Studies*. New York: M. E. Sharpe, 1984.

Brym, Robert. "Reevaluating Mass Support for Political and Economic Change in Russia." *Europe-Asia Studies* 48, no. 5 (July 1996).

264   Selected Bibliography

Brzezinski, Zbigniew. *The Permanent Purge*. Cambridge: Harvard University Press, 1956.

Bunce, Valerie. "The Political Economy of the Brezhnev Era: The Rise and Fall of Corporatism." *British Journal of Political Science* 13: 129–58.

Burawoy, Michael. "The End of Sovietology and the Renaissance of Modernization Theory." *Contemporary Sociology* 21 (Nov. 1992).

Burawoy, Michael. *The Politics of Production: Factory Regimes under Capitalism and Socialism*. London: Verso, 1985.

Burawoy, Michael. "Reflections on the Class Consciousness of Hungarian Steelworkers." *Politics and Society* 17, no. 1 (March 1989).

Burawoy, Michael, and Pavel Krotov. "The Soviet Transition from Socialism to Capitalism: Worker Control and Economic Bargaining in the Wood Industry." In *What About the Workers?* edited by Simon Clarke and Peter Fairbrother. London: Verso, 1993.

Burawoy, Michael, and Janos Luckacs. *The Radiant Past: Ideology and Reality in Hungary's Road to Capitalism*. Chicago: University of Chicago Press, 1992.

Calhoun, Craig J. "The Radicalism of Tradition: Community Strength or Venerable Disease and Borrowed Language?" *American Journal of Sociology* 88, no. 5 (1983).

Chamberlin, John. "Provisions of Collective Goods as a Function of Group Size." *American Political Science Review* 68 (1974): 707–16.

"Chetvertyi Konferentsiya Soyuza Trudyashchikhsya Kuzbassa," 18–19 November 1989, Novokuznetsk, published proceedings.

Clarke, Simon, Peter Fairbrother, and Vadim Borisov. *The Workers' Movement in Russia*. Aldershot, England: Edward Elgar, 1995.

Clarke, Simon, Peter Fairbrother, Vadim Borisov, and Petr Bizyukov, "The Privatization of Industrial Enterprises in Russia: Four Case Studies," *Europe-Asia Studies* 46, no. 2 (1994): 179–214.

Clarke, Simon, Peter Fairbrother, Michael Burawoy, and Pavel Krotov. *What About the Workers?: Workers and the Transition to Capitalism in Russia*. London: Verso, 1993.

Collier, David, and Ruth Berins Collier. *Shaping the Political Arena*. Princeton: Princeton University Press, 1992.

Connor, Walter. *The Accidental Proletariat: Workers, Politics and Crisis in Gorbachev's Russia*. Princeton: Princeton University Press, 1991.

Cook, Linda J. "Labor's Response to the Soviet Post-Communist Transition." Paper presented at the annual meeting of the American Political Science Association, September 1992.

Cook, Linda J. "Russia's Labor Relations: Consolidation Disintegration?" In *Russia's Future: Consolidation Disintegration*, edited by Douglas W. Blum. Boulder, Colo.: Westview Press, 1994.

Cook, Linda J. *The Soviet Social Contract and Why It Failed*. Cambridge: Harvard University Press, 1993.

Crawford, Beverly. "Post-Communist Political Economy: A Framework for the Analysis of Reform." In *Markets, State and Democracy: The Political Econ-*

omy of Post-Communist Transformation, edited by Beverly Crawford. Boulder: Westview Press, 1995.

Cronin, James E. "Theories of Strikes: Why Can't They Explain the British Experience?" *Journal of Social History* 12, no. 2 (1978–79).

Crouch, Colin. *Trade Unions: The Logic of Collective Action.* London: Fontana, 1982.

Crowley, Stephen. "The Kuzbass: Liberals, Populists and Labor." In *Russia's Protodemocracy in Action: Perspectives on the Election of 1993,* edited by Timothy Colton and Jerry Hough. Washington, D.C.: Brookings Institution Press, 1997.

Crowley, Stephen. "Between Class and Nation: Worker Politics in the New Ukraine." *Communist and Post-Communist Studies* 28, no. 1 (March 1995).

Crowley, Stephen F., and Lewis H. Siegelbaum. "Survival Strategies: The Miners of Donetsk in the Post-Soviet Era." In *Workers of the Donbass Speak: Survival and Identity in the New Ukraine, 1989–1992,* edited by Lewis H. Siegelbaum and Daniel J. Walkowitz. Albany: State University of New York Press, 1995.

Dimaggio, Paul J., and Walter W. Powell. *The New Institutionalism in Organizational Analysis.* Chicago: University of Chicago Press, 1991.

Dirks, Nicholas, Geoff Eley, and Sherry Ortner. *Culture/Power/History.* Princeton: Princeton University Press, 1994.

Doeringer, P., and M. J. Piore. *Internal Labor Markets and Manpower Analysis.* Lexington, Mass.: Heath, 1971.

Edwards, P. K. "A Critique of the Kerr-Siegel Hypothesis of Strikes and the Isolated Mass: A Study in the Falsification of Sociological Knowledge." *Sociological Review* 25 (August 1977).

Elster, Jon. *Ulysses and the Sirens.* Cambridge: Cambridge University Press, 1984.

Fantasia, Rick. *Cultures of Solidarity: Consciousness, Action and Contemporary American Workers.* Berkeley: University of California Press, 1988.

Feher, Ferenc. "Paternalism as a Mode of Legitimation in Soviet-Type Societies." In *Political Legitimation in Communist States,* edited by T. H. Rigby and Ferenc Feher. New York: St. Martin's Press, 1982.

Feher, Ferenc, Agnes Heller, and Gyorgy Markus. *Dictatorship Over Needs.* Oxford: Blackwell, 1983.

Filtzer, Donald. *Soviet Workers and the Collapse of Perestroika.* Cambridge: Cambridge University Press, 1994.

Filtzer, Donald. *Soviet Workers and De-Stalinization.* Cambridge: Cambridge University Press, 1992.

Frieden, Jeffrey. *Debt Development and Democracy.* Princeton: Princeton University Press, 1991.

Friedgut, Theodore. *Iuzovka and Revolution,* vol. 1. Princeton: Princeton University Press, 1989.

Friedgut, Theodore, and Lewis Siegelbaum. "Perestroika from Below: The Soviet Miners' Strike and Its Aftermath." *New Left Review* (summer 1990).

Friedrich, Carl J. "The Unique Character of Totalitarian Society." In *Totalitarianism.* Cambridge: Harvard University Press, 1954.

Gamson, W. A. *The Strategy of Social Protest.* Homewood, Ill.: Dorsey, 1975.

Gaventa, John. *Power and Powerlessness: Quiescence and Rebellion in an Appalachian Valley.* Urbana: University of Illinois Press, 1980.

Giddens, Anthony. *Central Problems in Social Theory: Action, Structure and Contradictions in Social Analysis.* London: Macmillan, 1979.

Gidwitz, Betsy. "Labor Unrest in the Soviet Union." *Problems of Communism* (November–December 1982).

Gimpelson, Vladimir. "Why There is No Mass Unemployment." Russian Research Center, Harvard University. Photocopy.

Glasman, Maurice. "The Great Deformation: Polanyi, Poland and the Terrors of Planned Spontaneity." *New Left Review,* no. 205 (May–June, 1994).

Godson, Joseph, and Leonard Shapiro, eds. *The Soviet Worker.* London: Macmillan, 1981.

Goldstone, Jack A. "Ideology, Cultural Frameworks, and the Process of Revolution." *Theory and Society* 20 (May 1991).

Gorbachev, Mikhail S. *Zhizn' i Reformi.* Moscow: Novosti, 1995.

Gordon, L. A. *Rabochii klass SSSR: tendentsii i perspektivy sotsialno-ekonomicheskogo razvitia.* Moscow, 1985.

Gordon, Leonid, E. Gruzdeva, and Viktor Komarovskii. *Shakhteri–92: Sotsialnoe soznanie i sotsialnnii oblik rabochei elity b poslesotsialisticheskoi Rossii.* Moscow: Progress-Kompleks, 1992. For English translation, see Leonid Gordon, "Russian Workers and Democracy," *International Journal of Sociology* (winter 1993–94): 3–99.

Gurr, T. R. *Why Men Rebel.* Princeton: Princeton University Press, 1979.

Hahn, Jeffrey W. "Continuity and Change in Russian Political Culture." *British Journal of Political Science* 21 (October 1991).

Hamilton, Richard F. *Affluence and the French Worker in the Fourth Republic.* Princeton: Princeton University Press, 1967.

Hardin, Russell. *Collective Action.* Baltimore: Johns Hopkins University Press, 1982.

Harris, Cheryl. "Modernization of the Soviet Steel Industry." In "Gorbachev's Economic Plans," vol. 1, study papers submitted to the Joint Economic Committee of Congress, Nov. 23, 1987. Washington, D.C.: U.S. Government Printing Office, 1987.

Hauslohner, Peter. "Gorbachev's Social Contract." *Soviet Economy* 3, no. 1 (1987).

Hewett, Ed A. *Reforming the Soviet Economy: Equality Versus Efficiency.* Washington, D.C.: Brookings Institution, 1988.

Hirschman, Albert. *Exit, Voice and Loyalty.* Cambridge: Harvard University Press, 1970.

Hoffman, Erik, and Robin F. Laird, eds. *The Soviet Polity in the Modern Era.* New York: Aldine, 1984.

Hyman, Richard. *Strikes,* 4th ed. London: Macmillan, 1989.

Inglehart, Ronald. "The Renaissance of Political Culture." *American Political Science Review* 82 (1988).

"In Russia's Far North, Inflation Destroys A Dream." *The Moscow Times,* 3 March 1993.

Johnson, James. "Symbolic Action and the Limits of Strategic Rationality: On the Logic of Working-Class Collective Action." In *Political Power and Social Theory*, vol.7, edited by Maurice Zeitlin. Greenwich, Conn: JAI Press.

Johnson, Simon, and Oleg Ustenko. "The Road to Hyperinflation: Economic Independence in Ukraine, 1991–1993." Paper presented to the conference "First Steps Toward Economic Independence: New States of the Postcommunist World," Stockholm, August, 1993.

Jung, Monika. "The Donbass Factor in the Ukrainian Elections." *RFE/RL Research Report*, no. 12 (25 March 1994).

Kagarlitsky, Boris. "Russian Trade Unions and the 1995 Elections." *Labour Focus on Eastern Europe*, no. 52 (autumn 1995).

Kalmyk, V., and T. Sil'chenko. "Sotsial'no-ekonomicheskaia obuslovennost' otnosheniie k mestu raboty." In *Otnoshenie k Trudu i Tekuchest' Kadrov*, edited by E. Antosenkov and V. Kalmyk. Novosibirsk, 1970.

Kazin, Michael. *The Populist Persuasion.* New York: Basic Books, 1995.

Kennedy, Michael. *Professionals, Power and Solidarity in Poland.* Cambridge: Cambridge University Press, 1991.

Kerr, Clark, and Abraham Siegel. "The Interindustry Propensity to Strike—An International Perspective." In *Labor and Management in Industrial Society*, edited by Clark Kerr. Garden City, N.Y.: Doubleday, 1964.

Kimeldorf, Howard. *Reds or Rackets?* Berkeley: University of California Press, 1988.

Kitschelt, Herbert. "The Formation of Party Systems in East Central Europe." *Politics and Society* 20, no. 1 (March 1992).

Kitschelt, Herbert. "Resource Mobilization Theory: A Critique." In *Research on Social Movements*, edited by D. Rucht. Boulder, Colo.: Westview Press, 1991.

Klandemans, Bert. "New Social Movements and Resource Mobilization: The European and the American Approach Revisited." In *Research on Social Movements*, edited by D. Rucht. Boulder, Colo.: Westview Press, 1991.

Koenker, Diane P., and William G. Rosenberg. *Strikes and Revolution in Russia, 1917.* Princeton: Princeton University Press, 1989.

Kohli, Atul, et. al. "The Role of Theory in Comparative Politics: A Symposium." *World Politics* 48 (October 1995).

Komarovskii, Viktor, and E. B. Gruzdeva. *Shakterskoe Dvizhenie.* Moscow: Institute of Problems of Employment and Ministry of Labor, 1992.

Kornai, Janos. *The Socialist System.* Princeton: Princeton University Press, 1992.

Kornai, Janos. *The Economic of Shortage.* 2 vols. Amsterdam, 1980.

Koropeckyj, I. S., ed. *The Ukrainian Economy.* Cambridge: Harvard University Press, 1992.

Kostyukovskii, Viktor. *Zharkoe leto 89–ogo: khronika, dokumenty, vpechetleniya ochevidtsa.* Moscow: Sovremennik, 1990.

Kotkin, Stephen. *Magnetic Mountain.* Berkeley: University of California Press, 1995.

Kotkin, Stephen. *Steeltown, USSR.* Berkeley: University of California Press, 1991.

Kravchenko, A. I., et al. "Zabastovki v SSSR: novaia sotsial'naya realnost'." *Sotsiologicheskie Issledovannia*, no. 1 (1989).

Laba, Roman. *The Roots of Solidarity: A Political Sociology of Poland's Working-Class Democracy.* Princeton: Princeton University Press, 1991.

Lacquer, Walter. *The Long Road to Freedom.* New York: Scribner's, 1989.

Laitin, David, and Aaron Wildalvsky. "Political Culture and Political Preferences." *American Political Science Review* 82, no. 2 (1988).

Lane, David. *Soviet Labour and the Ethic of Communism: Full Employment and the Labour Process in the Soviet Union.* Brighton, England: Harvester, 1987.

Lane, David. *The Soviet Industrial Worker.* London: Martin Robertson, 1978.

Laslett, John H. M., and Seymour Martin Lipset. *Failure of a Dream? Essays in the History of American Socialism,* rev. ed. Berkeley: University of California Press, 1984.

Leont'eva, E. "Obshchestvennyi konflikt." *Voprosy Ekonomiki,* no. 4 (1989): 120–29.

Levine, Richard M. "Mineral Industries of the USSR." *Mining Annual Review,* 1990.

Lijphart, Arend. "The Comparable-Cases Strategy in Comparative Research." *Comparative Political Studies* 8, no. 2 (July 1985): 158–77.

Lipset, Seymour Martin. *Political Man: The Social Bases of Politics,* enlarged ed. Baltimore: Johns Hopkins University Press, 1981.

Lockwood, David. "Sources of Variation in Working-Class Images of Society." *Sociological Review* 14, no. 1 (November 1966).

Lopatin, Leonid, compiler. *Rabochee Dvizhenie Kuzbassa: Sbornik Dokumentov i materialov.* Kemerovo, 1993.

Ludlam, Janine. "Reform and the Redefinition of the Social Contract Under Gorbachev." *World Politics* 43, no. 2 (1991).

Maksimova, Nina. "Zabastovka: shtrikhi k portretu yavleniya." *EKO,* no. 11 (1989).

Mandel, David. *Perestroika and the Soviet People: Rebirth of the Labour Movement.* Montreal: Black Rose Books, 1991.

Mandel, David. "The Russian Labour Movement and Politics." *Labour Focus on Eastern Europe,* no. 52 (autumn 1995).

Mandel, David. "The Rebirth of the Soviet Labor Movement: The Coal Miners' Strike of July 1989." *Politics and Society* (September 1990).

Marples, David. "Turmoil in the Donbass: The Economic Realities." *Report on the USSR* (12 October 1990).

Marples, David. "Ukraine after the Presidential Election." *RFE/RL Research Report* 3, no. 31 (12 August 1994).

Marples, David. "Ukraine, Belarus, and the Energy Dilemma." *RFE/RL Research Report* 2, no. 27 (2 July 1993).

Marples, David. *Ukraine under Perestroika: Ecology, Economics and the Workers' Revolt.* New York: St. Martin's Press, 1991.

Marshall, Gordon. "Some Remarks on the Study of Working Class Consciousness." *Politics and Society* 12, no. 3 (1983).

McAdam, D. *Political Process and the Development of Black Insurgency, 1930–1970.* Chicago: University of Chicago Press, 1982.

Metallurg (Organ of the Labor Collective of the Donetsk Metallurgical Factory, Donetsk). March 1989–May 1991.

Metallurg Zapsiba (Organ of the Labor Collective of the Western Siberian Metallurgical Combine, Novosibirsk). Jan. 1989–December 1993.

Ministerstvo Ugolnoi Promyshlennosti SSSR. "Osnovie pokazateli po ugol'." Moscow: October 1990.

Mitchell, Jay. "Macroeconomic Perspective of the Ukrainian Economy." Paper presented at the conference "Challenges of Transition for Ukraine's Economy," Washington, D.C., September 1993.

Mohr, Lawrence B. "The Reliability of the Case Study as a Source of Information." In *Advances in Information Processing in Organizations,* vol. 2. Greenwich, Conn.: JAI Press, 1985.

Moore, Barrington Jr. *Injustice.* White Plains, N.Y.: M. E. Sharpe, 1978.

Moore, R. S. *Pitmen, Preachers and Politics.* Cambridge: Cambridge University Press, 1974.

Morris, Aldon D., and Carol McClurg Mueller, eds. *Frontiers in Social Movement Theory.* New Haven: Yale University Press, 1992.

Morton, Henry W., and R. Stuart, eds. *The Contemporary Soviet City.* Armonk, N.Y.: M. E. Sharpe, 1984.

Nasha Gazeta (Independent Regional Newspaper, Kemerovo). 1989–94.

Nazimova, Alla. "Chelovek: konflikt na proizvodstve." *Politicheskoe Obrazovanie,* no. 10 (1989): 75–80.

North, Douglass. *Institutions, Institutional Change, and Economic Performance.* Cambridge: Cambridge University Press, 1990.

Oberschall, A. *Social Conflict and Social Movements.* Englewood Cliffs, N.J.: Prentice Hall, 1973.

Offe, Claus, and Helmut Wiesenthal. "Two Logics of Collective Action: Theoretical Notes on Social Class and Organizational Forms." In *Political Power and Social Theory,* edited by Maurice Zeitlin. Greenwich, Conn.: JAI Press, 1980.

Olson, Mancur. *The Logic of Collective Action: Public Goods and the Theory of Groups.* Cambridge: Harvard University Press, 1977.

Ost, David. "Labor, Class and Democracy: Shaping Political Antagonisms in Post-Communist Society." In *Markets, State and Democracy: The Political Economy of Post-Communist Transformation,* edited by Beverly Crawford. Boulder, Colo.: Westview Press, 1995.

Ost, David. *Solidarity and the Politics of Anti-Politics.* Philadelphia: Temple University Press, 1990.

Osterman, Paul, ed. *Internal Labor Markets.* Cambridge: MIT Press, 1984.

"Pervyi S'ezd Shakhterov SSSR," 11–15 June 1990, collected materials, Donetsk, parts 1 and 2.

Pipes, Richard. *Russia Under the Bolshevik Regime.* A. A. Knopf, 1993.

Polterovich, V. "Ekonomicheskaya reforma 1992 goda: bitva pravitelstva s trydovymi kollektivami." *Ekonomika I matematicheskiye metody,* no. 4 (1993).

Popkin, Samuel. *The Rational Peasant.* Berkeley: University of California Press, 1979.

Posusney, Marsha Pripstein. "Irrational Workers: The Moral Economy of Labor Protest in Egypt." *World Politics* 46 (October 1993).

Powell, Walter W., and Paul J. Dimaggio, eds. Introduction to *The New Institutionalism in Organizational Analysis*. Chicago: University of Chicago Press, 1991.

"Protokol o soglasovanikh merakh mezhdu regionalnim zabastovachnim komitetom kuzbassa i komissiei TsK KPSS, Soveta Ministrov SSSR, i VTsSPS." Unpublished document. Prokop'evsk, 17–18 July 1989.

Przeworski, Adam. *Democracy and the Market: Political and Economic Reforms in Eastern Europe and Latin America.* Cambridge: Cambridge University Press, 1991.

Przeworski, Adam. "Marxism and Rational Choice." *Politics and Society* 14, no. 4 (1985).

Pye, Lucian. "Political Science and the Crisis of Authoritarianism." *Political Science Review* 84 (1990).

Ragin, Charles. *The Comparative Method: Moving Beyond Qualitative and Quantitative Strategies.* Berkeley: University of California Press, 1987.

"Razgovor u barrakady." *Sotsiologicheskie Issledovania,* no. 6 (1990).

Reddy, William. *The Rise of Market Culture: The Textile Trade and French Society, 1750–1900.* Cambridge: Cambridge University Press, 1984.

Remnick, David. "Hammer, Sickle, and Book." *New York Review of Books* 43, no. 9 (23 May 1996).

Roemer, John. *A Future for Socialism.* Cambridge: Cambridge University Press, 1994.

Rogowski, Ronald. *Commerce and Coalitions.* Princeton: Princeton University Press, 1989.

Rueschemeyer, Dietrich, Evelyne Huber Stephens, and John D. Stephens. *Capitalist Development and Democracy.* Chicago: University of Chicago Press, 1992.

Rumer, Boris. *Soviet Steel: The Challenge of Industrial Modernization in the USSR.* Ithaca: Cornell University Press, 1989.

Rupnik, Jacques. "Totalitarianism Revisited." In *Civil Society and the State,* edited by J. Keane. London: Verso, 1988.

"Russian Federation: Restructuring the Coal Industry: Putting People First." *World Bank Report* No. 13187-RU, 2 vols., 12 December 1994.

Rutland, Peter. *Business Elites and Russian Economic Policy.* London: Royal Institute of International Affairs, 1992.

Rutland, Peter. "Labor Unrest and Movements in 1989 and 1990." *Soviet Economy* (December 1990).

Scott, James C. *The Moral Economy of the Peasant.* New Haven: Yale University Press, 1977.

Scott, James. *Weapons of the Weak: Everyday Forms of Peasant Resistance.* New Haven: Yale University Press, 1985.

Sewell, William. "A Theory of Structure: Duality, Agency, and Transformation." *American Journal of Sociology* 98, no. 1 (July 1992): 1–29.

Sewell, William. *Work and Revolution in France: The Language of Labor from the Old Regime to 1848.* Cambridge: Cambridge University Press, 1980.

Shorter, Edward, and Charles Tilly. *Strikes in France, 1830–1968.* Cambridge: Cambridge University Press, 1974.

Sieglebaum, Lewis. "We Haven't Seen Perestroika Yet: Behind the Soviet Miners' Strike." *Nation* 249, no. 13 (1989).

Siegelbaum, Lewis H., and Daniel J. Walkowitz. " 'We'll Remain in This Cesspool for a Long Time': The Miners of Donetsk Speak Out." *Oral History Review* 20, nos. 1 and 2 (spring–fall 1992).

Siegelbaum, Lewis H., and Daniel J. Walkowitz. *Workers of the Donbass Speak: Survival and Identity in the New Ukraine, 1989–1992.* Albany: State University of New York Press, 1995.

Snow, David, and Robert Benford. "Ideology, Frame Resonance, and Participant Mobilization." *International Social Movement Research* 1 (1988).

Snow, David, and Robert Benford. "Master Frames and Cycles of Protest." In *Frontiers of Social Movement Research,* edited by Aldon Morriss and Carol McClurg Mueller. New Haven: Yale University Press, 1992.

Soviet Energy Data Resource Handbook. Washington, D.C.: Government Printing Office, 1990.

Sperling, Valerie. "Society Organizes Itself: The Coal Miners' Strike Committees." Department of Government, Georgetown University. Photocopy.

Staniszkis, Jadwiga. *Poland's Self-Limiting Revolution.* Princeton: Princeton University Press, 1984.

Stark, David. "From System Identity to Organizational Diversity: Analyzing Social Change in Eastern Europe." *Contemporary Sociology* (1992).

Stark, David. "Organizational Innovation in Hungary's Emerging Mixed Economy." In *Remaking the Economic Institutions of Socialism: China and Eastern Europe,* edited by V. Nee and D. Stark. Stanford: Stanford University Press, 1989.

Stark, David. "Path Dependence and and Privatization Strategies in East Central Europe." *Eastern European Politics and Society* 6 (1992).

Stark, David. "Rethinking Internal Labor Markets: New Insights from a Comparative Perspective." *American Sociological Review* 51, no. 4 (1986): 492–504.

Stark, David, and Victor Nee. *Remaking the Economic Institutions.* Palo Alto: Stanford University Press 1989.

Stark, David, and Victor Nee. "Toward an Institutional Analysis of State Socialism." In *Remaking the Economic Institutions,* edited by David Stark and Victor Nee. Palo Alto: Stanford University Press 1989.

Stone, Katherine. "The Origin of Job Structures in the Steel Industry," *Review of Radical Political Economics* 6, no. 2 (summer 1974).

Swidler, Ann. "Culture in Action: Symbols and Strategies." *American Sociological Review* 51 (April 1986).

Szymanski, Albert. *The Capitalist State and the Politics of Class.* Cambridge, Mass.: Winthrop, 1977.

Tarrow, Sidney. "Mentalities, Political Cultures, and Collective Action Frames." In *Frontiers in Social Movement Theory,* edited by Aldon Morris and Carol McClurg Mueller. New Haven: Yale University Press, 1992.

Tarrow, Sidney. *Power in Movement: Social Movements, Collective Action, and Politics.* Cambridge: Cambridge University Press, 1994.

Tarrow, Sidney. *Democracy and Disorder: Protest and Politics in Italy, 1965–1975.* Oxford: Oxford University Press, 1989.

Taubman, William. *Governing Soviet Cities: Bureaucratic Politics and Urban Development in the USSR.* New York: Praeger, 1973.

Taylor, Michael. *The Possibility of Cooperation.* Cambridge: Cambridge University Press, 1987.

Teague, Elizabeth. "Perestroika and the Soviet Worker." *Government and Opposition* (spring 1990).

Teckenberg, Wolfgang. "Labour Turnover and Job Satisfaction: Indicators of Industrial Conflict in the USSR?" *Soviet Studies* 30, no. 2 (April 1978).

Thompson, E. P. "The Moral Economy of the English Crowd in the Eighteenth Century." *Past and Present,* no. 50 (February 1971).

Thompson, Paul. *The Nature of Work.* London: Macmillan, 1983.

Thornton, Judith. "Soviet Electric Power in the Wake of the Chernobyl Accident." In *Gorbachev's Economic Plans,* vol. 1, edited by John P. Hardt and Richard Kaufman. Washington, D.C.: Joint Economic Committee of Congress, GPO, 1987.

Ticktin, Hillel. *Origins of the Crisis in the USSR.* Armonk, N.Y.: M. E. Sharpe, 1992.

Tilly, Charles. *From Mobilization to Revolution.* Reading, Mass.: Addison Wesley, 1978.

Touraine, Alain, F. Dubet, M. Wieviorka, and J. Strzelecki. *Solidarity: Poland 1980–1981.* Cambridge: Cambridge University Press, 1983.

Trud v SSSR. Moscow: Financi I Statistiki, 1988.

Vasilyev, A., and M. Krans. "Konflict: chto za nim?" *Kommunist* 9 (1989).

Vujacic, Veljko. "Gennadiy Zyuganov and the 'Third Way.'" *Post-Soviet Affairs* 12, no. 2 (April–June 1996).

Walder, Andrew. *Communist Neo-Traditionalism: Work and Authority in Chinese Industry.* Berkeley: University of California Press, 1986.

Walder, Andrew. "Factory and Managers in an Era of Reform." *China Quarterly,* no. 118 (June 1989): 242–64.

Ward, Chris. *Russia's Cotton Workers and the New Economic Policy.* Cambridge: Cambridge University Press, 1990.

Warner, David, and Louis Kaiser. "Development of the USSR's Eastern Coal Basins." In *Gorbachev's Economic Plans,* vol. 1, edited by John P. Hardt and Richard Kaufman. Washington, D.C.: Joint Economic Committee of Congress, GPO, 1987.

Wesolowski, Wlodzimierz. *Classes, Strata and Power.* London: Routledge and Keagan Paul, 1979.

Westergaard, J. H. "The Rediscovery of the Cash Nexus." *The Socialist Register, 1970.* London: Merlin Press.

White, Stephen. "Economic Performance and Communist Legitimacy." *World Politics* 38, no. 3 (1986).

White, Stephen. *Political Culture and Soviet Politics.* London: MacMillan, 1979.

Wilson, Andrew. "The Growing Challenge to Kiev from the Donbass." *RFE/RL Research Report* 2, no. 33 (August 1993).

Winterton, Jonathan, and Ruth Winterton. *Coal, Crisis and Conflict: The 1984–1985 Miners' Strike in Yorkshire.* New York: St. Martin's Press, 1989.

Yanowitch, Murray, ed. *Soviet Work Attitudes.* White Plains, N. Y: M. E. Sharpe, 1979.

Yarrow, Michael. "The Labor Process in Coal Mining: The Struggle for Control." In *Case Studies in the Labor Process,* edited by Andrew Zimbalist. New York: Monthly Review Press, 1979.

"Zabastovka v SSSR: novaya sotsial'naya realnost'." *Sotsiologicheskie Issledovania,* no. 1 (1989).

Zald, Mayer, and J. D. McCarthy, eds. *Social Movements in an Organizational Society.* New Brunswick, N.J.: Transaction Books, 1987.

Zaslavsky, Viktor. "The Regime and the Working Class in the U.S.S.R." *Telos* (winter 1979–80).

Zemskov, V. N., compiler. *Rabochii klass SSSR 1917–1977.* Moscow: 1978.

Index